Balance of Payments and Exchange Rate Theories

Balance of Payments and Exchange Rate Theories

Norman C. Miller

Julian G. Lange Professor of Economics
Richard T. Farmer School of Business Administration
Miami University, Oxford, Ohio, U.S.A.

Edward Elgar
Cheltenham, UK * Northampton, MA, USA

© Norman C. Miller 2002

Published by
Edward Elgar Publishing Limited
Glensanda House
Montpellier Parade
Cheltenham
Glos GL50 1UA
UK

Edward Elgar Publishing, Inc.
136 West Street
Suite 202
Northampton
Massachusetts 01060
USA

A catalogue record for this book
is available from the British Library

Library of Congress Cataloguing in Publication Data

Miller, Norman C., 1939-
Balance of payments and exchange rate theories / Norman C. Miller.
    p. cm.
    Includes bibliographical references and index.
    1. Balance of payments. 2. Foreign exchange rates. I. Title.

HG3882 M555 2002
332.1'52'01—dc21

2002024584

ISBN 1-84064-954-2

Printed and bound in Great Britain by Bookcraft, Bath

Contents

Contents

Figures

Acronyms and symbols

CAPM	capital asset pricing model
CBP	commodity market approach to the balance of payments
CIP	covered interest parity
FDB	forward discount bias
FG	future goods
FX	foreign exchange
ID	home minus foreign nominal interest rate differential
IOL	intertemporal opportunity locus
ITL	intertemporal trade line
KBP	Keynesian approach to the balance of payments
LFER	loanable funds exchange rate theory
LOOP	law of one price
LT	long term
MBP	monetary approach to the balance of payments
MER	monetary approach to the exchange rate
M–F	Mundell/Fleming
M–L	Marshall-Lerner
MPK	marginal product of capital
OECD	Organization for Economic Cooperation and Development
PG	present goods
PPP	purchasing power parity
R1	regime 1 in the FX market
R2	regime 2 in the FX market
RE	rational expectations
RRIR	relevant real interest rate
SKF	stock-adjustment capital flow
ST	short term
UIP	uncovered interest parity

i	nominal rate of interest
f	log of the nominal forward exchange rate in home money per unit of foreign money
$f(\ )$	aggregate production function after a productivity shock
g	log of government expenditure
m	log of the nominal money supply
p	log of the price level
r	real rate of interest
s	log of the nominal spot exchange rate in home money per unit of foreign money

s^*	nominal fundamental exchange rate
s^e	expected future spot rate via recursive expectations
t	tax rate on domestic source income
t'	tax rate on foreign source income
tr_j	anticipated net transfer payments for the jth agent
$\underline{tr}_j$	actual net transfer payments for the jth agent
v_c	*ex ante* excess supply of commodities for one economic unit
$\underline{v}_c$	actual sales minus purchases of commodities
v_i	*ex ante* excess supply of good i by the jth agent
$\underline{v}_i$	actual sales minus purchases of good i by the jth agent
v_m	*ex ante* excess supply of money by the jth agent
$v(t)$	temporary shocks to the fundamentals in the FX market

$A(-1)$	lagged value of the net international asset position
$Aj(-1)$	lagged value of the jth agent's net asset position
A^*	foreign bonds held by home agents
$B(\ )$	behavioral function that determines the balance of payments
BP	*ex ante* and *ex post* balance of payments
BT	*ex ante* and *ex post* balance of trade
C	consumption
$C(\ )$	cost of transforming one unit of output into a capital good
CA	*ex ante* current account
Cd	FX purchases by ST-speculators or chartists
Cs	FX sales by ST-speculators or chartists
$E[\ ]$	expected value operator
Ex	exports
G	government purchases
$F(\ )$	aggregate production function
FBP	flow balance of payments
FKF	pure flow component of international capital flows
FX	foreign exchange
FX_i	*ex ante* flow excess supply of good i
$H[\ ]$	function determining the price of present goods
I	investment
Im	imports
J	FX market activities from the fundamental BP & some speculative actions
K	capital stock
KF	*ex ante* and *ex post* net capital flows
NX	*ex ante* and *ex post* net exports
P	price index for the composite good
P_{FG}	price of future goods

P_N	price of nontraded goods
P_{PG}	price of present goods
$Pr[\ ]$	probability
P_T	price of traded goods
Pay	total payments by home residents
$(Pay)h$	payments by home residents to home residents
Q	real exchange rate in home commodity units per foreign commodity unit
$\boldsymbol{Q}$	long run equilibrium real exchange rate
R	stock of international reserves
Rec	total receipts of home residents
$(Rec)h$	receipts of home residents from home residents
$RRIR$	relevant real interest rate
S	nominal exchange rate in home money units per foreign money
SKF	stock-adjustment capital flow
Sv	saving
$Sv - I$	optimum current account
SX_i	*ex ante* stock excess supply of good i
Tr	*ex ante* and *ex post* net international transfer payments
$U(\ )$	total utility function of the representative agent
$V[\ ]$	cumulative frequency distribution for temporary shocks to the fundamentals
V_A	total *ex ante* supply minus demand for bonds by home residents
$\underline{V}_A$	total *ex post* sales minus purchases of bonds by home residents
V_c	total *ex ante* supply minus demand for commodities by home residents
$\underline{V}_c$	total *ex post* sales minus purchases of commodities by home residents
V_M	total *ex ante* supply minus demand for money by home residents
V_i	total *ex ante* supply minus demand for good i by home residents
$\underline{V}_i$	total *ex post* sales minus purchases of good i by home residents
W	wealth
X	actual net income
$\boldsymbol{X}$	permanent net income
X_A	*ex ante* excess supply of home bonds
X_c	*ex ante* excess supply of home commodities
X_{FX}	*ex ante* excess supply of foreign exchange
X_i	*ex ante* excess supply of good i within a period framework
$\underline{X}_i$	*ex post* excess supply of good i within a period framework
X_M	*ex ante* excess supply of home money
$\underline{X}_M$	end of period or *ex post* excess supply of money
X_T	transitory net income
Y	total output

Z	net output available for home use
Z_0	permanent component of the fundamentals in the FX market

β	discount factor
χ	optimum ratio of foreign assets to total home wealth
Δm_j	*ex post* net flow of cash for the jth agent
ΔR	change in international reserves
ε	exchange rate prediction error
$\phi(\ )$	coefficient in the consumption function
λ	risk premium in the UIP condition
Λ	percentage of stock excess supply that generates buy or sell orders
Γ	FX purchases, (+), or sales, (−), by LT- speculators
η	long run price elasticity of home demand for imports
$\eta*$	long run price elasticity of foreign demand for home exports
η'	short run price elasticity of home demand for imports
$\eta*'$	short run price elasticity of foreign demand for home exports
μ	the risk premium for long term speculators
Π	profits
π	rate of decay in the interest rate differential
ρ	the subjective rate of discount
τ	tariff rate on imports
ψ	the weight given to fundamentals in recursive expectations
Ω	FX sales or purchases from profit taking by LT- speculators

An asterisk superscript on a term generally represents the foreign value for this variable.

Preface

This book attempts to provide a fresh perspective on balance of payments and exchange rate theories, including intertemporal models that focus on the optimum current account. To this end, it rigorously proves that any nonzero balance of payments must always be associated with a disequilibrium in either a commodity or an asset market. Important welfare and policy implications of this conclusion are explored.

Also, it develops: (a) a new theory of the balance of payments associated with commodity market disequilibrium; (b) a loanable funds theory of the exchange rate; and (c) a modern foreign exchange market theory of the exchange rate that rigorously incorporates capital flows. In addition, the book details 15 puzzling facts associated with open economies and the FX market. After reviewing many existing explanations to these puzzles, it shows how each of the above new theories provides new, often unified, solutions to these puzzles.

Although this is not a textbook, it reviews much about what is known and is not known. Hopefully it will be instructive for anyone who has had a good exposure to principles of economics, as well as an international economics course. However, a previous course in international economics is not needed if the reader is concurrently taking such a course. Most of the chapters have been used successfully as supplementary readings by MA students in economics, and by MBA students.

The book utilizes only elementary algebra and a bit of differential calculus. However, the level at which it is written is probably too high for all but the best undergraduates. To facilitate learning, every attempt is made to provide a logical explanation that is illustrated graphically for every conclusion that is obtained rigorously. Furthermore, each chapter ends with a detailed summary.

Much of the material was presented at various professional meetings and/or at seminars at the International Monetary Fund, Miami University of Ohio, the University of Pittsburgh, and West Virginia University. I am grateful for numerous suggestions that were made by a large number of people, especially Ron Balvers, Jim Cassing, Peter Clark, George Davis, and Steve Husted. Furthermore, Joshua Miller provided excellent computer support. Finally, I want to acknowledge the fact that the Richard T. Farmer School of Business Administration at Miami University of Ohio has provided an environment which allowed me to pursue an endeavor such as this.

1. Objectives, puzzles, and preview

1.1 OBJECTIVES

Balance of payments and exchange rate theories evolved steadily in the first 25 years after World War II, but the study of the balance of payments essentially ceased in the early 1970s. Undoubtedly the major reason for this was the demise of the fixed exchange rate Bretton Woods system. However, in recent years more than 40% of all countries have their currency pegged to one or more other currencies.[1] Consequently, the determinants of a nonzero balance of payments continue to be relevant for a large number of countries.

Since the work of Meese and Rogoff (1983a, 1983b) exchange rate theory has been in a state of disarray. Indeed, many scholars have given up trying to model movements in the exchange rate in the short to medium run. In addition, there exists a long list of puzzling stylized facts in the world of international finance and open economy macroeconomics. Section 1.3 lists and briefly explains 15 of these puzzles. One or more explanations have been offered for most of the puzzles, but this (implicitly) gives more than 15 different models or theories that try to explain the functioning of the international economy. It is explained below that many of the puzzles overlap. That is, they appear to be different aspects of one or more unknown dynamic processes for the exchange rate. If so, then the objective should be to develop a unified theory (or at least a small consistent set of models) that explain many of the puzzles simultaneously.[2]

In recent years the focus of research in international finance has switched to: (a) developing intertemporal open economy macro-models that analyze the **composition** of a zero balance of payments by exploring the underlying determinants of the current account and offsetting net capital flow;[3] (b) examining the institutional aspects of the foreign exchange (FX) market in the literature that is known as the micro-structure of the FX market;[4] (c) building and/or testing empirical models of the exchange rate, including those that: (i) are long run in nature,[5] or (ii) are strictly empirical, with no underlying theory, often in an attempt to ascertain the time series properties of the spot rate;[6] and (d) testing equilibrium relationships (rather than theories) such as uncovered interest parity (UIP) and purchasing power parity (PPP).[7]

The primary objective of this book is to provide a fresh perspective on balance of payments and exchange rate theories. This is accomplished in four ways. First, a careful examination is made of the causes of individual cash-flow imbalances. This leads to conclusions dealing with all possible causes for international payments imbalances, as well as the proper structure of models of the balance of payments and/or exchange rate. In the process we learn that a nonzero balance of payments must be associated with a disequilibrium in at least one market in addition to the FX market. Important theoretical and policy implications follow directly from this.

Second, the book develops and explores the open economy intertemporal model in a slightly different manner. This provides insights into the gains from intertemporal trade, and the determinants of the optimum composition of the balance of payments. Third, the book sketches a new theory of the balance of payments that is related to a nonclearing commodity market. Finally, the book formally develops two new theories of the exchange rate, namely: (a) a loanable funds sticky-price model, and (b) a modern FX market theory that incorporates international capital flows in a rigorous manner.

The development of theories within an abstract vacuum devoid of real world significance quickly becomes dry and boring. Consequently, a secondary objective of this book is to investigate the many puzzling stylized facts mentioned above. The chapters consider the extent to which existing theories (as well as the new ones developed here) are consistent with these facts or puzzles. In sum, this is a book about economic theory that attempts to keep an eye on reality by referring consistently to puzzling real world facts.

1.2 A BRIEF HISTORY OF EXISTING THEORIES[8]

1.2.1 The Foreign Exchange Market Approach

After World War II, the economics profession inherited the FX market theory of the exchange rate and balance of payments.[9] As is well known, in this approach the exchange rate is determined at the intersection of the demand and supply curves for FX. If the government uses FX market intervention to hold the exchange rate constant at a value other than its free market clearing value, then the resulting excess demand or supply of FX by private agents equals the *ex ante* balance of payments deficit or surplus.

Historically, the FX market approach very carefully derived the relationship between the spot rate and the FX value of exports and imports, with much attention given to some version of the Marshall–Lerner, M–L, condition that determines the conditions under which the FX market is stable. The crucial importance that this approach gave to the price elasticities of demand for exports and imports led to it being referred to as the 'elasticities approach'.

However, the traditional FX market theory handled international capital flows in a very nonrigorous manner. Typically, the magnitudes of capital flows were assumed to be independent of the current value for the spot rate. Some exogenous values for capital inflows and capital outflows were added in an *ad hoc* manner to the underlying demand and/or supply of FX associated with trade flows. This lack of rigor associated with capital flows is one reason why the FX market approach was discarded in scholarly work.

1.2.2 The 'Income Minus Absorption' and Mundell/Fleming Models

Alexander's (1952) income-absorption approach criticized the FX market theory for its failure to take account of macroeconomic principles. Its basic ideas were: (a) commodity market equilibrium requires the value for the trade balance to equal the difference between home output and absorption (i.e., consumption plus investment plus government purchases of goods and services); and (b) consequently, the FX market or elasticities approach can lead to incorrect conclusions because it does not take (a) into account. The original income-absorption approach was eventually synthesized with the elasticities approach by Alexander (1959).

Mundell (1962) and Fleming (1962) embedded Alexander's ideas in an open economy version of the IS/LM model. The Mundell/Fleming (MF) model quickly became the dominant approach to both exchange rate and balance of payments theory.[10] Even though it has been discarded in scholarly work, Krugman (1995) maintains that it continues to be the model of choice in policy discussions.

In the MF model, at a short run equilibrium such as at point A in Figure 1.1 (where IS intersects LM at a point above the positively sloped balance of payments equilibrium locus, BP) there is an international payments surplus. This arises because at all points above the BP curve the interest rate is too high (which means that the capital account is too strong) and home income is too low (yielding relatively low imports) for a zero balance of payments. Conversely, when IS intersects LM' at a point such as B (which lies below the balance of payments equilibrium locus) in Figure 1.1, then a balance of payments deficit exists.

In the flexible exchange rate version of the MF model, an incipient payments imbalance induces a variation in the spot rate that shifts the curves until IS intersects LM at a point on the BP curve. For example, at point A the incipient payments surplus induces an appreciation of home money, which worsens the trade balance and shifts the IS and BP curves to the left until IS intersects LM at a point on the BP curve.

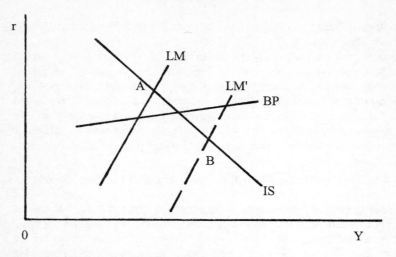

Figure 1.1 The Mundell/Fleming model

1.2.3 The Monetary and Portfolio Balance Approaches

In the late 1960s and during the 1970s, the MF model was challenged by the monetary approach to the balance of payments (MBP) and monetary approach to the exchange rate (MER).[11] These new approaches were very appealing because they: (a) ignored the complexities of a macro-model by focusing completely on the money market, and (b) were the first theories of the balance of payments and exchange rate that had any micro-foundations.[12] However, the MBP and MER reach conclusions that are precisely the opposite of those from both the old 'elasticities' approach and the MF model.

For example, in the latter two models an exogenous increase in home income stimulates imports and **worsens** the trade balance and balance of payments within a fixed nominal exchange rate system. Within a flexible exchange rate system, higher income leads to a **depreciation** of home money in order to prevent a deterioration in the trade balance and overall balance of payments.

On the other hand, the MBP focuses on the fact that an exogenous increase in home income increases the home demand for real money balances. Within a fixed exchange rate open economy, this can be satisfied via a balance of payments **surplus**, which increases the nominal money supply. In a flexible exchange rate system, the home excess demand for money is eliminated within the MER via an **appreciation** of home money. This reduces home prices, increases the home **real** money supply, and thereby eliminates the excess demand for money.

The MBP and MER also reach conclusions about the effects of variations in home prices or interest rates that are precisely the opposite of those obtained via other theories.[13] This created much confusion and controversy within the profession during the 1970s. The culmination of this was Kuska's (1978) provocative indictment of the MF model.[14]

During the late 1970s and early 1980s scholars developed the 'portfolio balance theory of the exchange rate'.[15] The main idea here is that FX is an asset, and its price (the exchange rate) can be modeled in a manner similar to the modeling of other asset prices. Thus, the portfolio balance theory contains only asset market equilibrium equations, such as those that specify the clearing of money markets and bond markets. It assumes that the volume of FX market transactions tied up with the trade balance and current account is too small (compared to the volume associated with capital flows) to exert any direct influence on the exchange rate. For this reason, both this (and the MER) represent asset market models of the exchange rate.

Also, during the late 1970s and early 1980s, Dornbusch's (1976) sticky price monetary model was developed.[16] This MF type of model assumes that commodity prices change slowly, which means that the commodity market can be out of equilibrium in the short run. In a true Keynesian fashion, it assumes that the interest rate is determined via the money market, both in and out of full macro-equilibrium. The model helps to explain exchange rate volatility by generating 'exchange rate overshooting' in response to monetary shocks, but not in response to real shocks such as changes in government spending.

1.2.4 The Meese and Rogoff Critique

Although various versions of the MBP, MER, and portfolio balance models were consistent with the data *ex post*, the work of Meese and Rogoff (1983a, 1983b) shocked the profession by showing that these theories had essentially no short run or medium run predictive power using out-of-sample data. More specifically, a random walk theory (which implies that the best predictor of the future spot rate is simply its current value) outperformed any existing theory for time horizons up to one year.[17]

Subsequent research by Wolff (1987), Schinasi and Swamy (1989), Throop (1993), and MacDonald and Taylor (1993, 1994) has come up with models that predict in the short run or medium run better than a random walk model. However, typically these studies focus on a small set of bilateral exchange rates, and/or use data covering a relatively brief time interval. In general, much empirical work has substantiated the results of Meese and Rogoff.[18] Perhaps an objective summary of this literature is that if we try hard enough we can come up with an exchange rate theory that predicts a specific bilateral exchange rate (over some limited time interval) slightly better than a random walk prediction. However, slightly outperforming a random walk model is no great accomplishment.

Because of this, Frankel and Dornbusch (1993, p.16) say that 'shorter term movements [in the exchange rate] remain completely unexplained'. Also, Taylor (1995) suggests that it might no longer be fruitful to try to explain short run movements in the exchange rate via models based solely on macroeconomic fundamentals. Finally, Frankel and Rose (1995, p.1708) state that 'no model based on standard fundamentals will ever succeed in explaining or predicting a high percentage of the variation in the exchange rate, at least at short or medium term frequencies'.

1.2.5 Some New Directions for Research

As pointed out above, the failure of short run and medium run exchange rate models has induced scholars to move in other directions. One direction has been the development of the intertemporal approach to open economy macro-models. The basic ideas of this approach have been around for some time via the work of Miller (1968), Connally and Ross (1970), and Webb (1970), each of whom apparently discovered the open economy intertemporal approach independently. Eventually, the ideas appeared in Heller's (1974) textbook. However, it was not until Sachs (1981) that the profession began exploring the intertemporal open economy model more fully.

The typical intertemporal open economy model as in Frenkel and Razin (1992) and Obstfeld and Rogoff (1995a, 1996) is for a small economy whose traded good is a perfect substitute for the foreign traded good. Thus, there is no real exchange rate in the traditional sense of the term, i.e., the relative price of the home and foreign commodities is always unity.[19] The large foreign country automatically buys or sells whatever quantity of the traded good that is necessary to clear the home market for the traded good. Consequently, the current account always equals the difference between domestic saving and investment.[20]

In the intertemporal open economy model, a representative agent maximizes an intertemporal utility function in two stages: (a) first, by deciding on the optimal level of investment, which in turn yields a value for current net income (i.e., the value for gross income minus investment and exogenous government spending); and then (b) by determining the optimal levels of saving and consumption, given the value for net income. Since the two steps in the optimization process are independent, it follows that an important characteristic of such models is that the levels of investment and saving need not be correlated.

Another property of such models is the implication that the current account balance does not depend on such variables as the nominal exchange rate, and home versus foreign prices or incomes, but rather on the underlying determinants of the home autarky rate of interest via the interaction of saving and investment.[21] One shortcoming of the open economy intertemporal models is that they have not been developed sufficiently to be useful in making policy decisions.[22]

A second direction in which scholarly research has moved is the careful investigation of the institutional details of the FX market. Among other things, this has provided insights into why the volume of FX market transactions is so large.[23] Another important aspect of this literature involves surveys of FX dealers in order to learn many details of their behavior, especially how they formulate their exchange rate expectations.[24]

In general, the surveys consistently find that fundamentals (such as prices, incomes, money supplies, and the trade or current account balance) become progressively less important in the determination of exchange rate expectations as the time horizon decreases. When the time horizon is very brief (e.g., from one day to perhaps one month) the importance of fundamentals is almost completely dominated by 'technical analysis'. The latter is a generic term that refers to all techniques (often employing the use of charts) that predict the exchange rate in the near future, based on its recent behavior.

A third direction in which scholarly research has moved in recent decades deals with empirical models of the exchange rate. Some of these explore the time series properties of the spot rate,[25] while others postulate exchange rate equations that tend to replicate observed exchange rate behavior.[26] In these cases, no underlying theoretical model is specified. On the other hand, Stein (1994), Williamson (1994), Isard and Faruqee (1998), and Clark and MacDonald (1999) attempt to provide a theoretical foundation for empirical models of the exchange rate in the long run. Such models appear to fit the in sample data reasonably well.

A fourth direction for recent research has been the testing of equilibrium relationships in international finance. This apparently represents an attempt to see 'if anything makes sense' (i.e., if the exchange rate is related at all to any fundamentals) and, in the process, provide some way to have at least a rough idea with regard to future values for the exchange rate. For example, uncovered interest parity for risk adverse agents (UIP) implies that the home minus foreign interest rate differential should equal the expected future change in the log of the spot rate. If expectations are rational, this implies that, in general, actual future changes in the exchange rate can be predicted by the current interest rate differential. As a second example, purchasing power parity (PPP) suggests that the nominal exchange rate (or changes in it) will approximately equal the ratio of home to foreign prices (or changes in it) in the long run. Therefore, to the extent that future relative prices can be predicted, PPP provides a mechanism for forecasting the future exchange rate. In sum, this fourth direction for new research has focused, on the extent to which the exchange rate is related to fundamentals at the most basic level.

1.3 PUZZLING STYLIZED FACTS

The following represents a list and brief explanation of the puzzling stylized facts that will be addressed in various parts of the book.[27] More detailed accounts of these facts as well as prominent existing explanations for them will be given in the chapters below. Before proceeding, however, a point of clarification is in order.

Since one or more explanations have been given for all of these puzzling stylized facts, it might be argued that such facts are no longer puzzles. This, however, presumes that these explanations are the correct ones. Unfortunately, there is usually a different model to explain every puzzle. Hence, we have a large number of competing theories with regard to the operation of open economies that utilize a flexible exchange rate system. Also, there are several completely different explanations for some of the puzzles (e.g., the forward discount bias). Consequently, it seems reasonable to suspect that perhaps some if not many of the existing explanations for the puzzles might not be the correct explanations.

1.3.1 Volatile Exchange Rates: Puzzle #1

It has been well known for many years that exchange rates are much more volatile than most (but not all)[28] of the fundamentals that are thought to affect them.[29] Mussa's 'magnification effect' suggests that this volatility arises at least in part because market participants often assume that a recent event (such as a larger than expected monetary growth rate) implies future events of a similar nature. Thus, the spot rate adjusts immediately much more than it would if everyone believed that the event was a one-shot affair. Dornbusch's (1976) exchange rate overshooting hypothesis represents another reasonable explanation for exchange rate volatility. However, the time series behavior of exchange rates exhibits characteristics that are not readily explained by the magnification effect or overshooting hypothesis. This is explained in the discussion of puzzles #2, #3, and #4 immediately below.

1.3.2 Discontinuous Jumps in the Spot Rate: Puzzle #2

Discontinuous jumps in the exchange rate have been observed frequently, especially for the currencies of the European Monetary Union during the last part of the 20th century. Akgiray and Booth (1988), Jorion (1988), Ball and Roma (1993), Bates (1996), and Malz (1996) have successfully modeled these via the use of jump diffusion models. Research along these lines, however, does not provide a theory as to why the random jumps occur.

In some cases the explanation is simply that a new official exchange rate was announced by a central bank within the EMU. On the other hand, in most cases the discontinuous jumps appear to have been caused by free market forces. Dornbusch's (1976) exchange rate overshooting model suggests that the exchange rate will jump discontinuously (in order for UIP to hold at all times) in response to an exogenous monetary shock. However, empirical evidence provided by Eichenbaum and Evans (1995) suggests that the exchange rate reacts slowly to monetary shocks in the United States.

1.3.3 Short Run Drifts and Long Swings: Puzzle #3

The existence of short run drifts in the exchange rate is obvious from most time series graphs of the major exchange rates. Also, the literature dealing with the existence of profits from short term speculation in the FX market (which is discussed in section 1.3.7 below) suggests that there have been predictable drifts or short term trends in the spot rate. Furthermore, as was just mentioned above, Eichenbaum and Evans (1995) have documented that short term drifts in the dollar's value occur in response to monetary shocks. Finally, the empirical work of Engel and Hamilton (1990) suggests that the spectacular rise in the value of the dollar during the first half of the 1980s is an example of a short term drift that developed into a long swing.

1.3.4 The Forward Discount Bias: Puzzle #4

As explained above, the existence of UIP implies that the home minus foreign interest rate differential should (adjusted for any risk premium) predict the future change in the log of the spot rate. If **covered** interest parity also holds, then the forward discount or premium always equals the home minus foreign interest rate differential. Consequently, the current period forward premium or discount should also predict future changes in the spot rate. Furthermore, any percentage change in the forward discount or premium (or in the interest rate differential) should lead to an equal percentage change in the future spot rate. The Forward Discount Bias (FDB) is tied up with the fact that none of these theoretical conclusions appear to hold in reality.

Since consistent and reliable data on the expected future change in spot rate do not exist, scholars use the actual future change in the spot rate as a proxy for them. Froot and Thaler (1990) point out that scores of studies find that: (a) the percentage change in the future spot rate is always less than the percentage change in the current period's forward premium or interest rate differential; and (b) in most cases, an increase in the forward premium, or in the interest rate differential, exerts a **negative** effect on the future change in the spot rate. In other words, when the forward rate rises relative to the current spot rate, then the spot rate falls in the future.

1.3.5 Heteroskedasticity and Volatility Clusters: Puzzle #5

Empirical evidence in Baillie and Bollerslev (1989), Hsieh (1991) and Hogan and Melvin (1994) indicates that frequency distributions for changes in the log of the spot rate exhibit heteroskedasticity when using very high frequency (daily or weekly) data, but not for lower frequency data. Furthermore, the spot rate often exhibits periods of relative tranquility that are interrupted by a brief period during which the exchange rate jumps up and down in a discontinuous and highly volatile manner.

1.3.6 Leptokurtic Frequency Distributions: Puzzle #6

Boothe and Glassman (1987), Akgiray *et al.* (1988), and Hsieh (1991) have shown that frequency distributions for changes in the log of the spot rate consistently have higher peaks and longer tails (implying relatively fewer medium size variations) than in a normal distribution. However, such distributions exhibit this leptokurtosis only for high frequency data such as daily, weekly, or monthly data. For annual data and for most quarterly data, the frequency distributions are approximately normal. It should be noted well that puzzles #5 and #6 are tied up with high frequency data.

1.3.7 Profitable Speculation: Puzzle #7

There are two parts to this puzzle, both of which deal with profits from FX market speculation. First, Dooley and Shafer (1984), Sweeney (1986), Gencay (1999), and Dewachter (2001) show that profits could have been earned in the FX market by speculating on a relatively short term basis via the use of various types of technical analysis. This suggests that short term movements in the exchange rate are, in part, predictable.

Second, Leahy (1995) and Neely (1998) have shown that during the flexible exchange rate era, it would have been profitable for speculators simultaneously to bet: (a) in the short run **against** the FX market activities of the US government, and (b) in the long run **with** the FX market activities of the US government. Most FX market intervention by the Fed and US Treasury tends to 'lean against the wind'. Thus, it follows that when the Fed **buys** FX (in response to what appears to be a decrease in the value of FX relative to its fundamental value) short term speculators could have profited by betting that the FX depreciation would continue, i.e., by **selling** FX. This is consistent with the results given in the paragraph immediately above. Surprisingly, however, the evidence shows that speculators also could have made a profit if they had bet (at the same time) on a **long term** basis **with** the Fed's purchases of FX. This suggests that the spot rate eventually has moved in the direction in which the Fed was nudging it, i.e., back toward its perceived fundamental value.

1.3.8 Extrapolative versus Recursive Expectations: Puzzle #8

As pointed out above, surveys of FX market dealers by Allen and Taylor (1990), Cheung and Chinn (1999a, 1999b, 2001), Cheung, *et al.* (2000), Lui and Mole (1998), and MacDonald and Marsh (1996) show that exchange rate expectations are formulated by most FX market dealers via the use of a combination of fundamentals and technical analysis. In general, short run expectations give essentially no weight to fundamentals, and are **extrapolative** in nature. That is, people expect short run drifts or trends in the spot rate to continue. In the long run, however, the forecasts of most agents are **recursive**, implying a belief that the spot rate will move in the long run toward its fundamental value. This appears to be consistent with puzzles #3, #7, and, perhaps also #4.

1.3.9 Fundamentals in the Short Run versus the Long Run: Puzzle #9

Section 1.2.4 pointed out that empirical models of the exchange rate based on fundamentals typically cannot predict short run and medium run variations in the exchange rate as well as a random walk model. Furthermore, empirical exchange rate models typically have unstable coefficients (when moving from one time interval to another) and often have coefficients with the wrong sign. In other words, in the short run and medium run there appears to be no stable relationship between fundamentals and the exchange rate. Obstfeld and Rogoff (2000) refer to this as the 'exchange rate disconnect puzzle'.

On the other hand, using an MER model, Mark (1995) finds that fundamentals such as income and prices appear to be useful in explaining exchange rates over two to three year time intervals. Other empirical studies that find evidence in support of an importance for one or more fundamentals in the long run are Baxter (1994), Chinn and Meese (1995), Flood and Taylor (1995), and Meredith and Chinn (1998). Also, as stated above, the long run models of Stein (1994), Williamson (1994), Isard and Faruqee (1998), and Clark and MacDonald (1999) appear to hold up fairly well empirically. Thus, the growing consensus is that fundamentals exert a progressively more significant effect on the exchange rate as the time horizon grows. Notice, furthermore, that puzzles #3, #7, #8, and #9 appear to be different aspects of the same underlying dynamics for the exchange rate.

1.3.10 Monetary Shocks and Interest Rates: Puzzle #10

The traditional liquidity preference theory of interest suggests that, in a world with sticky commodity prices, a positive monetary shock will initially cause interest rates to fall. This is referred to as the 'liquidity effect'. However, Stokes and Neuberger (1979) and Melvin (1983) found that the three month response of the nominal interest rate to a monetary shock in the US was positive during the 1970s. That is, a monetary expansion initially caused the interest rate to rise, not fall.

More recent empirical work by Christiano, *et al.* (1996, 1998) indicates that since that time, the short run effect of a monetary shock has been consistent with traditional thinking.[30] That is, a monetary expansion initially causes interest rates to fall in the US. Therefore, a puzzle exists as to why the short run response of the interest rate to a monetary shock was perverse during the 1970s. This puzzle does not appear in the literature.

1.3.11 The Correlation between Saving and Investment: Puzzle #11

As explained above, the open economy intertemporal model suggests that there need not be any correlation between domestic saving and investment. However, the well known work of Feldstein and Horioka (1980) and Feldstein (1983) found that these variables are highly correlated in a positive manner. Subsequent research by many others has confirmed the existence of this puzzle. These empirical results can be interpreted as an indictment of the open economy intertemporal model. That is, the latter concludes that saving and investment will be uncorrelated, but in reality they are highly correlated. Therefore, perhaps the intertemporal model is not a useful theory.

1.3.12 Relatively Low Consumption Correlations: Puzzle #12

According to the open economy intertemporal model, agents will use a nonzero current account to smooth consumption in response to temporary fluctuations in a country's output and income. Thus, home consumption will vary by less than home income. If foreign income and consumption vary very little, but home income varies in a more volatile manner, then (since home consumption varies less than home income) it follows that consumption levels between countries should be more highly correlated

than their income levels. However, empirical studies by Stockman and
Tesar (1990) and Backus, Kehoe, and Kydland (1992) and have found just
the opposite to be true.[31] This, too, can been interpreted to mean that the
intertemporal model is not relevant. That is, it might just be an elegant
theory that does not apply to the real world.

1.3.13 Relatively Small Current Account Imbalances: Puzzle #13

The open economy intertemporal model suggests that countries are apt to
have a nonzero current account (and offsetting net capital flow) on a regular
basis. Among the developed countries there appears to exist a high degree
of international capital mobility, which implies that net capital flows (and
the accompanying nonzero current account balances) could conceivably be
quite large. However, Obstfeld and Rogoff (1995a, 2000) point out that
current account imbalances as a percentage of GDP are much smaller than
one would expect when making reasonable assumptions about parameter
values within an intertemporal model.[32] The puzzle is that we do not know
if the relatively small current account imbalances imply that countries do
not optimize intertemporally or if the intertemporal model is not relevant.

1.3.14 Why Are Real Interest Rates Not Equal?: Puzzle #14

The apparently high degree of international capital mobility that exists
among the leading industrial countries suggests that real rates of interest
should be equalized among them. However, Mishkin (1984), and Cumby
and Mishkin (1986) present empirical evidence that, in general, this has not
occurred.[33] More specifically, the evidence suggests that it essentially never
holds among the G-7 countries for time horizons up to and including one
year.[34] This, too, can be taken as a criticism of the intertemporal approach.

1.3.15 The Huge Volume of FX Market Transactions: Puzzle #15

Economists have been perplexed by the unbelievably large volume of FX
market transactions. Currently, world trade is less than 10 trillion dollars per
year. However, estimates from bank data suggest that FX market
transactions are well over one trillion dollars per day and might be as high
as two trillion dollars per day.[35] Consequently, it follows that most FX
transactions must be tied up with financial transactions, presumably
international capital flows. Unfortunately, there are no published data on
gross capital flows. Governments publish data on the **net** flow of home
funds, and also on the net flow of foreign funds. From such data, it is
difficult to believe that the gross volume of capital flows is so large.

Burnham (1991) suggests three explanations for this puzzle.[36] First, the dollar is often used as an intermediate currency when market participants desire to exchange one less prominent currency for another. For example, suppose that a bank customer wishes to buy a large quantity of Mexican pesos with South Korean won. Doing so directly might move the 'won per peso' exchange rate in an unfavorable direction, because the market for these two currencies is relatively thin. Hence, the FX dealer who handles this transaction is likely to buy dollars with won, and then sell the dollars to buy pesos. Clearly, this doubles the volume of FX transactions involved in going from won to pesos. Note that this explanation for the high volume of FX market transactions need not involve any international capital flows if all transactions take place between residents of the same country.

Second, many FX market dealers are constrained by their employers to certain limits for their FX exposure at the end of each working day. They, however, might not be constrained in this manner during the day. Consequently, if dealers wish to speculate long term in favor of, say, the pound, then they do not buy pounds once and hold them for an extended period. Rather, they buy pounds at the beginning of each working day, and sell them at the end of that day.[37] Obviously, this can greatly increase the volume of FX market transactions. Again, however, such FX market transactions will not generate any international capital flows if the repeated speculative transactions take place between residents of the same country.

A third explanation for the huge volume of FX market transactions is called the 'hot potato' phenomenon. To explain, banks will automatically accept any FX deposits by a good commercial customer, even if the bank does not wish to take a position in this FX. Immediately after accepting the FX, the bank might sell most or all of it, often to 'correspondent banks' with whom the bank has prearranged agreements with regard to such activities. If these correspondent banks do not want the FX, then they will quickly unload part or all of it. This process could conceivably be repeated many times, thereby creating a 'FX transactions multiplier' that might be very large. Unfortunately, at this time no one has any idea about the magnitude of this multiplier. Finally, as before, 'hot potato' activities need not create any international capital flows if the banks who are involved are residents of the same country. In sum, the three explanations for the huge volume of FX market transactions appear to be reasonable. However, the profession awaits further work on this subject.

1.4 PREVIEW

Chapter 2 first uses budget constraints to ascertain every conceivable reason for individual cash-flow imbalances. In the aggregate this gives all possible causes for international payments imbalances. **The result is the important conclusion that a nonzero balance of payments must always be associated with at least one nonclearing market in addition to the FX market.** This leads to alternative theories of the balance of payments, each of which assumes that a different market is out of equilibrium. The chapter explores the important welfare and policy implications of this conclusion. Then it points out the possibility of a new theory of the balance of payments that is tied up with commodity market disequilibrium.

Chapter 3 develops a simple two period open economy Fisherian model, and emphasizes the parallel between the causes of and the gains from **intertemporal** trade and **temporal** trade. It then reviews several implications of the standard intertemporal model. Perhaps the most important one is that a current account surplus is not necessarily preferred to a current account deficit. The chapter explains that this implication arises because the intertemporal model assumes away all of the real world complexities that can make a current account deficit undesirable.

Chapter 4 carefully explores several real world circumstances that reduce the gains from intertemporal trade. These include tariffs and transportation costs, income tax rates that differ between countries, and changes in the relative price of traded versus nontraded goods. The chapter uses these theoretical results to explore the reasons for the existence of: (a) relatively small current account imbalances, puzzle #13, (b) the nonequalization of real interest rates internationally, puzzle #14, and (c) the positive correlation between saving and investment, puzzle #11.

Chapter 5 extends the open economy intertemporal framework to an infinite horizon model. Then it derives the 'fundamental equation for the optimum current account', and uses this to explore the underlying reasons for a nonzero current account. The present conventional wisdom from the work of Frenkel and Razin (1992), Obstfeld and Rogoff (1995a, 1996), and others is that a nonzero current account (and offsetting net capital flow) can arise for two reasons: first, if transitory net income is nonzero (i.e., the so-called 'consumption smoothing' function of the current account), and second, if the home subjective rate of discount does not equal the world real rate of interest (i.e., the so-called 'consumption tilting' aspect of the current account).

However, the original presentation of the intertemporal model by Miller (1968) and more recently by Dluhosch *et al.* (1996, p. 29) emphasizes that a nonzero net capital flow (and offsetting current account) will arise if the world real rate of interest does not equal what the home real interest rate would be in autarky. Chapter 5 reconciles this with the conventional wisdom described in the previous paragraph. Also, it uses the intertemporal model to investigate: (a) the low correlation between consumption levels internationally, puzzle #12, and (b) the 'saving versus investment' puzzle #11 .

Chapter 6 begins the development of a new theory of the balance of payments that is tied up with disequilibrium in the commodity market. This suggests that a balance of payments deficit can be associated with an excess **supply** of home commodities, as when home exports fall exogenously. Such an idea is just the opposite of traditional thinking that associates a payments deficit with an excess **demand** for home commodities. The chapter then explores the policy implications of a balance of payments deficit that exists in conjunction with an excess supply of home commodities. These include the conclusions that: (a) painful reductions in domestic absorption are not needed, and (b) on welfare grounds, tariffs can conceivably be a desirable tool for balance of payments adjustment.

Chapter 7 presents a sticky-price 'loanable funds theory of the exchange rate', sticky-price LFER, that is similar to the exchange rate overshooting model of Dornbusch (1976). However, in the latter the interest rate is always determined via the money market. On the other hand, the sticky-price LFER assumes that the bond market determines the interest rate when the economy is not experiencing full macro-equilibrium. It shows that the dynamics of the interest rate and exchange rate differ significantly if the interest rate is determined in the bond market, rather than in the money market. For example, within the sticky-price LFER the interest rate can initially **rise** in response to a positive monetary shock, as in puzzle #10. Also, Chapter 7 proves that within the sticky-price LFER theory of the exchange rate, fiscal shocks can cause exchange rate overshooting.

Chapters 8 and 9 begin the development of a modern FX market theory of the exchange rate. The model: (a) assumes that the Marshall–Lerner (M–L) condition is not satisfied in the short run but it is satisfied in the long run; this generates an unstable equilibrium that is bounded by two stable equilibria; (b) rigorously integrates long term portfolio capital flows into the FX market model; and (c) allows for extrapolative short run expectations but recursive long run expectations. The model is consistent with many of the puzzling stylized facts listed above.

More specifically, the FX market can jump discontinuously from one stable equilibrium to another (puzzle #2) with each jump initiating a slow drift or short term trend away from the fundamental value for the spot rate, as in puzzle #3. This provides a new explanation for puzzle #1, the high volatility of exchange rates. Since the short run jumps and/or drifts in the spot rate are likely to be reversed eventually, it follows that the jumps or drifts tend to cancel each other in the long run. Consequently, high frequency data will have relatively more large variations in the spot rate than will exist in lower frequency data, as in puzzle #6: leptokurtosis.

A short term drift can conceivably develop into a long term trend or swing (puzzle #3), but eventually such an event sows the seeds of its own destruction by altering the current account in a manner that is certain to 'burst the bubble'. Thus, fundamentals are relatively unimportant in the short run, but they always win in the long run, as in puzzle #9. The probability that a short term drift or trend in the spot rate will continue depends, in part, on the interest rate differential. This allows the model to generate the forward discount bias: puzzle #4. Next, this modern FX market model shows how volatility clusters, and hence heteroskedasticity, can arise via the profit taking activities of speculators. Finally, it explores the conditions under which it will be Muth rational to expect the spot rate to drift away from its fundamental value in the short run.

1.5 SUMMARY

1. The move from fixed exchange rates in the Bretton Woods system to flexible exchange rates induced scholars to switch their focus away from theories of the balance of payments and toward theories of the determination of the exchange rate. However, the extremely poor performance of empirical models of the exchange rate has prompted research to move in new directions, namely: (a) the development of open economy intertemporal models that investigate the composition of the balance of payments, i.e., the determinants of the optimum value for the current account and offsetting net capital flow; (b) examining the institutional aspects of the FX market, with an emphasis on how exchange rate expectations are formed; (c) building and/or testing empirical models of the exchange rate; and (d) testing equilibrium relationships such as UIP and PPP.

2. The primary objective of this book is to provide a fresh perspective on balance of payments and exchange rate theories. This involves: (a) the exploration of all possible reasons for payments imbalances, which, in turn, leads to the conclusion that the latter must always be associated with a disequilibrium in a market in addition to the FX market; it also provides the relevant Walrasian identity for various types of open economy macro-models; (b) the development and exploration of the open economy intertemporal model in a slightly different manner; this generates insights with regard to: (i) the gains from intertemporal trade, (ii) the underlying causes of nonzero current account balances, and (iii) several puzzling stylized facts; (c) an initial attempt to construct a theory of the balance of payments based on disequilibrium in the commodity market; (d) the development of two new theories of the

exchange rate, namely: (i) a sticky-price loanable funds theory, and (ii) a modern FX market theory.

3. A secondary objective of this book is to review and constantly relate existing and new theories to many puzzling stylized facts associated with the workings of the international economy.

4. The many puzzling stylized facts considered here are:

- puzzle #1: the high volatility of the exchange rate;
- puzzle #2: discontinuous jumps in the spot rate;
- puzzle #3: short run drifts and long swings in the spot rate;
- puzzle #4: the forward discount bias;
- puzzle #5: heteroskedasticity and volatility clusters;
- puzzle #6: leptokurtic frequency distributions
- puzzle #7: positive expected profits from FX market speculation;
- puzzle #8: extrapolative versus recursive exchange rate expectations;
- puzzle #9: the importance of fundamentals in the long run, but not in the short run;
- puzzle #10: the short run effect of a monetary shock on the interest rate;
- puzzle #11: the high correlation between saving and investment;
- puzzle #12: low correlations between consumption levels
- puzzle #13: surprisingly small current account imbalances;
- puzzle #14: why real rates of interest are not equalized internationally;
- puzzle #15: the huge volume of FX market transactions.

NOTES

1. See Aldcroft and Oliver (1998, p. 129), and International Monetary Fund (1997, p. 8).
2. Obstfeld and Rogoff (2000) suggest a common explanation for six puzzles in the field of open economy macroeconomics. Four of their puzzles are examined here, namely puzzles #9, #11, #12, and #13 in section 1.3 below.
3. For scholarly accounts of this see Frenkel and Razin (1992), Razin (1995), and Obstfeld and Rogoff (1995a).
4. See Flood (1991), Lyons (1993, 1995a, 1995b), and Frankel, Galli and Giovannini (1995).
5. See Stein (1994), Williamson (1994), Mark (1995), and Clark and MacDonald (1999).
6. Examples of this are: Akgiray and Booth (1988), Baillie and Bollerslev (1989) Bekaert (1995), Boothe and Glassman (1987), Hogan and Melvin (1994), and Hsieh (1991).
7. For references to tests of UIP see Froot and Thaler (1990) and Engel (1996). See Froot and Rogoff (1995) and Rogoff (1996) for the literature on PPP.
8. This section contains a brief sketch of balance of payments and exchange rate theories since World War II. See Taylor (1990, ch. 1) for a more thorough account of the history of balance of payments theory.
9. Cf Robinson (1937).
10. Visser (2000, ch. 2) contains an excellent presentation of IS/LM models for an open economy.

11. Cf. Frenkel and Johnson (1976).
12. These micro-foundations were provided by Johnson (1961). They are reviewed in Chapter 2 below.
13. The details of this are given in Chapter 2 below.
14. Chapter 2 contains a summary of Kuska's critique, and the profession's response to it.
15. Cf. Branson and Halttunen (1979), Branson (1983), and Branson and Henderson (1985). For advanced textbook accounts see Copeland (1994) and Visser (2000).
16. Dornbusch's paper stimulated a huge literature on the subject. Other important papers in this literature are Frenkel and Rodriguez (1982), and Levin (1986).
17. When Meese and Rogoff (1983b) placed constraints on the values for the coefficients in asset market models, the asset market models still failed to out-predict a random walk model for short run and medium run time periods. However, they 'beat' the random walk model for time horizons exceeding one year.
18. See Frenkel and Rose (1995) for a detailed account of (and many references to) empirical studies on exchange rates.
19. The model may or may not include a nontraded good. When it does, the relative price of the traded versus nontraded good is usually referred to as 'the real exchange rate'.
20. If home and foreign tradable goods are not perfect substitutes, then the *ex ante* value for the current account (as given by desired exports minus desired imports plus net international interest earnings and net international transfer payments) will differ from the *ex ante* value for saving minus investment, except when the real exchange rate is at its equilibrium value.
21. See Miller (1968, 1970).
22. See Krugman (1995). Note, however, that in recent years several scholars have begun to explore the effects of monetary policy within an intertemporal open economy framework. Cf. Sarno (2001).
23. Cf. Burnham (1991) and Lyons (1995a, 1997).
24. See Allen and Taylor (1990), Cheung and Chinn (1999a, 1999b, 2001), Cheung, Chinn, and Marsh (2000), Lui and Mole (1998), and MacDonald and Marsh (1996).
25. Cf. Akgiray, Booth, and Seifert (1988), Baillie and Bollerslev (1989), Bekaert (1995), Boothe and Glassman (1987), Engel (1994), and Hsieh (1991).
26. See Akgiray and Booth (1988), Ball and Roma (1993), Bates (1996), Dewachter (2001), Jorion (1988), and Malz (1996).
27. As mentioned above, Obstfeld and Rogoff (2000) examine six puzzles in open economy macroeconomics. Lewis (1995) contains another list of puzzles.
28. The exception is 'interest rates'.
29. See Mussa (1979) and MacDonald (1988)
30. Their empirical work begins in 1975 and they make no attempt to reproduce the results of Stokes and Neuberger (1979) and Melvin (1983).
31. Baxter (1995) provides a careful account of and many references to this subject.
32. Edwards (2001) summarizes the literature on this subject.
33. Darby (1986), and Koraczyk (1985) offer several explanations for this.
34. Note that the recent empirical work of Fujii and Chinn (2000) suggests that real interest rate parity does better for five and ten year time horizons
35. Cf. Bank for International Settlements (1998).
36. Lyons (1995a, 1997) develops the third explanation given in the text below.
37. This represents a simplified version of what Burnham describes. His scenario has the speculators also utilizing the forward market. Cheung and Chinn (1999b, p. 4) define the activities reported above in the text as 'jobbing' and indicate that jobbing represents 23 percent of the activities of FX dealers in the United States.

2. Balance of payments theory

2.1 INTRODUCTION

Chapter 1 pointed out that in the early 1970s, the economics profession was puzzled by the fact that the monetary approach to the balance of payments, MBP, and the monetary approach to exchange rates, MER, generated conclusions that were precisely the opposite of the conventional wisdom at that time. In particular, the standard FX market approach concluded that: (a) an increase in home income raises imports and worsens the balance of payments, or depreciates home money; (b) a higher domestic rate of interest improves the home capital account and, hence, improves the balance of payments or appreciates home money; and (c) higher home prices decrease exports, increase imports, and worsen the balance of payments or depreciate home money.

On the other hand, the MBP and MER suggest just the opposite, namely that: (a) an increase in home income raises the demand for money which, in turn, generates either a balance of payments surplus or an appreciation of home money; (b) higher home interest rates reduce the demand for money and create either a balance of payments deficit or a depreciation of home money; and (c) an increase in home prices reduces the real money supply, thereby creating an excess demand for money which generates a balance of payments surplus or appreciation of home money.

The controversy and confusion that the monetary approach created culminated in Kuska's (1978, 1982) indictment of Keynesian models of the balance of payments, i.e., the open economy IS/LM models of Mundell (1962) and Fleming (1962). Among other things, Kuska pointed out that Keynesian models generate a nonzero balance of payments, BP, if the IS curve (which depicts commodity market equilibrium) intersects the LM curve (which indicates money market equilibrium) at an interest rate and income that are not on the BP = 0 curve, as at points A or B in Figure 1.1 above.

However, the MBP (which Kuska took to be universally true) concludes that the balance of payments will be zero if the money market clears, i.e., if the economy is on its LM curve. Thus, he concluded that since the Keynesian models simultaneously have money market equilibrium and a nonzero balance of payments, they contain a logical contradiction. This stimulated papers by Buiter and Eaton (1981), Deardorff (1981), and Miller (1981, 1986a, 1986b).[1]

Section 2.2 uses budget constraints for each economic unit to obtain an identity that illustrates all possible reasons for an economic unit's cash-flow imbalances. Then section 2.3 sums this over all agents to obtain an open economy Walrasian identity that dictates the structure of open economy macro-models that utilize a period framework. **The most important idea is that a nonzero balance of payments cannot exist unless at least one market (in addition to the FX market) is out of equilibrium.**

Section 2.4 reviews the structure of open economy stock-flow models as well as asset market models, and shows that they generate the same conclusion with regard to the balance of payments and market disequilibrium. Then section 2.5 explores several important theoretical and policy implications of this conclusion. These include: (a) international payments imbalances have a deadweight loss associated with them, and the nature of this loss is similar for payments surpluses and payments deficits; (b) exogenous shocks such as economic growth, fiscal policy, and monetary policy can never generate a nonzero balance of payments within a full macro-equilibrium model; and (c) government policies to correct a balance of payments deficit or surplus should focus on the market that is out of equilibrium.

Next section 2.6 explains three alternative theories of the balance of payments. Each explicitly or implicitly assumes a different market to be out of equilibrium. These include the monetary approach, the so-called Keynesian approach, and a yet to be developed commodity market approach to the balance of payments. Section 2.7 explores several definitions of 'the excess supply of money', and the chapter ends with a summary in section 2.8.

2.2 CASH-FLOW IMBALANCES

2.2.1 Harry Johnson's Micro-Foundations

The first attempt to develop a microfoundation for international payments imbalances was apparently that of Harry G. Johnson (1961), whose ideas continue be very influential. They provide the micro-foundation for the widely accepted MBP and MER. Johnson pointed out that receipts of home residents from home residents, $(Rec)_h$, are always equal to payments by home residents to home residents, $(Pay)_h$, as in the first part of (2.1a) below. Also, by definition, receipts of home residents from foreigners, $(Rec)_f$, minus payments by home residents to foreigners, $(Pay)_f$, are the home balance of payments, BP, as in the second part of (2.1a). Summing both portions of (2.1a) indicates that the home balance of payments equals the difference between total home receipts, *Rec*, and total home payments, *Pay*, as in (2.1b).

$$(Rec)_h - (Pay)_h \equiv 0 \quad (Rec)_f - (Pay)_f \equiv BP \qquad (2.1a)$$

$$BP \equiv [(Rec)_h + (Rec)_f - (Pay)_h - (Pay)_f] \equiv Rec - Pay \qquad (2.1b)$$

$$Rec - Pay \equiv -X_M \qquad (2.1c)$$

Johnson reasoned that $(Rec - Pay)$ always equals minus the *ex ante* **beginning** of the period home excess supply of money, $-X_M$ in (2.1c), where X_M is defined as (the initial money supply) minus (the amount of money that people want to hold at the end of the time period). Allegedly, (2.1c) holds because home agents will not give up or accept money unless they are unhappy with their initial money balances. With this logic, a positive excess supply of home money, $X_M > 0$ in (2.1c), induces home agents to buy more internationally than they sell, $(Rec - Pay) < 0$, thereby generating a balance of payments deficit. Alternatively, an excess demand for money, $X_M < 0$ in (2.1c), prompts agents to deliberately sell more than they buy, $(Rec - Pay) > 0$. In the process, a balance of payments surplus arises. This logic is very persuasive, and it continues to be widely accepted, even though it is flawed.

2.2.2 Individual Cash-Flow Imbalances

Assume that the jth agent has a period framework *ex ante* budget constraint of the form:[2]

$$\Sigma \, v_i + v_m \equiv -tr_j - rA_j(-1) \qquad i = 1 \ldots m-1 \qquad (2.2a)$$

where:

- each of the v_i terms presents the agent j's *ex ante* excess supply, $s_i - d_i$, of the ith nonmonetary good;
- v_m is the *j*th agent's *ex ante* excess supply of money, $s_m - d_m$;
- tr_j is agent *j*'s anticipated net transfer payments, with $tr_j > 0$ for net receipts;
- $rA_j(-1)$ represents anticipated net interest earnings, with $A_j(-1)$ being the lagged value for the *j*th agent's net asset position, and r is the interest rate

Identity (2.2a) stipulates that any net excess of planned purchases over planned sales for nonmonetary goods, $\Sigma \, v_i < 0$, must always equal the *ex ante* excess supply of money, $v_m > 0$, if anticipated net interest and transfer payments are zero.

Also, within a period framework each agent faces an *ex post* budget constraint of the form:

$$\Sigma \underline{v}_i \equiv \Delta \underline{m}_j - \underline{tr}_j - \underline{rA}_j(-1) \qquad (2.2b)$$

where: (a) $\underline{v}_i = \underline{s}_i - \underline{d}_i$ is *ex post* or actual sales minus actual purchases of nonmonetary good i, (b) $\underline{tr}_j$ and $\underline{rA}_j(-1)$ are actual transfer payments and net interest income, and (c) $\Delta \underline{m}_j$ represents the jth agent's *ex post* cash flow surplus ($\Delta \underline{m}_j > 0$) or deficit ($\Delta \underline{m}_j < 0$). Identity (2.2b) tells us that agent j's actual purchases can exceed actual sales for nonmonetary goods, $\Sigma \underline{v}_i < 0$, only if there is an outflow of money, $\Delta \underline{m}_j < 0$, and/or a net receipt of gifts and/or interest earnings.

On the assumption that actual transfer and interest flows always equal their anticipated values, subtracting (2.2b) from (2.2a) yields the very useful identity

$$\Sigma [v_i - \underline{v}_i] + v_m \equiv -\Delta \underline{m}_j \qquad (2.2c)$$

which encompasses all possible reasons for cash flow imbalances.[3] First, a cash flow deficit, $\Delta \underline{m}_j < 0$, can arise even though all actual net nonmonetary transactions equal what were planned (i.e., $[v_i - \underline{v}_i] = 0$ for all i) provided that agent j initially has an *ex ante* excess supply of money, $v_m > 0$. Similarly, a cash flow surplus, $\Delta \underline{m}_j > 0$ in (2.2c), can arise because an economic unit initially has an *ex ante* excess demand for money, $v_m < 0$. Obviously, these cases relate to Harry Johnson's microfoundations for international payments imbalances.

On the other hand, an agent might be unable to sell as much of one or more nonmonetary goods as planned, i.e., $\Sigma[v_i - \underline{v}_i] > 0$. For example, let 'c' represent commodities, and assume that: (a) a firm's initial money balances are optimal, so that $v_m = 0$; (b) actual purchases and sales are equal for all goods other than commodities, and (c) the firm plans to sell 'x' commodity units more than it plans to buy; that is $v_c = x$;[4] however, (d) the firm ends up selling only $(x - \varepsilon)$ commodity units more than it buys, i.e., actual net sales fall short of planned net sales by $\varepsilon > 0$. In this case, $\underline{v}_c = x - \varepsilon$, and (2.2c) becomes

$$[v_c - \underline{v}_c] + 0 \equiv [x - x + \varepsilon] \equiv -\Delta \underline{m}_j > 0 \qquad (2.2d)$$

With $\varepsilon > 0$, the firm must reduce its money balances below their initially optimal level by the magnitude of the shortfall in sales. In more formal terminology, the firm's **secondary** demand for money is less than its initial or **primary** demand for money via a **spillover effect**. In plain words, the firm will draw down its money balances in order to pay its bills.

Clearly then, a cash flow deficit can occur even though money balances are initially at their optimal level. In general, such a situation might induce the firm to borrow a portion of the funds it needs, rather than financing the cash flow shortfall completely out of money balances. However, none of the important conclusions reached below are affected by following the 'buffer-stock' approach to monetary theory and assuming that **all** spillover effects go entirely to the money market.[5]

Other causes of cash flow deficits include: (a) some or all of the funds from a planned loan are not obtained, (b) an agent is unable to sell some assets, and (c) an agent has unexpected expenditures that require the drawing down of money balances. Conversely, a cash flow surplus can arise because of: (a) an initial *ex ante* excess demand for money, as in Harry Johnson's microfoundations, (b) the inability to purchase as much of one or more nonmonetary goods as was planned, or (c) actual sales of one or more nonmonetary goods are larger than planned sales.

2.3 AN OPEN ECONOMY WALRASIAN IDENTITY WITHIN A PERIOD MODEL

Define V_i as the sum of the *ex ante* v_i over all agents within an economy, and $\underline{V}_i$ as the sum of the *ex post* $\underline{v}_i$ over all agents. If there are 'm' goods (with $i = 1 \ldots m-1$ nonmonetary goods), and 'n' economic units, then (2.2c) can be summed over all economic units within an economy to obtain an open economy Walrasian identity within a period framework.

$$\Sigma \, [V_i - \underline{V}_i] + V_M \equiv - \Sigma \, \Delta \underline{m}_j \quad \{\, i = 1 \ldots m-1; \; j = 1 \ldots n \,\} \quad (2.3a)$$

V_i represents the *ex ante* supply minus demand for good i by home residents. In an open economy it does not equal the total market *ex ante* excess supply of good i, except for nontraded goods. V_M is total home supply minus home demand for money. On the assumption that agents hold only the money of their country (i.e., there is no currency substitution) it follows that V_M also represents the total market *ex ante* excess supply of home money. $\underline{V}_i$ is *ex post* home sales minus home purchases of good i.

The right hand side, rhs, of (2.3a) is minus the *ex post* balance of payments. Consequently, the *ex post* balance of payments can be in deficit, $- \Sigma \, \Delta \underline{m}_j > 0$, if: (a) there is initially an *ex ante* excess supply of money by home agents, $V_M > 0$, or (b) home agents cannot sell all the nonmonetary goods that they desire, or (c) home agents unexpectedly buy more nonmonetary goods than they planned.

In cases (b) and (c) we have $\Sigma [V_i - \underline{V}_i] > 0$ in (2.3a). For example, let V_A represent net planned sales of nonmonetary financial assets, or bonds, and assume that home agents plan to have net sales of bonds with a value of 20, i.e., $V_A = +20$. If, however, actual net sales of bonds are only 18, i.e., $\underline{V}_A = +18$, then home agents experience a shortfall of incoming funds, i.e., $V_A - \underline{V}_A = +2$. This will force them to draw down their money balances by 2.[6] In the aggregate, a country's money balances can decrease only via an *ex post* balance of payments deficit, $- \Sigma \Delta \underline{m}_j = +2$.

Identity (2.3a) contains the *ex post* balance of payments on the rhs, but open economy macro-models deal with the *ex ante* balance of payments. Therefore, in order to obtain a Walrasian identity that is useful for open economy model building, it is necessary to make an assumption with regard to the relationship between the *ex ante* and the *ex post* balance of payments.

The analysis here follows the vast majority of open economy macro-models by assuming that *ex ante* international transactions are demand determined. Also, it assumes that all *ex ante* international transactions are always realized *ex post*. That is, the *ex post* balance of payments, $\Sigma \Delta \underline{m}_j$ in (2.3a), always equals the *ex ante* balance of payments, BP. The latter is defined as [foreign *ex ante* demand for home exports plus their *ex ante* cumulative (over one time interval) flow demand for home assets] minus [home agents' *ex ante* demand for imports plus their *ex ante* cumulative (over one time interval) flow demand for foreign assets].

Next, assume that there are only three goods, namely: commodities, C, bonds, A, and money, M.[7] Thus, (2.3a) becomes (2.3b).

$$[V_C - \underline{V}_C] + [V_A - \underline{V}_A] + V_M \equiv - BP \qquad (2.3b)$$

$$V_C + V_A + V_M \equiv - Tr - rA(-1) \qquad (2.3c)$$

The $\underline{V}_C$ term is the *ex post* value for net exports, and, with our assumptions, it also represents *ex ante* net exports, NX. Similarly, $\underline{V}_A$ represents the *ex post* and *ex ante* private net international capital flow, KF.

It will prove useful later to add $NX + KF$ to both sides of (2.3b) in order to obtain (2.3c).[8] Identity (2.3c) is the home country's aggregate budget constraint. It represents the sum (over all agents) of the individual *ex ante* budget constraints as given by (2.2a). Each term on the left hand side, lhs, of (2.3c) is the *ex ante* total home supply minus home demand for that good. In a closed economy these must sum to zero, because the rhs of (2.3c) will be zero.

However, in an open economy net interest and net transfer payments can be nonzero. Consequently, the V_i in (2.3c) need not sum to zero. Also, in a closed economy, each term on the lhs of (2.3c) represents the *ex ante* total market excess supply of good *i*. However, in an open economy this (in general) is not true, because the *ex ante* total market excess supply of any good '*i*' is determined by V_i plus or minus the *ex ante* value for net international transactions in this good.

If we substitute *ex ante* net exports, *NX*, for the *ex post* value of net international transactions in commodities, $\underline{V_C}$, and substitute *ex ante* net capital flows, *KF*, for $\underline{V_A}$ in (2.3b), the result is

$$[V_C - NX] + [V_A - KF] + V_M \equiv - BP \qquad (2.3d)$$

Each term of the lhs of (2.3d) amounts to the **ex ante total market excess supply** for good *i*, represented here by X_i, with '*i*' equal to *C* for commodities, *A* for bonds, and *M* for money. Thus, we can rewrite (2.3d) as (2.4a) below.[9] If all planned international transactions generate an *ex ante* demand or supply for FX, then the *ex ante* balance of payments is also the *ex ante* excess supply of foreign exchange, X_{FX}, and (2.4a) can be rewritten as (2.4b).

$$X_C + X_A + X_M \equiv - BP \qquad (2.4a)$$

$$X_C + X_A + X_M + X_{FX} \equiv 0 \qquad (2.4b)$$

These identities represent the relevant Walrasian identity within a three good open economy period model for a small economy. In addition, (2.3d) is an equivalent Walrasian identity. Clearly, (2.4b) is exactly as one would expect, namely that the sum of all the *ex ante* excess supplies must equal zero. The important point here is that an open economy Walrasian identity must include the FX market.

2.4 THE STRUCTURE OF STOCK-FLOW AND ASSET MARKET MODELS

Open economy macro-models of the traditional variety often utilize a stock-flow framework. Within a stock-flow framework each agent has two budget constraints: (a) one that constrains the **flow** of income and other **flow** sources of funds to equal the sum of the **flow** demands for commodities and assets; and (b) one that constrains the sum of all **stock** demands for assets to equal the **stock** of existing wealth. The flow and stock aggregate budget constraints can be used to generate two open economy Walrasian identities within a stock-flow framework, one involving flows and the other involving stocks.[10]

Let FX_i represent the *ex ante* total market excess supply of good i in **flow** terms. For example, the *ex ante* flow excess supply of commodities, FX_C, equals home output minus absorption $(C + I + G)$ minus net exports, *NX*. Also, let SX_i represent the *ex ante* total market excess supply of asset i in **stock** terms. In a model with three goods (commodities, bonds, and money) the two open economy Walrasian identities are:

$$FX_C + FX_A + FX_M \equiv -[NX + rA(-1) + Tr] + FKF \equiv -FBP \quad (2.5a)$$

$$SX_A + SX_M \equiv -SKF \quad (2.5b)$$

where *FBP* is the flow balance of payments, and the *SKF* and *FKF* terms refer to the 'stock-adjustment' net capital flow, and the 'pure flow' component of net capital flows, respectively.

To explain, Miller and Whitman (1970, 1972, and 1973) use the work of Willett and Forte (1969) who point out that if: (a) optimal *ex ante* home holdings of foreign bonds, A^*, equal some optimum portfolio ratio, χ, multiplied by total home wealth, W, as in (2.6a); then (b) the *ex ante* change in home demand for foreign assets is given by the total derivative of A^* with respect to time, as in (2.6b).

$$A^* = \chi W \quad (2.6a)$$

$$dA^*/dt = \chi \, dW/dt + W \, d\chi/dt \quad (2.6b)$$

The $W \, d\chi/dt$ term represents a 'stock-adjustment' capital flow associated with variations in the optimum portfolio ratio. This type of capital flow is inherently temporary in nature, because it ends when existing wealth is reallocated optimally. If $W \, d\chi/dt$ is combined with a similar term for the foreign country, then the result is the stock-adjustment net capital flow, *SKF*, in (2.5b).

On the other hand, the $\chi dW/dt$ term in (2.6b) is tied up with the fact that home agents allocate a portion of any new saving to foreign bonds. If this is combined with a similar term for the foreign country, then the result is the 'pure-flow' net capital flow, *FKF*, in (2.5a). This component of total capital flows is inherently persistent provided that saving occurs in each period. When *FKF* is added to the current account balance on the rhs of (2.5a), this yields the 'flow balance of payments', *FBP*.

Walrasian identities (2.5a) and (2.5b) govern the structure of one country stock-flow models. On the other hand (2.5b) alone governs the structure of one country asset market models of the balance of payments[11] or exchange rate. In such models, the balance of payments and excess supply of FX is determined solely by the stock-adjustment capital flow, *SKF*, because of the assumption that pure flow magnitudes (such as the current account and *FKF*) are miniscule compared to *SKF*.

A stock identity similar to (2.5b) holds for the foreign country, as in (2.7a). Since $SKF \equiv -SKF^*$, it follows that (2.7a) and (2.5b) yield (2.7b).[12] This represents the relevant open economy Walrasian identity in two country asset market models of the balance of payments or exchange rate.

$$SX_{A^*} + SX_{M^*} \equiv -SKF^* \qquad (2.7a)$$

$$SX_A + SX_M + SX_{A^*} + SX_{M^*} \equiv 0 \qquad (2.7b)$$

The overall balance of payments within a stock-flow framework is the sum of the flow balance of payments, *FBP* in (2.5a), and the stock-adjustment net capital flow in (2.5b), multiplied by a term Λ. The latter represents that portion of any difference between the stock supplies and stock demands for assets that generates bids to buy or sell in the asset market within one time interval.[13] This converts the stock term *SKF* into a flow term, ΛSKF, that can be meaningfully added to the flow balance of payments. Using this notation, (2.5a) and (2.5b) can be summed to obtain

$$FX_C + [FX_A + \Lambda SX_A] + [FX_M + \Lambda SX_M] \equiv -FBP - \Lambda SKF \qquad (2.8)$$

Clearly, this generates the main conclusion reached via the use of the open economy Walrasian identity within a period model, (2.4a), namely that a nonzero balance of payments must always be accompanied by a disequilibrium in at least one market in addition to the FX market. However, (2.8) makes it clear that asset market equilibrium within a stock-flow framework (wherein the SX_i stock excess supplies have been converted to hybrid flows via the Λ term) means that any nonzero FX_i is offset by a nonzero ΛSX_i. **Furthermore, from (2.8), a zero balance of payments means that the flow balance of payments is offset by the net stock-adjustment capital flow (adjusted for Λ).**

2.5 THEORETICAL AND POLICY IMPLICATIONS

Identity (2.4b) tells us that a nonzero *ex ante* balance of payments, $X_{FX} \neq 0$, must always be accompanied by disequilibrium in at least one market in addition to the FX market. This conclusion is the equivalent of the conclusion that individual cash flow imbalances can arise either because: (a) agents are initially unhappy with their money balances, which in the aggregate yields $X_M \neq 0$ in (2.4b); or (b) agents do not buy or sell all that they had planned of one or more nonmonetary goods, which in the aggregate gives a nonzero value for X_C and/or X_A in (2.4b).

The fact that a nonzero balance of payments always involves market disequilibria has important welfare implications, as well as implications for open economy macro-economic theory and policy. Historically, governments typically have shown much less concern for a balance of payments surplus than for a payments deficit. This is because the latter drains the central bank's stock of international reserves, and/or is taken to imply that the home country is not competitive in world markets, thereby creating a political embarrassment.

However, it is well known that a market disequilibrium decreases the sum of total consumers' and sellers' surpluses. Logically, any output that is less than the competitive equilibrium output yields a marginal social benefit that exceeds the marginal social cost. Conversely, any output that exceeds the competitive equilibrium output gives a marginal social benefit that is less than the marginal social cost. In both cases, the market disequilibrium generates a deadweight loss.

Since a nonzero excess supply of FX is always accompanied by a disequilibrium in another market, it follows that **the general level of wellbeing within a country is decreased when the balance of payments is nonzero. This applies to both payments surpluses and payments deficits.** Consequently, there are good reasons for government policies to eliminate payments imbalances in addition to those associated with the loss of international reserves and/or the political embarrassment associated with payments deficits.

Much scholarly research has been devoted to how the balance of payments is affected by monetary policy, fiscal policy,[14] and/or by economic growth.[15] However, the open economy Walrasian identity tells us that the balance of payments effects from any shock will be zero if all markets clear. **Consequently, monetary policy, fiscal policy, and/or economic growth will have no effect on the balance of payments within a full macro-equilibrium framework.**

All theoretical work on this subject has (usually implicitly) assumed that a particular market does not clear, and that a nonzero balance of payments is tied up with this disequilibrium. In such cases, all theoretical conclusions about how an exogenous shock affects the balance of payments amount to conclusions about how that shock affects the magnitude of the disequilibrium in the nonclearing market.

These important ideas must be explored further. From the aggregate budget constraint, (2.3c), it follows that any **domestic** shock (which, by definition, does not directly affect the rhs of (2.3c), the aggregate budget constraint) must initially alter two or more the V_i such that the sum of the V_i remains unchanged. Consequently, from the Walrasian identity (2.3d) this means that the initial impact of a **domestic** shock on the *ex ante* balance of payments must always be zero. Such a shock can create a nonzero balance of payments only if: (a) it induces variations in endogenous variables (such as prices, interest rates, etc.) that alter the *ex ante* balance of payments; and then (b) transactions occur when one or more markets (in addition to the FX market) are out of equilibrium.

On the other hand, an exogenous shock to any component of the balance of payments on the rhs of (2.4a) can simultaneously create one or more market disequilibria on the lhs of this identity. For example, if foreign *ex ante* demand for home exports decreases exogenously, then the *ex ante* value for the balance of payments falls. Such an event also creates an excess supply of the home commodity, $X_c > 0$ in (2.4a). Alternatively, if foreign demand for home bonds increases exogenously, this creates a positive *ex ante* balance of payments and an excess demand for home bonds, $X_A < 0$, in (2.4a).

In reality instantaneous market clearing cannot possibly exist in all markets. Thus, it follows that the severity of payments imbalances in response to exogenous shocks will be a negative function of the speed with which markets clear. This, in turn, suggests that economies are likely to be plagued by balance of payments problems if their laws and institutions encourage price rigidities, inhibit the free market determination of interest rates or other asset prices, and/or place controls on the movement of capital and other resources.

For example, if government policies prevent domestic interest rates from rising sufficiently to clear the home bond (or credit) market, then such an economy is likely to experience chronic payments **deficits** that are accompanied by excess **supplies** of the home bond. Consequently, it follows that, in general, an excellent government policy toward international payments imbalances is to create an environment for efficient, rapidly clearing markets throughout the economy. Furthermore, if it is clear which market disequilibrium is associated with a nonzero balance of payments, then it seems logical that government balance of payments adjustment policies should focus on this nonclearing market.

2.6 ALTERNATIVE THEORIES OF THE BALANCE OF PAYMENTS

2.6.1 Introduction

For review, the open economy Walrasian identity (2.4a) requires that a nonzero *ex ante* balance of payments (or FX market disequilibrium) always be accompanied by at least one other nonclearing market. Alternative theories of the balance of payments differ according to which market is assumed not to clear when a payments imbalance exists. This section explains three alternatives, namely: (a) the MBP, (b) Mundell/Fleming models that can be interpreted as implicitly assuming that the bond market does not clear, and (c) the yet to be developed 'commodity market' disequilibrium theory of the balance of payments.

Although model builders can arbitrarily assume that any market is out of equilibrium, presumably the relevant nonclearing market should depend on the characteristics of the country whose international payments imbalances are being modeled. For example, if a country has poorly functioning asset markets, with government controls on interest rates and/or capital flows, then alternative (b) above might be most appropriate. On the other hand, if asset markets function well, but commodity prices are very sticky in the short run, then perhaps a commodity market approach, alternative (c), is best.

Another consideration might be the type and frequency of shocks typically experienced by a country. For example, if a central bank continually pumps up the nominal money supply, and always sterilizes any effects of a nonzero balance of payments on the monetary base, then perhaps a nonclearing money market is most likely. On the other hand, if a country often experiences shocks to the demand for its exports, then the assumption of a nonclearing commodity market might be most appropriate.

Casual empiricism suggests that during the Bretton Woods era: (a) countries frequently experienced a nonzero balance of payments, and (b) payments imbalances of the same sign were often persistent. When combined with the conclusion that a nonzero balance of payments must be associated with a least one nonclearing market, these facts suggest that: (a) markets are often out of equilibrium when transactions take place, and (b) market disequilibria can be persistent.

For those (including this author) who find it difficult to believe that prices and/or other endogenous variables do not, in general, move to clear most markets relatively quickly, it is important to obtain a proper perspective on these inferences. The length of time it takes a market to adjust to an exogenous shock is (in itself) completely irrelevant. The speed of adjustment must be compared with the frequency of shocks to that market.

For example, assume that market j always clears within a fraction, $1/n$, of one time interval, with n being much larger than unity. If market j is disturbed by a shock only once per time period, then it is probably reasonable to model market j as though it is always in equilibrium. On the other hand, if this market faces exogenous shocks 'k' times per period, and if 'k' is much larger than 'n', then it is likely that the market is always in a state of disequilibrium, even though it is continually moving toward a new equilibrium. In sum, sluggish inefficient markets are not needed to generate persistent market disequilibria. All that is needed is a sufficiently high relative frequency for exogenous shocks.

Furthermore, a proper perspective on the idea of persistent commodity market equilibrium can be obtained if we drop the assumption of only one commodity, and realize that in reality there are thousands of different types of commodities. In this case, it is possible for an exogenous shock to a particular commodity market to be transmitted (via linkage and multiplier effects) slowly to other types of commodity markets. Consequently, even though each of the commodity markets might clear very quickly, there can conceivably be a persistent disequilibrium if we consider the aggregate supply versus aggregate demand for commodities.

2.6.2 The Monetary Approach to the Balance of Payments: MBP

The monetary approach to the balance of payments, MBP, can be constructed within a period framework, a stock/flow framework, or within an asset market framework. The analysis here utilizes a period framework for a small open economy, whose structure is governed by (2.4a). The MBP requires that all nonmonetary markets clear quickly, as would occur if all prices (including those of financial assets) are perfectly flexible.

Equivalently, the MBP becomes relevant in a three good model if: (a) the home country is small compared to the rest of the world, and (b) the home commodity and bond are perfect substitutes for their foreign counterparts. These assumptions mean that the rest of the world automatically buys or sells whatever quantities of commodities or bonds that are needed to clear the home markets for these goods, i.e., $V_C - NX \equiv 0$ $\equiv V_A - KF$ in (2.3d). If all nonmonetary markets clear quickly, then (2.3d) becomes simply (2.9a).

$$V_M \equiv - BP \tag{2.9a}$$

$$X_M \equiv - BP \equiv - \Delta R \tag{2.9b}$$

In other words, if commodity market and bond market excess supplies in (2.4a) are always zero, then (2.4a) reduces to (2.9a), which is equivalent to (2.9b), where ΔR is the current period change in international reserves. Note that (2.9a) and (2.9b) are equivalent, because V_M always equals X_M here.[16] Both (2.9a) and (2.9b) reflect Harry Johnson's micro-foundations for payments imbalances. That is, the **beginning** of period *ex ante* excess supply of money, X_M or V_M, determines the *ex ante* balance of payments.

It is now possible to explain why the MBP generates counter-intuitive conclusions, such as the fact that the home balance of payments **improves** if the home interest rate **falls** or the home price level **increases**. For simplicity, assume that initially all markets are in equilibrium, and that $V_C = 0 = V_A$. This means that net exports, NX, and net capital flows, KF, are also zero initially. Also, assume that net international transfer payments and net interest earnings are constant in order to rewrite the home budget constraint (2.3c) in total differential form as (2.10a).

$$dV_C + dV_A + dV_M \equiv 0 \qquad (2.10a)$$
$$(-) \qquad (+) \qquad (-)$$

$$dNX + dKF + dX_M \equiv 0 \qquad (2.10b)$$
$$(-) \qquad (+) \qquad (-)$$

A lower home interest rate will stimulate money demand and, thereby create an excess demand for money, $dV_M < 0$ in (2.10a), as indicated by the (−) sign under dV_M. Since V_M always equals X_M, it follows that dX_M in (2.10b) is negative by the same magnitude. Also, a lower interest rate will increase home demand for home commodities, $dV_C < 0$ in (2.10a). If home and foreign commodities are identical and if the home country is small, then this automatically causes net exports, NX, to decrease equally. This is indicated in (2.10b) by the minus sign under dNX. Furthermore, a decrease in the home interest rate will increase the quantity of home bonds supplied and decrease the quantity of bonds demanded by home residents, thereby causing $dV_A > 0$ in (2.10a). This, in turn, instantaneously improves net capital flows by an equal amount, $dKF = dV_A > 0$.

The signs of the terms in (2.10b) imply that the magnitude of the induced improvement in the capital account dominates the deterioration in net exports. Consequently, the home *ex ante* balance of payments **improves** when the home interest rate **decreases** temporarily. (Any drop in the home interest rate exists only momentarily because home and foreign bonds are perfect substitutes. Thus, they must have the same interest rate in equilibrium.) In sum, the home balance of payments improves when the home interest rate decreases, because of the (implicit) assumption that foreigners will automatically buy the resulting excess supply of home bonds.

Similarly, within the small country MBP, an increase in the home price level **improves** the home balance of payments, because of the assumption that the rest of the world will automatically buy or sell any amount of commodities that home agents desire. For example, assume that an exogenous increase in the home price level generates an increase in home supply and a decrease in home demand for commodities. This generates an excess supply of home commodities, $dVc > 0$ in (2.11a). Thus, home net exports instantaneously improve by an equal amount in (2.11b). Also, a higher home price level reduces the home real money supply, thereby creating an excess demand for money, $dVm < 0$ in (2.11a) and $dXm < 0$ in (2.11b). These changes are indicated by the signs under each variable.

$$dV_C + dV_A + dV_M \equiv 0 \qquad\qquad (2.11a)$$
$$\;(+) \quad\; (?) \quad\;\; (-)$$

$$dNX + dKF + dX_M \equiv 0 \qquad\qquad (2.11b)$$
$$\;(+) \quad\;\; (?) \quad\;\; (-)$$

The effect of a higher home price level on the home bond market and net capital flow does not matter. The home *ex ante* balance of payments improves regardless of the sign of dV_A and dKF. To see this, assume that an increase in the home price level creates a positive excess supply of bonds. Foreigners will automatically buy this excess supply of home bonds, thereby improving the net capital flow by an equal amount. Thus, in this case, both net exports and net capital flows increase, and this ensures that the balance of payments improves when the home price level rises.

Alternatively, assume that an increase in the home price level creates an excess demand for home bonds, i.e., a negative excess supply. In this case, foreigners will automatically sell bonds to home agents, thereby worsening the home capital account. In this case, the order of the signs in (2.11b) would be $(+)$, $(-)$, $(-)$. Since all of the terms in (2.11b) must sum to zero, it follows that the improvement in net exports dominates the deterioration in net capital flows. Hence, again, the home balance of payments improves when the home price level rises (temporarily).[17]

In sum, within a **small** country model, the counter-intuitive conclusions reached by the MBP arise because of the implicit assumption that home commodities and bonds are perfect substitutes for their foreign counterparts. It remains to be seen as to whether such an assumption is approximated in reality. The relevance of the MBP for a **large** country, on the other hand, depends on the degree of flexibility of prices and interest rates within the economy, which affect how fast the commodity and bond markets clear.

2.6.3 The Keynesian Approach to the Balance of Payments: KBP

The profession has used the term 'Keynesian approach to the balance of payments' to refer to any model that contains an equation defining the balance of payments as equal to the current account (usually represented simply by exports minus imports) plus net private capital flows. We prefer, however, to follow Kuska (1979, 1982) by defining the fixed exchange rate Mundell/Fleming model as the 'Keynesian approach to the balance of payments', referred to hereafter as the KBP,

KBP models usually contain three goods (commodities, bonds, and money) and utilize either a period framework or a stock/flow framework. The same conclusions can be generated from either type of model. Within a period model, the relevant open economy Walrasian identity is (2.4a), which is rewritten for convenience as (2.12a) below. The KBP models contain equations of the type given in (2.12b), which specify commodity market and money market equilibrium. Also, the *ex ante* balance of payments is not constrained to zero, and is determined via a behavioral function, $B(\ )$.

$$X_C + X_A + X_M \equiv - BP \qquad (2.12a)$$

$$X_C = 0 \qquad X_M = 0 \qquad BP = B(\ ) \qquad (2.12b)$$

Graphically, the KBP uses the familiar IS/LM graph, as in Figure 1.1 above. Recall that if the economy is at the intersection of IS and LM at a point above the $BP = 0$ curve (as at point A in Figure 1.1), then there is a balance of payments surplus. Conversely, if IS and LM' intersect at a point below the $BP = 0$ curve (as at point B in Figure 1.1), then a balance of payments deficit exists.

Clearly, from (2.12a), it follows that when the money and commodity markets are simultaneously in equilibrium (as at the intersection of the IS and LM curves) then

$$X_A = - BP \qquad (2.12c)$$

Therefore, the KBP implicitly assumes that any nonzero balance of payments is associated with a nonclearing bond market. A payments deficit is accompanied by a positive excess supply of bonds, and a payments surplus is associated with a negative excess supply of bonds, i.e., an excess demand for bonds.

Section 2.2 pointed out that Kuska (1978) suggested that the KBP contains a logical contradiction, because: (a) the economy always moves to a short run equilibrium where IS intersects LM; (b) if IS intersects LM at a point that is not on the BP equilibrium locus, then the balance of payments will not be zero; however, (c) if the economy is on its LM curve, then the money market is in equilibrium; (d) the balance of payments is always zero if the money market is in equilibrium. Therefore, (b) contradicts (d).

We now know that the error is in the MBP's assertion (d). That is, the KBP is logically consistent, because a nonzero balance of payments can exist even though the money market is initially in equilibrium, provided that some nonmonetary market (such as the bond market) is in a state of disequilbrium.

For simplicity in macro-model building, the bond market is often assumed to be the only nonmonetary asset market. However, in reality there is a very large number of nonmonetary assets. In countries where all asset markets always clear efficiently, the KBP is never relevant. It remains to be seen if this applies to any real world economy. On the other hand, the KBP is likely to be relevant in countries wherein bond and other asset markets are not well developed, and/or where the government imposes controls on interest rates and/or lending.

Identity (2.12c) provides valuable insights with regard to government balance of payments policies in cases wherein the KBP is relevant. For example, assume that a country's government has controls on domestic interest rates and on capital flows, and that these create a persistent excess supply of bonds (or demand for loanable funds). This country is likely to experience chronic balance of payments deficits. If home output is below its potential level, then the traditional policy prescription for a payments deficit within KBP models is an expenditure switching policy (such as a depreciation of home money).

However, identity (2.12c) implies that if the KBP is relevant, then no government policy to correct a payments deficit will do any good unless it reduces the size of the bond market excess supply. It seems problematic as to whether currency depreciations will accomplish this. At any rate, this is an important issue that needs to be explored in a scholarly manner. The obvious policy response to a balance of payments deficit that is associated with an excess supply of home bonds is to remove the controls on home interest rates and/or international capital flows that are the underlying cause(s) of the nonclearing bond market.

2.6.4 A Commodity Market Approach to the Balance of Payments: CBP

From the open economy Walrasian identity (2.4a) it is conceivable that a nonzero balance of payments can be associated with a nonclearing commodity market, i.e., a 'commodity market approach to the balance of payments', CBP. Unfortunately, no such theory exists, but it seems logical that there are circumstances wherein shocks to the commodity market, along with sticky commodity prices, cause the commodity market to be out of equilibrium when transactions take place.

Chapter 7 below represents a first step in the development of a CBP. It points out that the CBP might be the relevant theory if frequent shocks to home exports take the commodity market out of equilibrium. In addition, it shows that (contrary to traditional thinking): (a) a balance of payments deficit within the CBP can be reduced by a bond financed **increase** in government expenditure; and (b) import tariffs can conceivably be a desirable tool for balance of payments adjustment.

2.7 THE CORRECT TIME DIMENSION FOR THE MONEY SUPPLY

As pointed out above, the *ex ante* excess supply of money, X_M, that appears in (2.4a) and (2.4b) utilizes the **beginning** of period money supply, and this is the same concept as that used by Harry Johnson in (2.1c). To repeat Johnson's logic, if people are unhappy with their beginning of period money holdings, then they will run a balance of payments deficit or surplus so that the **end** of period money supply becomes optimal.

Buiter (1980) points out that asset demands in period models refer to **end** of period magnitudes. Consequently, he asserts that asset market equilibrium equations must use **end** of period asset supplies. Hence, Buiter maintains that the only correct way to specify money market equilibrium is to use the **end** of period money supply, which equals the beginning of period money supply plus any change in international reserves during that period.

Denote the **end** of period excess supply of money within a period model by $\underline{X}_M$. Using this definition, money market equilibrium is given by (2.13).

$$\underline{X}_M = X_M + \Delta R = 0 \qquad (2.13)$$

Buiter is absolutely correct about the proper way to specify money market equilibrium. However, this does not mean that open economy macro-models must contain a money market equation of the form $\underline{X}_M = 0$. Any model that contains (2.13) is implicitly assuming that an international payments imbalance, $\Delta R \neq 0$, always equals minus the beginning of period *ex ante* excess supply of money. That is, $\underline{X}_M = 0$ is really just a rearranged version of $X_M = -\Delta R$. Therefore, (2.13) is the appropriate money market equation only if a payments imbalance is always associated with a beginning of period *ex ante* excess supply of money, i.e., only if the MBP is relevant.

On the other hand, if the model builder believes that a nonzero balance of payments is associated with a disequilibrium in a nonmonetary market, then (2.13) cannot appear in the model. In this case, the appropriate money market equation within a period framework is $X_M = 0$. If the balance of payments is nonzero, then the change in international reserves that occurs in the current time period will take the money market out of equilibrium by the end of that period. This in no way, however, violates any principles of model building.

2.8 SUMMARY

1. Harry Johnson provided the first micro-foundation for international payments imbalances. His logic was that a balance of payments surplus or deficit requires an inflow or outflow of money, and this cannot occur unless home agents initially have an excess demand for (or supply of) money. That is, the beginning of period home money supply does not equal what people desire to hold.

2. The MBP generates conclusions that are the opposite of those reached via more traditional models. Within the MBP, the home balance of payments will improve if home prices are higher, home interest rates are lower, or home income is higher.

3. The conclusions generated by the MBP led to Kuska's (1979, 1982) indictment of Keynesian models of the balance of payments. Allegedly, the KBP contains a logical contradiction, because it allows for a nonzero balance of payments even though the economy is on its LM curve, i.e., even though the money market is in equilibrium. Kuska's provocative work prompted scholars to explore the structure of open economy macro-models.

4. In general, an economic unit can have a cash flow imbalance because: (a) its initial money balances are suboptimal, as in Johnson's micro-foundations; or (b) actual purchases or sales of commodities or bonds do not equal what were planned.

5. In the aggregate, (4a) above is related to the MBP. However, (4b) relates to other reasons for payments imbalances other than an initial disequilibrium in the money market.

6. Within a period model that contains only three goods, namely commodities, C, bonds, A, and money, M. The open economy Walrasian identity is given by $Xc + X_A + X_M \equiv - BP$, where Xi is the total market *ex ante* excess supply of good i. This identity tells us that a nonzero balance of payments must be associated with at least one nonclearing market in addition to the FX market.

7. This conclusion implies that: (a) there are welfare costs associated with both a payments surplus and a deficit that arise via the well known dead-weight loss from a market disequilibrium; (b) monetary shocks, fiscal shocks, and/or exogenous economic growth will have no effect on the balance of payments if all markets are in equilibrium when transactions occur; and (c) in general, it seems reasonable to believe that a desirable balance of payments policy is to ensure that all markets function as efficiently as possible.

8. The Bretton Woods system appears to have been characterized by frequent payments imbalances that were often persistent. This implies that market disequilibria existed and that they were often persistent.

9. A market can often be out of equilibrium even though it always moves quickly toward a new equilibrium. All that is needed is for there to be a sufficiently high frequency for exogenous shocks.

10. In reality there is a huge number of different commodity markets. Thus, an exogenous shock to one market might be transmitted slowly to many others. In this case, the aggregate commodity market can be in a state of persistent disequilibrium even though each individual commodity market clears relatively quickly.

11. Alternative theories of the balance of payments differ according to which market is assumed to be out of equilibrium. These include: (a) the MBP which assumes that the money market is initially out of equilibrium; (b) the Mundell/Fleming or Keynesian model, KBP , that can be interpreted as assuming a nonclearing bond market; and (c) the yet to be developed CBP wherein the commodity market is out of equilibrium.

12. Open economy models need not include an equation that specifies equilibrium in the money market via the equating of the end of period money supply (that includes any current period variations in international reserves) with money demand. Models that do this are implicitly assuming that the MBP is the relevant theory. Some versions of the Mundell/Fleming model are like this.

NOTES

1. This chapter owes much to this literature, especially Miller (1986a, 1986b). Note that Miller (1976) anticipated this literature.

2. Within a period framework, all magnitudes are defined in stock (as opposed to flow) terms. Therefore, income is cumulative income over one time interval. This allows the budget constraint to sum the excess supplies of commodities and assets in a meaningful manner.

3. Obviously, (2.2c) does not include the possibility that a cash-flow imbalance can arise via a divergence between the actual and *ex ante* magnitudes of net interest and/or net transfer payments.

4. This example implicitly assumes that the price of commodities is unity.

5. See Laidler (1984) for an account of the buffer-stock approach. This assumption is more likely to conform to reality as the duration of one time interval becomes smaller.

6. This example continues to use the assumption that all spillovers from any nonclearing market go entirely to the money market.

7. The omission of the labor market here implies that we are implicitly constraining it to be either in equilibrium or in a constant state of disequilibrium. This, in turn, implies that all behavioral functions utilized here are of the 'effective' rather than the 'notional' variety.

8. In order to obtain (2.3c) from (2.3b), note that $BP = NX + Tr + rA(-1) + KF$.

9. Hahn (1977) correctly postulates a similar identity within a two good (commodities and money) framework as $Xc + X_M \equiv -NX$. However, he incorrectly writes the three good (commodities, bonds, and money) version of the identity as $Xc + X_A + X_M \equiv -NX$.

10. For a derivation of these results see Miller (1986b).

11. Three examples of asset market models of the balance of payments are: Kouri and Porter (1974), Frenkel and Johnson (1976), and Taylor (1990, ch. 4).
12. $SKF' \equiv -SKF^{*\prime}$ because of the assumption that *ex ante* and *ex post* net capital flows are demand determined.
13. This idea comes from Foley (1975).
14. For a scholarly account of fiscal policy within a Mundell/Fleming model see Frenkel and Raxin (1992, chs. 1–3).
15. See, for example, Komiya (1969), Dornbusch (1980, ch.4), Miller and Askin (1976), Luan and Miller (1978), and Miller (1980), Chakraborty and Miller (1988), and Chakraborty, *et al.* (1996).
16. Recall the assumption here that agents hold only the money of their country.
17. The temporary nature of any increase in the home price level is tied up with the assumption that the home country is small and that home and foreign commodities are perfect substitutes.

3. The optimum balance of payments composition

3.1 INTRODUCTION

The gains from **temporal** trade along comparative advantage lines have been known for over 150 years, and they formed the theoretical underpinnings for the tremendous growth in world trade during the post World War II portion of the 20th century. On the other hand, the gains from **intertemporal** trade were not pointed out rigorously until the 1960s, and they have been less well known. More recently, the intertemporal open economy model has gradually become the theoretical model of choice for many scholars.[1]

Nevertheless, the welfare aspects of this model are typically given little attention. This chapter utilizes a simple **two period** open economy model of the Fisherian variety to illustrate the gains from intertemporal trade. The standard intertemporal model implicitly or explicitly assumes that all markets clear. Consequently, a zero balance of payments exists at all times. This means that the standard model cannot be used to investigate the causes of international payments imbalances. Rather, the intertemporal approach generates a rigorous theory of the **composition** of the balance of payments, i.e., the optimum current account and net capital flow.[2]

The presentation here and in the next chapter uses the fact that the analysis of the gains from temporal trade can easily be modified to investigate the gains from intertemporal trade. For example, tariffs or transportations costs create a divergence between home and foreign relative prices, and thereby reduce the gains from temporal trade. Chapter 4 shows that this is also true with regard to intertemporal trade.

Section 3.2 develops a two period Fisherian closed economy model. Section 3.3 extends this to an open economy, and does so in a way that makes it clear that the optimum current account equals the difference between domestic saving and investment. Also, it explains why saving and investment should be uncorrelated within a such a model.

Section 3.4 explores several implications of the intertemporal model. Perhaps the most important of these is that a current account deficit is not necessarily undesirable. However, it explains that the standard intertemporal model assumes away all of the real world reasons why a current account deficit might be viewed in a negative manner. Section 3.5 offers a 'perspective' on the open economy intertemporal model, and explains why the latter is a general **equilibrium** macro-model, even though it does not explicitly contain any market clearing equations. The chapter ends with a summary in section 3.6.

3.2 A CLOSED ECONOMY INTERTEMPORAL MODEL

3.2.1 Introduction

The open economy intertemporal model developed in section 3.3 amounts to either a simple extension of Fisher's (1930) closed economy theory of capital to an open economy, or, equivalently, the application of Leontief's (1933) classic article on the gains from temporal trade along comparative lines to intertemporal trade. As pointed out in Chapter 2, this appears to have been done independently by Miller (1968), Connally and Ross (1970), and Webb (1970).

The idea appeared in Heller's (1974) textbook, and later in Sachs' (1981) scholarly work. During the 1980s an extensive literature dealing with the current account was developed via the intertemporal approach.[3] The open economy intertemporal model has become much more widely known via the scholarly work of Frenkel and Razin (1992) on fiscal policy, and Obstfeld and Rogoff's (1996) comprehensive presentation of open economy macroeconomic theory.

3.2.2 An Endowment Economy

Fisher's closed economy intertemporal model encompasses only two periods. Consumption in each period is denoted by C_1 and C_2. Net income is defined as output available for consumption, and it equals output minus investment and government purchases. For simplicity, assume initially that no investment activities occur, and that output and income in each period, Y_1 and Y_2, are exogenous endowments. In addition, government spending in each period, G_1 and G_2, is exogenous and fully funded via lump sum taxes, so that net income in each period is given by $Y_1 - G_1$ and $Y_2 - G_2$.

Assume a well behaved homothetic and separable intertemporal utility function, $U(\ )$, represented by

$$U(\ ) = U(C_1) + \beta U(C_2) + U(G_1) + \beta U(G_2) \qquad (3.1a)$$

where $\beta = 1/(1 + \rho)$ is the discount factor with the subjective rate of discount, ρ. For simplicity, this chapter makes the typical assumption that ρ equals the real rate of interest, r. Since government spending is exogenous, the last two terms on the rhs of (3.1a) can be treated as a constant that has no effect in the optimization process.

This utility function yields a set of intertemporal indifference curves between C_1 and C_2, as in Figure 3.1, whose slopes are given by:

$$- U_1/U_2 \; = \; - U'(C_1)/ \beta U'(C_2) \qquad\qquad (3.1\text{b})$$

Figure 3.1 measures current period output (less government purchases) and consumption of present goods, PG, on the horizontal axis and second period output (again net of government purchases) and consumption of future goods, FG, on the vertical axis.

With the exogenously given **net incomes** of $Y_1 - G_1$ and $Y_2 - G_2$, wealth, W, is defined as the sum of current net income and the present value of the second period's net income.

$$W = (Y_1 - G_1) + (Y_2 - G_2)/(1+r) \qquad\qquad (3.1\text{c})$$

The intertemporal budget constraint restricts current consumption plus the present value of future consumption to equal the value of wealth.

$$C_1 + C_2/(1+r) = W \quad or \quad C_2 = W(1+r) - (1+r)C_1 \qquad (3.1\text{d})$$

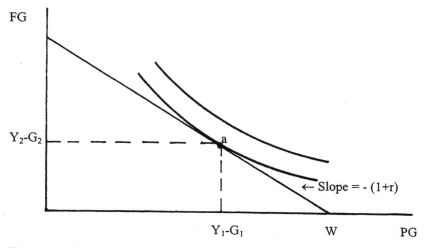

Figure 3.1 Optimum consumption

This constraint assumes that all resources are consumed by the end of the second period, and is represented by the intertemporal budget line in Figure 3.1. From the first version of (3.1d), it is clear that the horizontal intercept of this budget line indicates the value for wealth. The second version of (3.1d) clearly indicates that the slope of the budget line in a two period model is − $(1+r)$. In an endowment economy with exogenous government purchases, the intertemporal budget line passes through point a, which depicts current period net income, $Y_1 - G_1$, and future net income, $Y_2 - G_2$.

In general, the optimum combination of C_1 and C_2 is found by maximizing (3.1a) subject to the intertemporal budget constraint, (3.1d). A first order condition for this optimum is[4]

$$U'(C_1)/\beta U'(C_2) = (1+r) \qquad (3.2a)$$

(3.2a) implies that an indifference curve is tangent to the intertemporal budget line.

In a **closed endowment** economy, wherein current and future net incomes are given exogenously, consumers are constrained to consume these net incomes, as at point a in Figure 3.1. In this case, (3.2a) determines the home economy's real interest rate plus unity via (minus) the slope of the intertemporal indifference curve that passes through point a.

In the general case of a non-endowment economy, the assumption that the subjective rate of discount equals the real rate of interest means that (3.2a) becomes

$$U'(C_1) = U'(C_2) \qquad (3.2b)$$

The optimum combination of C_1 and C_2 requires their marginal utilities to be equal. This, in turn, implies that C_1 must equal C_2. In this case, the consumption function can be obtained directly from the budget constraint, (3.1d), by assuming $C_1 = C_2 = C$, and solving for C to get:[5]

$$C = [1/(1+\beta)]W \qquad (3.2c)$$

3.2.3 Allowing for Production and Investment

The supply side of the Fisherian model focuses on the trade-off between current and future consumption, as represented by the negatively sloped **Intertemporal Opportunity Locus**, IOL, in Figure 3.2. The IOL is the intertemporal equivalent to a production possibilities curve. It depicts the combinations of present goods, PG, and future goods, FG, that are available for consumption.[6] Current output (which is produced by an exogenously given existing capital stock) equals $0Y_1$. All of the existing capital stock is used up in the production of $0Y_1$.

Hence, if period 1 consumption equals period 1 output, then there will be no output available in period 1 for investment in capital goods. In this case, period 2 output will be zero. On the other hand, if none of current output in

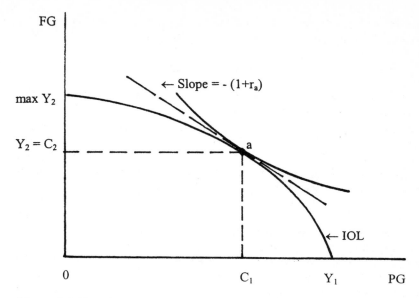

Figure 3.2 Closed economy intertemporal equilibrium

Figure 3.2 is used for consumption, then this frees all of current output for investment. The IOL indicates that this yields a future output of max Y_2

In order to obtain an expression for the IOL, note first that the relationship between current period investment and future output is determined by the production function given by (3.3a), where K represents capital inputs that experience diminishing returns. Presumably, there are other inputs, but they are ignored on the assumption that they are constant. (Ignore expressions (3.3b) and (3.3c) for now.)

$$Y = F(K,...) \qquad F' > 0, \; F'' < 0 \qquad\qquad (3.3a)$$

$$\Pi = F(I)/(1+r) - I \qquad\qquad (3.3b)$$

$$F' = 1 + r \qquad\qquad (3.3c)$$

The representative agent faces the two budget constraints below. Consumption in period 1 must equal net income in that period, $Y_1 - I - G_1$, as in (3.4a). Similarly, consumption in period 2 equals net income in that

$$C_1 = Y_1 - I - G_1 \qquad\qquad (3.4a)$$

$$C_2 = F(I) - G_2 \qquad\qquad (3.4b)$$

period. In a model with only two periods, investment is zero in period 2. Solving (3.4a) for I and inserting this into (3.4b) yields

$$C_2 = = F(Y_1 - C_1 - G_1) - G_2 \qquad (3.4c)$$

This makes it clear that C_2 depends negatively on C_1, as illustrated by the intertemporal opportunity locus, IOL, in Figure 3.2.

Profits, Π in (3.3b) above, are defined as the difference between the present value of future output, $Y_2/(1+r)$ or $F(I)/(1+r)$, and the capital stock that is used to produce this output, $K_2 = I.$[7] The optimum capital stock (and, hence, level of investment) is obtained by maximizing (3.3b) with respect to I, which gives the first order condition (3.3c) above.

Within a small **open** economy, the rate of interest is given **exogenously** by the interest rate abroad, and the representative agent can determine the optimum level of investment via (3.3c) independently of optimum consumption. However, the rate of interest is determined **endogenously** within a closed economy. Therefore, in a closed economy, the representative agent determines the optimum levels of consumption, saving, and investment simultaneously. Consequently, saving and investment are perfectly correlated.

Autarky equilibrium is found by maximizing (3.1a) subject to the intertemporal budget constraint, (3.4c). In order to do this, use (3.4c) to substitute for C_2 in (3.1a). Then differentiate with respect to C_1, and set the resulting expression equal to zero to obtain:

$$- U'(C_1)/\beta U'(C_2) = - F' = - (1+r) \qquad (3.4d)$$

The second equality in (3.4d) comes from the profit maximization condition, (3.3c). The first equality in (3.4d) tells us that intertemporal optimization occurs when the marginal rate of substitution between present and future consumption equals minus the marginal product of capital. In this framework the latter equals minus (unity plus the real rate of interest).

Graphically, the autarky optimum combination of C_1 and C_2 occurs at the point of tangency between the IOL and an intertemporal indifference curve, as at point a in Figure 3.2. At point a: (i) current consumption is $0C_1$, (ii) current period saving and investment are C_1Y_1, and (iii) future output and consumption are $Y_2 = C_2$. The absolute value of the slope of the IOL and of the indifference curve at point a are given by unity plus the **autarky** real rate of interest, $(1+ r_a)$. Of particular importance, here, is the fact that a closed economy restricts the representative agent to choose only those present goods and future goods that can be produced domestically.

3.3   A SMALL OPEN ECONOMY

3.3.1 Assumptions, Definitions, and Budget Constraints

The objective here is to maximize: (a) profits in (3.3b), and (b) the utility function (3.1a) subject to the first period and second period budget constraints facing a representative agent in a small **open** economy. The country is small in the sense that it cannot affect the foreign price level or foreign real rate of interest. We need to obtain expressions for the two budget constraints. First, however, several definitions are in order. Furthermore, we complicate the algebraic version of the model slightly by allowing for the flow of net interest internationally, rA_o, where A_o is the exogenous balance of international indebtedness for the home country, and where the home real interest rate, r, equals the foreign rate, r^*.

Assume that: (a) home and foreign commodities are perfect substitutes, implying that the rest of the world will automatically buy or sell whatever quantity of this commodity that is needed in order to clear the home commodity market; and (b) home and foreign bonds are perfect substitutes, implying that net capital flows, KF, adjust instantaneously to keep the home bond market in equilibrium. The second assumption means that if there are no market imperfections then, in equilibrium, home and foreign bonds must pay the same real rate of interest.

Next define the *ex ante* current account, CA, as the sum of: (a) net trade in present goods, or the balance of trade, BT,[8] (b) net international interest payments, rA_0, and (iii) net unilateral transfer payments, Tr, that is

$$CA = BT + rA_0 + Tr \tag{3.5}$$

From equation (2.3c) in Chapter 2, the home budget constraint in period 1 for a model wherein money does not exist as a separate good is given by (3.6a), where (for review) each V_i represents home supply minus home demand for that good.

$$V_c + V_A \equiv -rA_0 - Tr_1 \tag{3.6a}$$

$$V_c \equiv Y_1 - C_1 - I - G_1 \tag{3.6b}$$

$$V_A \equiv S_A - D_A \tag{3.6c}$$

$$X_c + X_A \equiv -BP \tag{3.6d}$$

$$X_c \equiv V_c - BT \qquad X_A \equiv V_A - KF \tag{3.6e}$$

48   *Balance of payments and exchange rate theories*

Definition (3.6b) says that V_c equals income minus absorption, $C + I + G$. Also, (3.6c) defines V_A as the value of bonds (home and foreign) held by home agents at the **beginning** of the period, S_A, minus the value of bonds that home agents plan to hold at the end of the period, D_A.

The sum of the home excess supplies of commodities, Vc, and bonds, V_A, must equal zero in a closed economy. However, (3.6a) indicates that in an open economy they equal the sum of minus net interest earnings and net transfer payments. Therefore, if the home country **receives** net interest and transfer payments from abroad, then the sum of planned home purchases of commodities and bonds can exceed the sum of income and initial bond holdings.

The standard intertemporal model does not have money as a separate good, but simply as a unit of account. Consequently, from identity (2.4a), the relevant open economy Walrasian identity in these intertemporal models is given by (3.6d). Recall that each X_i represents the total market *ex ante* excess supply of good i. The precise definitions of the excess supply of the home commodity, X_c, and of home bonds, X_A, are given by (3.6e). Full macro-equilibrium, of course, exists when each X_i is zero, and (by Walras' Law) the balance of payments equals zero. In an open economy, this requires that each V_i equals the net international transactions in good i.

The assumption that the home commodity and bond are perfect substitutes for their foreign counterparts, as well as the assumption that the home country is small, means that the standard open economy intertemporal model assumes that the home commodity and bond markets are always in equilibrium. Inserting (3.6b), (3.6c), and the second part of (3.6e) into (3.6a), and solving for minus the net capital flow, $-KF_1 = Ao - A_1$, in period 1 gives

$$[-KF_1 = A_1 - A_0] = [(Y_1 + rA_0 + Tr_1) - C_1 - G_1] - I = Sv - I \quad (3.7a)$$

which makes use of the standard definition of saving, $Sv = (Y_1 + rAo + Tr_1) - C_1 - G_1$. This version of the period one budget constraint tells us that net purchases of foreign assets, $-KF = A_1 - A_0$, always equal saving minus investment if the bond market is in equilibrium. For example, if domestic saving exceeds domestic investment, then home agents will be net buyers of foreign bonds. This represents a net capital outflow, $KF < 0$.

Since the home commodity market also clears instantaneously, the term $(Y_1 - C_1 - I - G_1)$ in (3.7a) always equals the balance of trade in period 1, BT_1, so that (3.7a) becomes

$$-KF_1 = BT + rAo + Tr_1 = CA_1 \quad (3.7b)$$

$$CA_1 + KF_1 = 0 \quad (3.7c)$$

Expression (3.7c) illustrates what was stated above, namely that in the standard intertemporal open economy model the balance of payments is always zero. This can also be seen directly from the Walrasian identity, (3.6d). If equilibrium always exists in the commodity market, $X_c = 0$, and in the bond market, $X_A = 0$, then the balance of payments is always zero.

The budget constraint in an open economy for the second period is of the form of (3.6a) with period 2 magnitudes inserted. As stated above, within a two period Fisherian model, there is no investment in period 2, i.e., $I_2 = 0$, because there is no opportunity to reap the benefits from this in future periods. Also, neither country will want to have a positive net international asset position at the end of the second period. The reason is that this would mean that consumption was forgone in period 2 (in order to buy the other country's bonds) with no possibility of an increase in future consumption. Consequently, the home country's terminal net asset position, A_2, is zero. This also implies that in period 2 home agents consume all of their net international asset position that existed at the end of period 1, A_1. Thus, from (3.6a), the aggregate budget constraint for the second period is

$$Y_2 - C_2 - G_2 + A_1 = -Tr_2 - rA_1 \qquad (3.8)$$

3.3.2 Open Economy Equilibrium

As pointed out previously, in a closed economy the optimum levels of consumption, saving, and investment are determined simultaneously, but in an open economy the optimization process takes place in two steps. By convention in the literature, the representative agent first determines the optimum level of investment in period 1. Then the agent determines the optimum levels of current consumption and saving, and, hence, of future consumption. As pointed out in Chapter 1 this two step optimization procedure suggests that domestic saving and investment need not be correlated within an open economy intertemporal model.

In the first step, the optimum level of investment is determined according to (3.3c) by setting the marginal product of capital equal to $(1+r)$, where $r = r^*$ because of the joint assumptions that the home country is small, and its bonds are perfect substitutes for foreign bonds. In Figure 3.3, the value for the exogenous foreign real rate of interest, r^*, is given by the absolute value of the slope of the intertemporal trade locus, ITL, minus unity. The optimum amount of domestic investment occurs at point T where the ITL is tangent to the intertemporal opportunity locus. This gives domestic investment of XY_1, which generates a period 2 output of $0Y_2$.

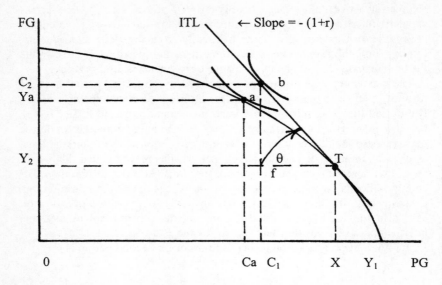

Figure 3.3 Open economy intertemporal equilibrium

With the optimum level of investment (and, hence, also Y_2) determined via the first step, the representative agent then decides on the optimum combination of current and future consumption. The first order conditions for this optimum are found by: (a) solving the second period's budget constraint, (3.8) for A_1; (b) inserting this into the version of the first period's budget constraint given by (3.7a),[9] and solving the resulting expression for C_2; (c) substituting the expression for C_2 into the utility function (3.1a); (d) differentiating with respect to C_1; and (e) setting this derivative equal to zero. This yields:

$$-U'(C_1)/\beta U'(C_2) = -F' = -(1+r) \qquad (3.9)$$

which is the same as the first order condition for the closed economy given by (3.2a), except that now the real interest rate is determined exogenously abroad.

Thus, the optimum combination of C_1 and C_2 is found at the point of tangency between an indifference curve and the relevant budget line, just as before. However, in a closed economy the budget line is the **intertemporal opportunity locus**, IOL, in Figure 3.2. On the other hand, in an open economy the budget line is the **intertemporal trade linte**, ITL, in Figure 3.3.

Figure 3.3 assumes that in autarky the home economy would be at point a, with: (a) present consumption of 0Ca; (b) future output and consumption as given by 0Ya; and (c) domestic investment equal to CaY_1.[10] This graph assumes that the world rate of interest exceeds the autarky home rate of interest at point a, i.e, the ITL is steeper than a tangent to the IOL at point a. Since these slopes indicate the opportunity cost of present goods in terms of future goods, dFG/dPG, it follows that in this case the home country has: (a) a lower opportunity cost for present goods, and, hence, (b) a comparative advantage in present goods.

Consequently, the level of wellbeing at home can be enhanced if the home country: (a) specializes in and becomes a net exporter of present goods, and (b) becomes a net importer of future goods by buying foreign bonds, which are claims on foreign future output. In Figure 3.3, the intertemporal open economy consumption equilibrium occurs at point b, where an indifference curve is tangent to the ITL. Present consumption rises from 0Ca to $0C_1$, while future consumption rises from 0Ya to $0C_2$.

Current output is $0Y_1$ in Figure 3.3; investment is XY_1; present period consumption is $0C_1$; and government spending is zero. Therefore, it follows that the home commodity market clears only if the balance of trade equals C_1X. This represents a home **current account** surplus, since transfer payments and net interest earnings are zero here.

The absolute value for the home country's current account surplus of C_1X equals the net capital outflow in Figure 3.3. To see this, recall from identity (3.7a) that saving minus investment always determines the net capital flow. Home saving equals home income minus consumption and government spending (and the latter is zero here). Thus, in Figure 3.3 home saving is simply current output, $0Y_1$, minus current consumption, $0C_1$, and this equals the distance C_1Y_1. However, only XY_1 units of home saving are needed for domestic investment. Thus, saving exceeds investment by the distance C_1X, and this equals the value for the net capital outflow.[11]

3.4 IMPLICATIONS OF THE INTERTEMPORAL MODEL

Within the standard intertemporal open economy model, the underlying causes of current account imbalances are the factors that create differences between the home **autarky** real rate of interest, r_a, and the real interest rate abroad, r^*. If r_a is less than r^*, then it is optimal for home agents to invest abroad, and conversely if r_a exceeds r^*.[12] Therefore, in the most general way, current account imbalances arise via international differences in intertemporal preferences, technologies, and/or relative factor endowments, all of which can create a difference between the autarky real rate of interest and the real interest rate abroad.

For example, in Figure 3.3, the slope at the autarky tangency point would be flatter (i.e., r_a will be lower) if the intertemporal indifference curves were, in general, flatter. This would occur if home agents have a relatively stronger preference for future goods, i.e., a lower subjective rate of discount.[13]   Hence, they would save a larger portion of current net income, as Japan has done for many decades. In this case, the home country will experience persistent net capital outflows that are offset by current account surpluses, as illustrated in Figure 3.3.

Alternatively, if the home subjective discount rate is relatively high, then home intertemporal preferences favor current consumption over future consumption. In this case, the intertemporal indifference curves will be steeper, thereby yielding a higher autarky rate of interest. This makes it more likely that r_a exceeds r^*, in which case it pays the rest of the world to invest in the home country. Consequently, the home country will experience persistent capital inflows that are offset by current account deficits, which are not shown here. Since intertemporal preferences in developing countries appear to be of this nature, this provides one reason for the chronic current account deficits experienced by many developing countries.

Another reason why the autarky interest rate might exceed the interest rate abroad is that the home intertemporal opportunity locus, IOL, in Figure 3.3 is relatively steeply sloped. As in the previous paragraph, if r_a exceeds r^*, then the home country will experience a net capital inflow and current account deficit. A steeply sloped IOL implies that the home marginal product of capital is relatively high, as when the home country has many workers per unit of capital (as in developing countries). Therefore, the intertemporal model suggests that current account deficits are apt to occur in developing countries, for two reasons, namely: (a) a high subjective rate of discount, that generates a relatively high demand for current consumption; and (b) a high marginal product of capital as a result of a low capital to labor ratio.

Conversely, countries with a high capital/labor ratio are more likely to experience a relatively lower marginal product of capital and lower autarky rate of interest. In such a case, the intertemporal model suggests that it will pay to invest abroad, thereby yielding net capital outflows and current account surpluses. There is, however, an important caveat here. If a country with a higher capital/labor ratio also possesses an advanced level of technology, then its marginal product of capital and real interest rate in autarky might still be high enough to induce a net capital inflow.

It is well known that the volume of and the gains from **temporal** trade increase as home relative commodity prices (in autarky) differ more from relative prices abroad. Similarly, the volume of and the gains from **intertemporal** trade will increase as the home country's autarky rate of interest differs more from the world rate of interest. This leads to the prediction by the intertemporal model that (for countries of similar size) the absolute value of bilateral net capital flows and bilateral current account balances will be larger between countries whose autarky real interest rates differ more. This, in turn, suggests that, in general, the absolute value of bilateral net capital flows and current account balances will be larger between developing and advanced economies (of similar size) than between countries with similar stages of development.

Exceptions to this conclusion arise if: (a) one advanced economy has a vastly superior technology to another advanced economy, or (b) an advanced economy is much larger than a developing country. In the latter case, the net capital flow and offsetting current account balance between two large advanced countries (wherein the autarky interest rates differ only slightly) can be relatively large. However, the net capital flow and offsetting current account balance between a large advanced country and a small developing country (wherein the autarky interest rates differ significantly) can be relatively small.

Finally, and perhaps most importantly, is the implication of the open economy intertemporal model that there is nothing inherently 'good' or 'bad' about current account surpluses or deficits. If agents act freely in well functioning markets, then the sign and magnitude of a country's current account will be determined **optimally**. Consequently, a current account deficit (if it arises via intertemporal optimization) is just as 'good' as a current account surplus. This point of view is in sharp contrast to the 'old' view that current account deficits are 'bad' because they imply that the home country is 'weak' and is not competitive in world markets.

This 'new' view was made early on by Sachs (1981), who emphasized that it is quite appropriate for a country to incur a current account deficit, if the country has a high marginal product of capital that stimulates domestic investment. This point has also been made more recently by Corden (1994). The new perspective on current account deficits implies that the latter do not necessarily reflect a weak domestic economy, but a strong economy with a high return on investment. However, the standard open economy intertemporal model does not take account of several important real world complexities.

First, at the theoretical level, the standard intertemporal model is a full employment equilibrium model, which means that there is no way for an economy to be 'weak' within such a framework. Also, as stated above, the standard intertemporal model assumes that the home traded good is a perfect substitute for the foreign traded good. This means that the rest of the world always buys or sells whatever quantity of this good is needed to clear the home commodity market. Consequently, there is no way in the standard intertemporal model for the home commodity to be uncompetitive in world markets.

On the other hand, if we allow for the possibility that the home commodity is not a perfect substitute for the foreign commodity, then it becomes logically possible for there to be a lack of competitiveness for home products in world markets. This can simultaneously: (a) decrease foreign demand for home exports, (b) create a current account deficit, and (c) reduce domestic output in a Keynesian type of model.[14] In this case, the current account deficit will be associated with a weak domestic economy whose products are not competitive internationally, as in the 'old' point of view. **In other words, the 'new' perspective provided by the intertemporal approach is a consequence of its dual assumptions of full employment equilibrium and of home and foreign commodities being perfect substitutes.**

Second, persistent current account deficits can be associated with huge inflows of financial capital, especially into the home banking sector. This can lead to a relaxation of credit standards if home banks have so much to lend that they extend loans to high risk borrowers. Such activities will gradually deteriorate the quality of bank assets, and, in the process, sow the seeds of a banking crisis. Furthermore, even if bank balance sheets do not deteriorate, a cumulatively huge inflow of financial capital can put a country at risk, because such capital flows can be reversed quickly.[15]

Third, persistent current account deficits progressively deteriorate a country's balance of international indebtedness. At some point the home country might become unable to service its debt, as was the case for Brazil and Mexico in the 1980s. However, long before a debt crisis arises, world financial markets might lose confidence in the home country's ability to service its debt in the future. In this case, a currency crisis can arise, as in Mexico and East Asia in the 1990s. Indeed, scholarly studies of currency crises by Corsetti, *et al.* (1998), Radelet and Sachs (2000), and Edwards (2001) suggest that persistently high current account deficits as a percent of GDP make it more likely that a currency crisis will occur.[16]

In sum, the open economy intertemporal model provides a valuable insight into the welfare aspects of current account imbalances. Clearly, the 'old' view is not always correct. Current account deficits need not imply that the home economy is weak or uncompetitive. Indeed, they might arise because the home economy is very strong, with high rates of return from investment. However, the 'new' view ignores real world complications associated with unemployment, a lack of competitiveness, and potential banking or currency crises. The profession awaits theoretical research that builds these complications into an open economy intertemporal model in a rigorous manner.

3.5 A PERSPECTIVE

The open economy intertemporal model will probably be developed extensively in the near future, and eventually be the model of choice for both scholarly work (as it has recently become) and for policy decisions. The elegance and rigorous nature of the model make it easy to ignore its extremely simple structure. As pointed out in section 3.3, the standard small country intertemporal model (wherein nontraded goods and money do not appear as separate goods) is simply a two good (bonds and traded commodities) model.

The home bond market clears instantaneously via the assumption that home bonds are perfect substitutes for foreign bonds. Instantaneous bond market clearing is typically not made explicit, but rather is implied by the assumption that the home real rate of interest equals the foreign rate. The model is implicitly solved only for commodity market equilibrium. This equilibrium condition, however, is usually not apparent. That is, explicitly it appears as though the intertemporal model is solved only for the first order conditions (subject to the appropriate intertemporal budget constraint) for optimum consumption and investment. However, from Arrow and Debreu's second principle of welfare economics, it follows that such an optimum is equivalent to a Walrasian general equilibrium wherein all markets clear.

This is best understood via Figure 3.2 above that illustrates **autarky** equilibrium at point a. Algebraically, this equilibrium is found via the first order conditions for optimum consumption over time, with the constraint given by the intertemporal opportunity locus, IOL, in Figure 3.2. However, at the autarky optimum point a, current output, $0Y_1$,[17] is given by the horizontal intercept of the IOL. Current period consumption, $0C_1$, plus investment, C_1Y_1, equals this net output. That is, **the home commodity market is in equilibrium when investment and consumption are at their optimal levels.** Indeed, the optimization process includes a budget constraint, (3.4a), that amounts to a commodity market equilibrium condition. By Walras' law in a two good closed economy, the bond market also clears.

A similar conclusion holds for an open economy, as in Figure 3.3. The intertemporal optimum conditions are satisfied with consumption at point b, and domestic investment at point T. Output in the current period is $0Y_1$. This equals the sum of current period consumption, $0C_1$, domestic investment, XY_1, and the trade balance surplus of C_1X. **Consequently, intertemporal optimization again implies commodity market equilbrium.**

Also, it was proven via (3.7c) that the *ex ante* balance of payments is always zero within the standard intertemporal model. Therefore, from the Walrasian identity (3.6d) it follows that the bond market is also in equilibrium when intertemporal optimization exists. Therefore, the open economy version of the intertemporal model implicitly assumes that all markets clear. This means that both the closed and open economy versions of the intertemporal model represent full macro-equilibrium models, even though they do not appear so explicitly.

3.6 SUMMARY

1. Existing intertemporal models assume that the balance of payments is always zero. They have been used to investigate rigorously the **composition** of the balance of payments, i.e., the optimum net capital flow and offsetting current account balance.
2. The open economy intertemporal model suggests that countries can enhance their level of wellbeing (i.e., have more present goods and more future goods) by running nonzero current accounts with offsetting net capital flows if their autarky rate of interest differs from the real interest rate abroad. In this case, they have a comparative advantage either in present goods or future goods.
3. Within an intertemporal **closed** economy, consumption, saving, and investment decisions are made simultaneously. Consequently, saving and investment will be perfectly correlated. On the other hand, the intertemporal **open** economy model suggests that there will be no necessary correlation between domestic saving and investment, because optimization occurs in two steps: (a) first the optimum level of investment is determined; (b) then the optimum values for consumption and saving are determined.
4. The underlying cause of a nonzero current account is a home real autarky rate of interest that differs from the real interest rate abroad. Thus, it follows that current account imbalances arise via international differences in intertemporal preferences, technologies, or factor endowments.
5. The intertemporal model suggests that less developed countries are likely to experience current account deficits, because: (a) their time preferences lean toward consuming present goods, i.e., they have a relatively high subjective rate of discount; and (b) their autarky marginal product of capital are likely to be relatively high, because of a low ratio of capital to labor.

6. Similar logic leads to the conclusion that highly developed countries are likely to experience current account surpluses, unless they possess a vastly superior technology.

7. The model suggests that the gains from intertemporal trade will be larger and, hence, the observed bilateral net capital flows and current account imbalances will also be larger between developing and advanced countries than between countries at a similar stage of development. Exceptions to this can arise if one advanced economy has a much superior technology than another advanced economy, or if countries are of vastly different sizes.

8. The standard intertemporal model implies that current account surpluses are not necessarily preferred to current account deficits. This is in contrast to the 'old' point of view that current account deficits reflect a weak uncompetitive home economy. However, the intertemporal model assumes away many real world complexities that represent an integral part of the old point of view.

9. The standard open economy intertemporal model has an extremely simple structure, with two goods (tradable commodities and bonds). The relevant Walrasian identity within a period framework specifies that the sum of the excess supplies for commodities and bonds always equals minus the balance of payments.

10. Intertemporal open economy models appear to ignore the concepts of markets and market clearing. However, these models are equivalent to a two good (commodities and bonds) macro-equilibrium model.

NOTES

1. For example see: Frenkel and Razin (1992), Razin (1995), Obstfeld and Rogoff (1995a), and Obstfeld and Rogoff (1996, chs 1–3).
2. Miller (1972) emphasizes that the open economy intertemporal model is a theory of the composition of the balance of payments.
3. See, for example, Sachs (1981), Obstfeld (1982), Svensson and Razin (1983), and the many references in the survey by Obstfeld and Rogoff (1995a).
4. (3.2a) is obtained by: (a) solving (3.1d) for C_1, and substituting the resulting expression into (3.1a); (b) differentiating (3.1a) with respect to C_1; and (c) setting this derivative equal to zero, and solving for $(1+r)$.
5. This consumption function differs from the more familiar one, $C = (1-\beta)W$, that is relevant within an infinite horizon model. Cf. Sargent (1987).
6. More precisely, the IOL indicates what is available for consumption after government purchases have been subtracted from home output. For simplicity, the discussion assumes that government purchases are zero.
7. Since all of the initial capital stock is used up in producing the current output, it follows that the capital stock for the second period is equal to the level of investment in the first period. Thus, output in the second period is given by $F[I]$.

8. Since home and foreign commodities are perfect substitutes, there is no two way trade here. The balance of trade is simply the one way flow of present goods into or out of the home country.

9. At this stage we obtain the aggregate intertemporal budget constraint: $C_1 + I_1 + C_2/(1+r) = [(Y_1 - G_1) + rAo + Tr_1 + Ao] + (Y_2 - G_2 + Tr_2)/(1+r)$ which says that the sum of present consumption, investment, and the discounted value of future consumption must equal all sources of funds.

10. For simplicity, Figure 3.3 assumes that government spending, transfer payments, and the initial net international asset position are zero.

11. Alternatively, a zero balance of payments follows from the fact that the present value of the home claims on foreign future goods equals the current account surplus. To see this, first note that in Figure 3.3 the home country will produce $0Y_2$ units of output in the second period, and it will consume $0C_2$. This implies that it will import foreign goods in period 2 whose value equals the distance Y_2C_2. This, in turn, means that in the first period, the home country buys claims (foreign bonds) on Y_2C_2 units of future foreign output. The value for this net capital outflow in period 1 is given by the present value of Y_2C_2 commodity units in period 2. The latter is simply $Y_2C_2/(1+r)$. In triangle fbT in Figure 3.3, $tan\ \theta = fb/fT = Y_2C_2/C_1X = (1+r)$. Therefore, $C_1X = Y_2C_2/(1+r)$. The current account surplus of C_1X exactly offsets the net capital flow.

12. This was pointed out initially by Miller (1968), and recently by Dluhosch, *et al* (1996, p. 29). Chapter 5 reconciles this perspective on the causes of current account imbalances with the present conventional wisdom that focuses on the fact that a nonzero current account will arise when home transitory net income is not zero.

13. Obviously, the discussion here has dropped the simplifying assumption (used in the algebraic version of the model) that the home subjective rate of interest equals the market real rate of interst.

14. In order to generate an output at less than full employment, the intertemporal model must assume sticky prices and/or wages, as in Obstfeld and Rogoff (1996, ch. 10).

15. Calvo (2000) points out that the essence of the problem here is that the maturity of bank liabilities is much shorter than the maturity of its assets. This is true for all banks, but it becomes especially problematic when bank assets are primarily domestic in nature, while bank liabilities have a large international component to them.

16. Not everyone agrees with this. For an excellent set of articles on currency crises see those edited by Krugman (2000).

17. Recall that for simplicity Figure 3.2 assumes that $G_1 = 0$.

4. Reductions in gains from intertemporal trade

4.1 INTRODUCTION

This chapter continues the investigation of the intertemporal approach to open economy macroeconomics. One objective here is to use what is well known with regard to the welfare aspects of **temporal** trade in order to investigate what decreases the gains from **intertemporal** trade. For example, a standard conclusion is that tariffs or transportation costs associated with temporal trade will create a wedge between home and foreign relative commodity prices, and, thereby, reduce the gains from temporal trade. It is proven below that this is also true with regard to the gains from intertemporal trade. They are diminished via tariffs or transportation costs associated with imports of present goods, which create a wedge between the home and foreign real rates of interest.

This chapter also shows that the gains from intertemporal trade are diminished if a different income tax rate applies to domestic versus foreign source income. Such a distortion takes domestic investment away from its optimal value. A third cause of decreases in the gains from intertemporal trade deals with variations in the relative price of traded versus nontraded goods. This makes the relevant real interest rate at home diverge from the rate abroad.

The analysis of causes for decreases in the gains from intertemporal trade helps to explain puzzle #14 in Chapter 1, i.e., why real rates of interest among advanced countries are not consistently equalized via capital flows. It also provides a possible solution for puzzle #13, the surprisingly small values for net capital flows and current account balances. Finally, it is relevant for puzzle #12, the relatively low correlation between consumption levels internationally.

Section 4.2 shows in a general way why any divergence between the home real rate of interest and the foreign interest rate serves to reduce the gains from intertemporal trade. Section 4.3 uses the results of this investigation to explore the effects of import tariffs or transportation costs. Then section 4.4 looks at the effects of different income tax rates on home and foreign source income. Section 4.5 investigates the effects on the gains from intertemporal trade from variations in the relative price of traded versus nontraded goods. The implications of sections 4.3 through 4.5 with regard to puzzles #13 and #14 are pointed out along the way. Then, section 4.6 turns to an investigation of why consumption correlations are lower than income correlations internationally, puzzle #12. The chapter ends with a summary in section 4.7.

4.2 DISTORTIONS AND THE GAINS FROM INTERTEMPORAL TRADE

4.2.1 Puzzle #13

This section reviews in a general manner how the existence of a distortion reduces the gains from intertemporal trade. This provides the background for the next three sections that examine specific reasons for such distortions. First, however, a brief review of puzzle #13 and attempts to solve it is in order. Obstfeld and Rogoff (1995a, pp.1747–8) use a standard intertemporal model of a small open country whose autarky rate of interest is consistently higher than the real interest rate abroad. Thus, the country optimally borrows internationally (a net capital inflow) and simultaneously runs a current account deficit. This means that in the long run, the country must have trade balance surpluses in order to service its debt.

Using reasonable assumptions about the values for the parameters, they calculate an optimum value for net foreign debt as a percentage of GDP equal to 20.[1] In order to service this debt, the economy will need (in the long run) a trade balance surplus in each period equal to 80% of GDP. In a similar manner, Obstfeld and Rogoff (1996, p.119) make a set of calculations with slightly different assumptions about parameter values, and find that the optimum ratio of foreign debt to GDP is 15. The required trade balance surplus that is needed to service this debt in the long run is 45% of GDP.

Real world (foreign debt)/GDP ratios almost never exceed 0.50, and current account imbalances exceeding 5% of GDP are rare.[2] This represents a puzzle that has two aspects to it. First, if the calculations that fall out of the standard intertemporal model are somewhere 'in the ballpark', then why are real world debt percentages so low? Do countries not optimize intertemporally? Second, are the calculations totally 'off the mark'? If so, what real world complications must be added to the standard intertemporal model in order to generate optimum debt percentages of the order of magnitude observed in reality?

Earlier research by Blanchard (1983) provides a partial solution to this puzzle. His intertemporal model assumes that investment has **installation costs** associated with it. When the model is simulated using parameter values that resemble the Brazilian economy, the result is an optimum ratio of foreign debt to GDP equal to 3, and a required long run trade surplus (to service the debt) of 10% of GDP. These are considerably lower than the percentages calculated by Obstfeld and Rogoff, but still much larger than those observed in reality.

Fernandez de Cordoba and Kehoe (2000) calibrate a standard intertemporal model with parameter values that are appropriate for Spain. They calculate an optimum current account deficit of 60% of GDP in response to financial reform, whereas Spain actually ran a deficit of about 3.5% under such circumstances. Then they assume that factor mobility across sectors is low and costly. This reduces their calculated value for the optimum current account deficit, but it remains unrealistically high.

Obstfeld and Rogoff (1995, p. 1748) point out that the standard intertemporal model makes no allowance for default risk. That is, the standard model assumes that a small country can borrow all that it desires at the fixed real interest rate that exists abroad. If there is the risk of default on its debt, then a debtor country will have to pay an interest rate that is in excess of the world rate. Furthermore, this rate will rise as the ratio of foreign debt to GDP increases. Both of these facts would reduce the optimum amount of debt, and, hence, also reduce the steady state trade surplus needed to service the debt.

4.2.2 Intertemporal Distortions in General

Now turn to the general effects of intertemporal distortions on the gains from intertemporal trade. Figure 4.1 illustrates the case of a country that exports future goods (a net capital inflow) and imports present goods (a current account deficit). By assumption, its autarky position is at point a, where the home real rate of interest exceeds the world real interest rate, as given by the absolute value of the slope (minus unity) of the solid ITL line.

With perfect capital mobility and no impediments to the free flow of capital and commodities, the optimum intertemporal equilibrium in Figure 4.1 has production at point T and consumption at point b. The home country produces more future goods at point T than it consumes at point b. Therefore, it exports C_2Y_2 of future goods. Also, domestic investment at point T equals XY, and at point b it consumes 0C present goods. This yields a current account deficit equal to the distance XC.

Now suppose that something prevents the home marginal product of capital from falling completely from its autarky value at point a to the value given by $(1+r^*)$ associated with the solid ITL curve. This is illustrated in Figure 4.1 by assuming that: (a) the home marginal product of capital (plus unity) is represented by the absolute value of the slope of the line labeled MPK, and (b) the MPK curve is steeper than the ITL curve.

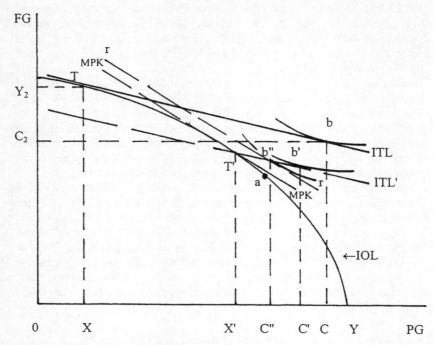

Figure 4.1 The effects of intertemporal distortions

In this situation, optimum domestic investment occurs at point T', where the MPK line is tangent to the IOL, and investment falls to X'Y. The new relevant intertemporal trade line,[3] ITL', passes through point T'. This means that the home country's consumption opportunities have been reduced, i.e, ITL' lies southwest of ITL. Consequently, if neither present goods nor future goods are considered to be inferior, then the new consumption equilibrium on ITL' will have fewer present goods and fewer future goods than at point b. This occurs at point b' in Figure 4.1. Hence, a divergence between the home marginal product of capital and $(1+ r^*)$ reduces the gains from intertemporal trade.

Domestic wellbeing will decline more because of the consumption effects of any divergence between the home rate of interest and the foreign rate. Figure 4.1 shows the case where the home interest rate equals the marginal product of home capital, both of which are lower than r^*. If ITL' represents the relevant intertemporal trade line, then (as just stated) optimum consumption is found initially at point b'. However, if the home interest rate is above the foreign rate, then consumption equilibrium occurs on ITL', where an indifference curve is tangent to the home interest rate line, r r, in

Figure 4.1. The r r line is steeper than the ITL' curve by the amount of the interest rate differential.[4]

In Figure 4.1 the new consumption equilibrium occurs at point b", which lies on a lower indifference curve than does point b'. In sum, the gains from intertemporal trade will be lower as a consequence of the inability of international capital flows to equate the home and foreign real rates of interest, and/or to equate the home marginal product of capital with the foreign real rate of interest.

The results here provide a reason why the absolute values of current account imbalances are much smaller than what the standard intertemporal model suggests will be optimum. In Figure 4.1, the current account deficit with no intertemporal distortions is given by XC, which equals domestic saving, CY, minus domestic investment, XY.

However, when a distortion creates a divergence between the home marginal product of capital and $(1+r^*)$, then the current account deficit decreases to X'C', which equals the new value for saving, C'Y, minus the new value for investment, X'Y. Then, when a divergence also exists between the home and foreign real rates of interest, the consumption point moves from point b' to b". This reduces the size of the home current account deficit even more to X'C". Therefore, anything that creates an intertemporal distortion will reduce the absolute value of current account imbalances.

4.3 IMPORT TARIFFS AND TRANSPORTATION COSTS[5]

This section shows that import tariffs or transportation costs for imports reduce the gains from intertemporal trade.[6] The home opportunity cost of present goods in terms of future goods, dFG/dPG, can be thought of as the ratio of the money (as a unit of account) price of present goods, P_{PG}, to the money price of future goods, P_{FG}. This opportunity cost is given by 'unity plus the home rate of interest', $1+r$. Similar definitions hold for the foreign country. That is,

$$dFG/dPG = P_{PG}/P_{FG} = 1+r \qquad (4.1a)$$

$$dFG^*/dPG^* = P^*_{PG^*}/P^*_{FG^*} = 1+r^* \qquad (4.1b)$$

If there is perfectly free trade in future goods with essentially no transactions costs, then arbitrage will equate the home price of future goods with the foreign price of future goods.

$$P_{FG} = P^*_{FG^*} \qquad (4.1c)$$

Now let there be either: (a) a home country tariff of τ percent on imports of foreign present goods, or (b) transportation costs on the foreign present good (home imports) that are τ percent of the value of imports.[i] If the home country is a net importer of present goods, then the home price of present goods will be given by (4.2a) below. The home price of present goods exceeds the foreign price of present goods by the amount of the tariff or transportation costs. When (4.2a) is combined with (4.1a) through (4.1c) the result is (4.2b).

$$P_{PG} = (1 + \tau)P^*{}_{PG*} \tag{4.2a}$$

$$(1 + r) = (1 + \tau)P^*{}_{PG*} / P^*{}_{FG*} > 1 + r^* \tag{4.2b}$$

An import tariff or the existence of transportation costs creates a wedge between the home and foreign real rates of interest. In order to understand the economic logic of this conclusion, recall that a country will experience a net import of present goods (i.e, a current account deficit) if it concurrently has a net capital inflow. The latter occurs if its autarky rate of interest exceeds the real interest rate abroad. The net capital inflow brings the home interest rate down to equal the world rate.

However, if a tariff exists on imports of present goods, then fewer present goods will be imported. Thus, the current account deficit will be smaller, which means that the net capital inflow will be reduced. This, in turn, implies that the home interest rate will not fall as much, thereby yielding a divergence between home and foreign real rates of interest. Of much significance is the fact that this conclusion holds even though capital flows are uninhibited.

This is important for three reasons. First, it means that impediments to **temporal** trade reduce the gains from both temporal trade and **intertemporal** trade. Second, it means that the free flow of capital internationally will not equalize real rates of interest if tariffs or transportation costs exist. Thus, the existence of import tariffs and/or transportation costs helps to explain puzzle #14, the fact that real interest rates are (in general) not equalized internationally between advanced economies, even though capital appears to move freely between them. Third, it means that the absolute size of current account imbalances will be reduced, as in puzzle #13, by the existence of import tariffs and/or transportation costs. Anything that creates a wedge between the foreign real interest rate and the home interest rate, serves to create a suboptimal amount of intertemporal trade, thereby yielding current account imbalances that are smaller than optimal.

4.4 DIFFERENCES IN INCOME TAX RATES

A second possible cause of intertemporal distortions is a difference in the tax rate on home versus foreign income. Figure 4.2 illustrates a country whose autarky real rate of interest at point a is assumed to be lower than the world rate of interest as given by the absolute value of the slope of the ITL minus unity. If there are no income taxes, then with the free flow of present goods and future goods consumption equilibrium is at point A, with saving equal to CY. Also, the optimum level of investment at point T equals XY.

This implies that the home country experiences a current account surplus of CX that is accompanied by a net capital outflow of the same magnitude. In this situation, the home marginal product of capital, as given by F' from the aggregate production function (3.3a), equals unity plus the world rate of interest. The latter equals the foreign marginal product of capital, F*', on the assumption that there is no income tax abroad. That is, initially

$$F' = (1+r) = (1+r^*) = F^{*\prime} \tag{4.3a}$$

where F*' is the marginal product of capital abroad.

Now assume that the home government levies an income tax of t% on income derived from domestic investment, and a tax rate of t'% on foreign source income. (The foreign country still has no income taxes.) Home agents will determine the optimum quantities of domestic versus foreign investment by equalizing the after-tax marginal products of home and foreign capital, as indicated by (4.3b) below. This and the condition $F^{*\prime} = 1+r^*$ yields (4.3c).

$$F^{*\prime}(1-t') = F'(1-t) \tag{4.3b}$$

$$F' = (1+r^*)[(1-t')/(1-t)] \tag{4.3c}$$

Clearly from (4.3c), the home marginal product of capital equals $(1+r^*)$ only if tax rates are identical on home and foreign source income. On the other hand, if foreign source income is taxed at a higher rate, then from (4.3c) the home marginal product of capital ends up lower than $(1+r^*)$. Intuitively, the higher tax rate on foreign source income induces home agents to invest less abroad and more domestically, thereby reducing the home marginal product of capital.

This case is illustrated in Figure 4.2 where the absolute value of the slope of the r r line (which depends on $1+r$) is less than the slope of the ITL (which depends on $1+r^*$) by the magnitude of $(1-t')/(1-t)$. In this case, optimum domestic investment occurs at point T', where the rr line is tangent to the IOL. Consequently, domestic investment rises above its ideal value of

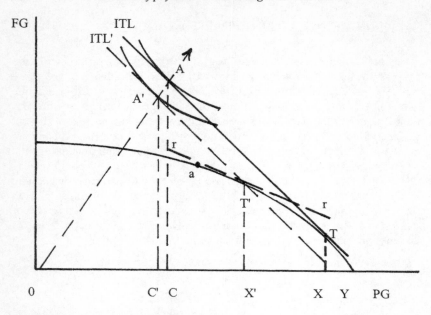

Figure 4.2 Differences in income tax rates

XY at point T to X'Y at point T'. Because of this, the relevant intertemporal trade locus (which always passes through the point on the IOL that indicates the value for domestic investment) shifts down and to the left to ITL'. Optimum home consumption falls from point A to point A', which has fewer PGs and fewer FGs than at point A. Also, the optimum current account surplus falls from CX to C'X' in Figure 4.2.

In sum, unequal income tax rates reduce the gains from intertemporal trade.[8] Furthermore, unequal income tax rates mean that the home real rate of interest will not equal the foreign real rate, even if capital moves freely internationally, and if there are no tariffs or transportation costs. Finally, unequal income tax rates reduce the absolute size of current account imbalances. As pointed out above, all of these conclusions arise if anything creates a divergence between the home and foreign real rates of interest.

4.5 THE RELATIVE PRICE OF NONTRADED GOODS

A third possible cause of intertemporal distortions deals with changes in the relative price of nontraded goods. For simplicity nontraded goods have not been included in our intertemporal model, but they do not need to be added formally in order to understand how they affect the gains from intertemporal trade. The basic idea, which comes from Dornbsuch (1983), is that a change in the relative price of traded versus nontraded goods creates a divergence between the world rate of interest and the relevant real interest rate, RRIR, at home.

To understand why, assume that: (a) home and foreign traded goods continue to be perfect substitutes, and (b) the world rate of interest in terms of the traded good is fixed exogenously at r^*, but (c) each country has a nontraded good. Then define the composite good price index for domestic present goods in period t, $P_{PG}(t)$, as in (4.4a). This composite good price index is a positive function, $H[\ ]$, of the money prices of the current period home price of the numeraire tradable present good, $P_T(t) \equiv 1$, and the current period price of the home nontradable present good, $P_N(t)$.[9] Expression (4.4a) implies that an increase in the relative price of the nontraded good serves to raise the composite price index.

$$P_{PG}(t) = H[P_T(t),P_N(t)] = H[1, P_N(t)/P_T(t)] \quad H_2 > 0 \qquad (4.4a)$$

$$(1 + RRIR) = (1 + r^*)\, P_{PG}(t)/P_{PG}(t+1) \qquad (4.4b)$$

RRIR is defined by (4.4b), which shows that RRIR can differ from the foreign real rate of interest, r^*, even though there are no impediments to trade in present goods or future goods.[10] For example, if the relative price of the nontraded good rises between period t and period $t+1$, then: (a) the composite price index in (4.4a) increases, (b) $P_{PG}(t)/P_{PG}(t+1) < 1$ in (4.4b), and (c) *RRIR* is less than r^*.

The intuition is best explained via a numerical example. Suppose that the real rate of interest abroad in terms of the traded good is 0.06, and that the relative price of the nontraded good is initially unity. Thus, one unit of the traded good trades for one unit of the composite good now. If the relative price of the nontraded good is constant from period 1 to period 2, then: (a) one unit of the traded good now will trade for 1.06 units of either the traded good or the nontraded good in the next period; and (b) one unit of the composite good now will also trade for 1.06 units of the composite good in the next period. Thus, *RRIR* = r^* = 0.06 here.

As a second case, let the relative price of the nontraded good be unity initially, and assume that real interest rate with regard to the traded good remains at 0.06. However, now let the relative price of the nontraded good rise from unity to above unity from one period to another. This means that in period 2, it takes more of the traded good to buy one unit of the nontraded good, and, also, of the composite good. Consequently, (a) one unit of the traded good still trades for 1.06 units of the traded good in the next period; but (b) one unit of the traded good now will trade for less than 1.06 units of the composite good in the next period. Therefore, one unit of the composite good in period 1 will trade for less than one 1.06 units of the composite good in period 2. *RRIR* has fallen below 0.06.

Domestic saving and investment decisions are based on *RRIR*. Firms will invest domestically until the home marginal product of capital equals (1 + *RRIR*), and consumers will equate the slope of an indifference curve with (1 + *RRIR*). Consequently, both investment and consumption will be affected by the variations in the relative price of the nontraded goods. As with any divergence between (1+*r**) and (1+*r*), this will yield a lower level of wellbeing compared to the case where the relative price of the nontraded good is constant. Furthermore, this provides another possible explanation as to why real world current account balances are smaller in absolute value than the simple intertemporal model predicts.

4.6 CONSUMPTION CORRELATIONS

As was pointed out in Chapter 1, time series correlations between consumption magnitudes in different countries are lower than the correlations between the incomes of those countries, i.e., puzzle #12.[11] This represents a puzzle, because the intertemporal model suggests that each country will use a nonzero current account to smooth out consumption in response to temporary fluctuations in income.[12] This implies that consumption correlations will exceed correlations between incomes.

To explain, assume first that two countries have identical intertemporal preferences and identical (both permanent and temporary) shocks to their incomes. This would give a perfect correlation between their incomes, and between their consumption and saving levels. Assume, next, that only the home country experiences **temporary** fluctuations in income, so that home and foreign incomes will be less than perfectly correlated. Home consumption will vary much less than home income, because of the well known conclusion from an intertemporal model that temporary fluctuations in net income exert a trivial effect on consumption. This is possible within an open economy because home agents use a nonzero current account to smooth consumption in response to temporary variations in home income. Therefore, in this case, the consumption correlation will continue to be almost perfect, and, hence, will exceed the correlation between incomes. However, in reality just the opposite is true.

One possible explanation for the relatively low consumption correlations deals with variations in the relative price of traded versus nontraded goods, as in the previous section. Assume again that home and foreign outputs and incomes are perfectly correlated, both in terms of permanent and temporary fluctuations in them. This suggests that home and foreign consumption levels will also be perfectly correlated. However, any variation in the relative price of the home nontraded good (holding the relative price of the foreign nontraded good constant) will alter the home *RRIR*. This in turn will affect the optimal levels of domestic saving and consumption. Consequently, home and foreign consumption levels will not be perfectly correlated (even though their incomes are) if the relative price of the home nontraded good varies.[13]

A second explanation for the relatively low international consumption correlations deals with variations in the foreign real rate of interest. Figures 4.3a and 4.3b illustrate the determination of interest rates and net capital flows in a simple manner. Figure 4.3a contains a positively sloped foreign saving curve, S^*_v, and a negatively sloped foreign investment curve, I^*. On the assumption that the foreign country is large compared to the home country, its equilibrium real rate of interest, r^*_1, is determined at point A. By assumption, this initial value for the world's real interest rate in Figure 4.3a exceeds the home autarky rate of interest at point a in Figure 4.3b. However, the free flow of capital internationally eventually brings the home real interest rate up to equal the foreign rate r^*_1. When this occurs, the value for home saving, S_v at point c in Figure 4.3b, exceeds domestic investment at point b by the distance bc. Consequently, home agents invest bc of their saving abroad. If all markets clear, then this capital outflow is matched by a current account surplus of equal value.

Next assume that an exogenous decrease in foreign consumption occurs via a decrease in the foreign rate of time preference. This means that foreign saving increases, which shifts the S^*_v curve in Figure 4.3a to the right to $S^{*'}_v$. Thus, the equilibrium foreign real interest rate falls to r^*_2. In Figure 4.3b, this lower world real interest rate reduces home saving to S_v' at point c', which implies that home consumption increases. Thus, home consumption **rises** when foreign consumption **falls**, thereby reducing the correlation coefficient between consumption levels, even though incomes are perfectly correlated.

A third possible explanation for consumption correlations that are lower than income correlations deals with the fact that consumption depends on wealth, which, in turn, equals the present value of current and future values for **net** income $(Y - G - I)$, and not **total** income. Assume that home and foreign total incomes are perfectly correlated. However, let differences in home versus foreign investment or in home versus foreign government expenditure yield a less than perfect correlation between home and foreign **net** incomes. In such a case, the correlation between home and foreign consumption levels will be lower than the correlations between total incomes, as observed in reality. This explanation might completely solve the consumption correlation puzzle. Obstfeld and Rogoff (2000, Table 5) find that the average of all correlation coefficients between growth rates of per capita private consumption among France, Germany, Italy, Japan, UK, and

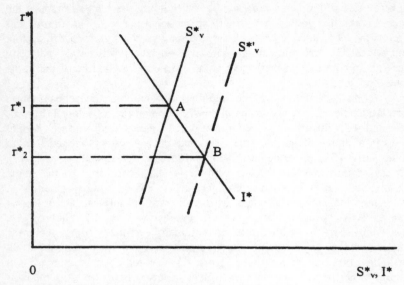

Figure 4.3a An exogenous shock to foreign saving

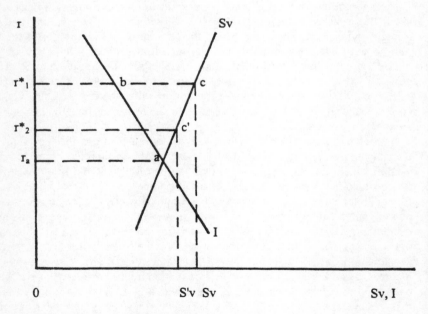

Figure 4.3b A lower world interest rate

the US over the 1973-1992 interval is 0.40. On the other hand, the average of the correlation coefficients for **net** incomes is only 0.17, which means that there is no consumption correlation puzzle when using the correct measure of incomes. In sum, it is possible that the consumption correlation puzzle is caused simply by using the wrong measure of income (**actual** income instead of **net** income) when calculating correlation coefficients between the incomes of different countries, and that this puzzle is more apparent than real.

4.7 SUMMARY

1. A lack of restrictions on international capital flows does not in itself mean that net capital flows and offsetting current account balances will be at their ideal levels.
2. If anything creates a wedge between the home real rate of interest and the real interest rate abroad, then both domestic investment and consumption of present goods will be affected in a suboptimal manner.
3. There are many reasons why the gains from intertemporal trade have not been maximized in reality. These include: (a) tariffs and transportation costs associated with imports; (b) income tax rates that differ between domestic and foreign source incomes; (c) changes in the relative price of the traded versus nontraded goods.
4. The first two factors above also help to explain: (a) why real rates of interest are usually not equal among the leading countries, puzzle #14; (b) why ratios of current account imbalances to GDP are lower than what is suggested as optimal from the standard intertemporal model, puzzle #13.
5. The standard intertemporal model suggests that consumption levels will be smoothed over time by running current account imbalances. This, in turn, implies that international correlations between consumption levels will be higher than correlations between incomes.
6. However, just the opposite is observed in reality, puzzle #12. This can conceivably be the result of: (a) divergent (between the home and foreign country) changes in the relative price of the traded versus nontraded good; (b) exogenous shocks to foreign saving and consumption that alter the world's real rate of interest in a manner that induces an opposite movement in home consumption; (c) measuring income incorrectly, i.e., using **actual** income data rather than **net** income data, as required by the intertemporal model. It is possible that the latter totally solves puzzle #12.

NOTES

1. The procedure makes assumptions about the world's real rate of interest and the rate of growth at home. Then it calculates the value for (foreign debt)/GDP that will yield a constant burden for servicing the debt, as measured by the ratio (net exports)/GDP

2. Cf. Edwards (2001) for a comprehensive set of data on current account imbalances.

3. Graphically, at point T' the slope of the IOL equals that of the MPK curve. Then the intertemporal trade line, ITL', passes through this point.

4. Graphically, point b" is found by sliding the rr curve along ITL' until rr is tangent to an indifference curve at a point on ITL'.

5. The ideas in this subsection are closely related to the analysis of one puzzle in Obstfeld and Rogoff (2000). This is the puzzle associated with the strong home bias in holdings of equities. This is similar to puzzle # 13, i.e., current account balances and their offsetting net capital flows are much smaller than what appears to be optimal.

6. Connally and Ross (1970) were the first to explore the welfare effects of tariffs within an intertemporal open economy model.

7. Since transportation costs will also exist for the home present good, τ can be thought of as the difference between foreign and home transportation costs as a percentage of the price of imports.

8. This idea is referred to as 'the residence principle in international taxation'. Cf. Gordon and Varian (1989), Frenkel, Raxin, and Sadka (1991), and Razin, Sadka, and Yuen (1996).

9. Most scholars maintain that such a price index can be constructed only if the utility function is homothetic. Their logic is that if this is not true, then the relative consumption quantities for tradables and nontradables will vary with wealth. In such a case, a simple fixed weighted average of $P_T(t)$ and $P_N(t)$ will not be acceptable, because their weights in the price index, must vary with wealth. It, however, seems logical that the function H[ ] in (4.4a) could contain weights which depend on wealth, W, in an appropriate manner. For example, let the wealth elasticity of demand for tradables exceed the wealth elasticity for nontradables. In this case, the price index given by $PPG(t) = aP_T(t) + (1-a)P_N(t)$ will be appropriate provided that the weight 'a' is given by $a = a(W)$ with $a' > 0$.

10. See Obstfeld and Rogoff (1995a, p.1753).

11. See Baxter (1995) for documentation of this puzzle, and an excellent review of the literature on this subject.

12. Also, if the world experienced complete contingent markets in the Arrow–Debreu sense then home and foreign agents would end up having their disposable incomes vary identically. This would yield consumption correlations of unity. This would be true even if home and foreign incomes were not perfectly correlated, because all agents would own equal claims to home and foreign incomes. Even though the literature on complete markets represents a useful theoretical exercise, clearly they do not exist in reality. Baxter (1995) contains a thorough discussion of the implications of the complete markets model.

13. If the relative price of the foreign nontraded good also varies, but by a different amount, then the *RRIR* abroad will differ from that at home. Hence, home and foreign consumption levels will differ.

5. An infinite horizon intertemporal model

5.1 INTRODUCTION

The two period model of Chapter 3 is an excellent simple framework for presenting the basic ideas of the intertemporal model. However, it cannot adequately investigate some important aspects of the underlying causes of current account imbalances or of the effects of temporary versus permanent shocks to the economy. An infinite horizon model is better suited for the analysis of these and other topics. Thus, the first task here is to extend the two period model to one with an infinite horizon.

The literature on the open economy intertemporal model contains a so-called 'fundamental equation' for the current account, that indicates what causes saving minus investment to be nonzero.[1] The main ideas obtained from this equation (which are the current conventional wisdom on the subject) is that a nonzero current account arises: (a) if actual net income differs from permanent net income, and/or (b) if the home subjective discount rate does not equal the real rate of interest in world markets. However, the main conclusion from the two period intertemporal model in Chapter 3 was that a nonzero current account is caused by differences in intertemporal preferences, technologies, and/or factor endowments. These cause the home autarky rate of interest to differ from the rate abroad. Consequently, one objective of this chapter is to reconcile these apparently different reasons for current account imbalances.

Section 5.2 extends the Fisherian two period open economy model of Chapter 3 to an infinite horizon model, and adds the complication that the subjective discount rate need not equal the real rate of interest. Section 5.3 uses the infinite horizon model to derive a new version of what we call 'the fundamental equation for the optimum current account'.[2] This is used to illustrate how a nonzero current account can facilitate consumption smoothing (allowing consumption to vary less in the short run than net income) and consumption tilting (allowing consumption to be consistently less than or greater than net income). Then, section 5.4 relates this fundamental equation to the underlying causes of current account imbalances as given in Chapter 3.

Section 5.5 is devoted to Feldstein and Horioka's (1980) finding of a high positive correlation between domestic saving and investment: puzzle #11.

Since this is just the opposite of what the intertemporal model appears to suggest, it represents a potentially serious criticism of the intertemporal approach. Section 5.5 reviews several well known explanations that have been offered as solutions to this puzzle. It, also, suggests a new explanation. The chapter ends with a summary in section 5.6.

5.2 EXTENDING THE INTERTEMPORAL MODEL

The model here is similar to the two period Fisherian model, except that consumers have an infinite time horizon. In an open economy, the representative agent still optimizes in two stages: first, the optimum level of investment is determined; then optimum consumption and saving for each period are decided. In the process, the difference between saving and investment determines the optimum value for the current account, just as in the two period model. We continue to use the assumption that home and foreign commodities are identical, as are home and foreign bonds.

The optimum level of investment for each period is found by maximizing the profits from that investment, where the latter are defined as: (a) the present value of the future output stream (net of depreciation) from investment, $F[I]/r$, minus (b) the cost of this investment, which equals the commodities used for investment purposes, I, plus the cost of transforming a unit of output to a capital good, $C(I)$.

$$\text{Max } \Pi = F[I]/r - I - C(I) \quad C', C'' > 0 \qquad (5.1a)$$

where $F[\ ]$ is the production function that indicates the future output per period (net of depreciation) in perpetuity, and r is the home real rate of interest. The first order condition for maximum profits from each period's investment is given by:

$$F' = (1+C')\, r \qquad (5.1b)$$

Thus, the marginal product of capital must exceed the real rate of interest when adjustment costs exist. This means that the level of investment in each period will be less than what is needed to equate the marginal product of capital with the real interest rate. Consequently, investment in each period moves the capital stock toward its long run optimum value, but it can take much time to actually attain the optimum.[3] This means that we can write the investment function as a negative function of the real rate of interest.

$$I = I[r] \qquad I' < 0 \qquad (5.1c)$$

The representative agent has a homothetic, intertemporally separable, utility function that includes current and all future consumption magnitudes.[4]

$$U[\ ] = U[C_1] + \beta U[C_2] + \beta^2 U[C_3] + \ldots \beta^n[C_{n+1}] \tag{5.2a}$$

$$\beta = 1/(1+\rho) \qquad U'[Cn] > 0 \qquad U''[Cn] < 0 \tag{5.2b}$$

where C_i is consumption in period 'i', and ρ is the subjective rate of discount.

Next define X as the permanent value for any variable X, where X is the constant value for X per period in perpetuity that yields the same present value as the perhaps nonconstant infinite time series of values for X. That is,

$$X/r \equiv X_2/(1+r) + X_3/(1+r)^2 + \ldots X_n/(1+r)^{n-1} \tag{5.3a}$$

Expression (5.3b) below defines actual **net** income, X, in the same way as in Chapter 3, namely as gross income minus what is used for investment, I, and government expenditure, G. Gross income is composed of income produced via home production, Y, plus net interest income, $rA(-1)$, where $A(-1)$ is the lagged value for the home country's net international asset position, plus net international transfer payments, Tr.

Expression (5.3c) defines **actual** net income, X, as the sum of **permanent** net income, X, and **transitory** net income X_T. Permanent net income is defined by (5.3d) as permanent gross income minus the permanent values for investment, *I,* and government expenditure, **G**. The components of transitory net income are given in (5.3e) as the components of actual net income minus their corresponding permanent values. Finally, wealth, W in (5.3f), is the sum of current net income and the present value of permanent net income.

$$X \equiv Y + rA(-1) + Tr \ -I - G \tag{5.3b}$$

$$X \equiv X + X_T \tag{5.3c}$$

$$X \equiv Y + rA(-1) + Tr - I - G \tag{5.3d}$$

$$X_T \equiv (Y-Y) + (r-r)A(1) + (Tr - Tr) - (I - I) - (G-G) \tag{5.3e}$$

$$W \equiv X + X/r \tag{5.3f}$$

The representative agent maximizes utility as given by (5.2a) subject to the intertemporal budget constraint (5.6).

$$C_1 + C_2/(1+r) + C_3/(1+r)^2 \ldots + Cn/(1+r)^{n-1} \equiv W \qquad (5.6)$$

which requires the present value of all consumption to equal wealth. This yields a set of first order conditions which gives (5.7a) for any two consecutive periods, k and k+1. For periods 1 and 2, (5.7a) reduces to (5.7b), which is identical to the first order condition, (3.2a) in the two period intertemporal model. Planned consumption is optimal only if the marginal utility of consuming **now** equals the marginal utility (appropriately discounted) of waiting and consuming more **later**.

$$U'[C_k] = \beta (1+r)U'[C_{k+1}] \qquad (5.7a)$$

$$U'[C_1] = \beta(1+r)U'[C_2] \qquad (5.7b)$$

Chapter 3 followed the lead of most open economy intertemporal models by utilizing the simplifying assumption that the subjective rate of discount, ρ, equals the real rate of interest, r.[5] In this case, $\beta(1+r) = 1$, and, thus, from (5.7a) the marginal utility of consumption in any two consecutive periods must be the same. This, in turn, means that consumption must be constant over time.

Denote this constant level of consumption by C, and rewrite the intertemporal budget constraint, (5.6), as (5.8a). Solving this for C yields (5.8b); substituting ρ for r in (5.8b) and rearranging slightly gives (5.8c), which is the familiar consumption function found in many infinite horizon intertemporal models.[6] Using (5.3f) to substitute for wealth in (5.8c) yields (5.8d), which generates the well known conclusion that (when $\rho = r$) consumption will equal permanent net income, X, when transitory net income, X_T, is zero. Also, since $(1-\beta) = r/(1+r)$, it follows that variations in transitory net income, X_T, exert a very small effect on consumption in (5.8d). That is, changes in transitory net income primarily affect saving.

$$C + C/(1+r) + C/(1+r)^2 + C/(1+r)^3 \ldots + C/(1+r)^{n-1} \equiv W \qquad (5.8a)$$

$$C = [r/(1+r)] W \qquad (5.8b)$$

$$C = (1-\beta) W \qquad (5.8c)$$

$$C = X + (1-\beta)X_T \qquad (5.8d)$$

Apparently, no one has come up with a general consumption function (that does not constrain ρ to equal r) which yields (5.8c) or (5.8d) as special cases. The standard practice when $\rho \neq r$ is to assume some specific utility function, and then solve the first order conditions and budget constraint for a specific consumption function that includes that utility function's parameters. Unfortunately, this can yield a cumbersome consumption function, and, more importantly, it makes the model less than perfectly general.

To remedy this, assume a consumption function of the form given by (5.9a) and, equivalently, (5.9b) below. These are alternative versions of the typical infinite horizon consumption functions, (5.8b) or (5.8d), multiplied by a term, $\phi(t+n)$. By assumption, $\phi(t+n) = 1$ if the home subjective discount rate equals the real rate of interest.

In this case, the consumption functions given by (5.9a) and (5.9b) reduce to (5.8b) or (5.8d), respectively. Furthermore, it is assumed that $\phi(t+n)$ is less than or greater than plus unity as r is greater than or less than ρ. In these cases, consumption will be greater or less than permanent net income when transitory net income is zero.

These relationships are spelled out formally via (5.9c) through (5.9e). Expression (5.9c) says that ϕ is a negative function of $\beta(1+r)$, and a function of the time period, t+n.

$$C(t+n) = \phi(t+n)\,[r/(1+r)]W \tag{5.9a}$$

$$C(t+n) = \phi(t+n)\,\{X + [r/(1+r)]X_T\} \tag{5.9b}$$

$$\phi(t+n) = \phi[\beta(1+r),\, t+n] \quad \phi_1 < 0 \tag{5.9c}$$

$$\phi[1,\, n] \equiv 1 \quad \text{for} \ n = 0 \ldots \infty \tag{5.9d}$$

$$\{\phi < 1 \text{ for all n if } \beta(1+r) > 1\} \quad \phi_2 > 0 \text{ if } \beta(1+r) > 0 \tag{5.9e}$$

$$\{\phi > 1 \text{ for all n if } \beta(1+r) < 1] \quad \phi_2 < 0 \text{ if } \beta(1+r) < 0 \tag{5.9f}$$

Equation (5.9d) indicates that if the subjective rate of discount equals the real rate of interest, i.e., $\beta(1+r) = 1$, then $\phi = 1$ in all time periods.

Before investigating the cases where ρ and r are not equal, it is necessary to impose a transversality condition, i.e., a constraint on the country's net asset position as time approaches infinity. We follow the usual practice, as in Obstfeld and Rogoff (1996, pp. 64–5), and constrain the present value of the net international asset position, $A(t+n)$, to approach zero as n approaches infinity. This allows the home country conceivably to borrow or lend indefinitely, but the rate of change in $A(t+n)$ must be less than the real rate of interest. In this case, even though the absolute value of $A(t+n)$ grows over time, it does so slowly enough that its present value approaches zero assymptotically. There, however, is a logical difficulty in that it is conceivable that the home country might own or borrow all of the wealth in the world, long before 'n' approaches infinity. We follow the conventional practice of stating this problem and then ignoring it.

Now assume that ρ is **less than** r, so that $\beta(1+r) > 1$. A relatively low value for ρ implies a strong propensity to save. In this case, (5.7b) implies that the marginal utility of consumption in period 1 must exceed the marginal utility of consumption in period 2; consequently, C_1 has to be lower than C_2.

Similarly, in this case, condition (5.7a) requires the marginal utility of consumption to fall steadily over time, which, in turn, means that consumption must **rise** steadily over time. Condition (5.9e) gives $\phi < 1$ in this situation; this means that consumption in (5.9b) will always be less than permanent net income when transitory net income is zero. Furthermore, (5.9e) indicates that in this case $\phi_2 > 0$, which means that ϕ will rise over time. Thus, when the subjective discount rate is below the real rate of interest, and when transitory net income is zero, then the general consumption function (5.9b) gives consumption that is always less than permanent net income, even though it rises over time.

On the other hand, if the subjective rate of discount exceeds the real rate of interest, then $\beta(1+r) < 1$. A relatively high value for the subjective discount rate implies a high propensity to consume. In this case, from (5.7a) the marginal utility of consumption must rise over time. This implies that consumption must fall steadily, albeit perhaps very slowly. Expression (5.9f) tells us that in this case we have $\phi(\ ) > 1$ always. Consequently, the general consumption function, (5.9b), generates consumption in excess of permanent net income, whenever transitory net income is zero. Also, from (5.9f) consumption will fall slowly over time in this situation.[7] In sum, both forms of the general consumption function, as given by (5.9a) and (5.9b), allow us to neatly ascertain how differences between the subjective rate of discount and the real rate of interest affect consumption.

5.3 THE FUNDAMENTAL EQUATION FOR THE OPTIMUM CURRENT ACCOUNT

As in Chapter 3, the difference between domestic saving, Sv, and investment, I, determines the **optimum** current account. For review, saving is total income minus consumption, C, and government expenditure, G. As before: (a) the home country is small, and (b) home and foreign commodities are perfect substitutes, as are home and foreign bonds. These assumptions imply that the rest of the world automatically buys or sells any commodities that the home country desires, which means that, with these assumptions, the actual current account automatically equals its optimum value given by $(Sv - I)$.

Using (5.9b) for consumption, and the standard definition of saving, yields a general version of the **fundamental equation for the optimum current account** as:

$$Sv - I = [1 - r/(1 + r)]\phi X_T + (1 - \phi)X \qquad (5.10a)$$

In the simple case where the subjective rate of discount equals the real rate of interest (so that $\phi = 1$), this reduces to simply

$$Sv - I = \beta X_T \qquad (5.10b)$$

which tells us that the optimum current account will be nonzero only when transitory net income is positive or negative. This corresponds to the well known **consumption smoothing** function of the current account.[8]

For example, if transitory net income is **positive**, then home agents save most of this temporarily higher net income and invest it abroad. This generates a net capital outflow for the home country, thereby requiring a positive current account balance in (5.10b). This optimum current account surplus and matching net capital outflow allow consumption to rise in future periods, because the home country obtains claims on future foreign output. Thus, a positive current account helps to raise consumption slightly in all future periods when income rises temporarily above its permanent net level.

On the other hand (still assuming that $\rho = r$ so that $\phi = 1$), any negative value for transitory net income induces a decrease in saving and an optimum current account deficit in (5.10b). When home output falls temporarily, home agents prevent consumption from falling very much by importing present goods. This planned current account deficit requires them to borrow internationally and/or to sell assets to foreigners, both of which worsen their net international asset position. The latter means that foreigners obtain claims on future home output, thereby reducing home consumption in all future periods. Thus, a current account deficit allows the consumption effects of any temporary decrease in home net income and output to be spread out over many years.

In the general case wherein $\rho \neq r$, and, thus, $\phi \neq 1$, (5.10a) indicates that the optimum current account will be nonzero even when transitory net income is zero. This represents the **consumption tilting** function of the current account. For example, if $\rho < r$ and, hence, $\phi < 1$, then home agents always consume less than their permanent net income if transitory net income is zero. This generates a tendency to have persistently **positive** optimum current account balances in (5.10a).

In this case, from (5.10a), the size of this current account surplus depends positively on: (a) the magnitude of permanent net income; and (b) the value for ϕ, which depends, in part, on how much the real rate of interest exceeds the subjective discount rate. If interest rates and permanent net income are constant over time, then (5.10a) suggests that this optimum current account surplus will decrease each period, due to the fact that ϕ grows larger over time. However, if permanent net income grows over time, then it is clear from (5.10a) that the positive optimum current account could remain constant or even grow over time. This yields the empirically testable conclusion that countries with persistent current account surpluses will have these surpluses be a positive function of that country's growth rate of permanent net income.

In general, countries with a relatively low ρ (which implies that they are high saving countries) are apt to have persistent current account surpluses. Thus, the current account performs a **consumption tilting** function. Furthermore, we know that ϕ remains less than unity as long as $\rho < r$. Therefore, the home current account remains in surplus over time, even though consumption is rising over time. Consequently, we obtain the important conclusion that in this case **home residents never reap the benefits (via a surplus of imports) from investing some of their saving abroad each year. They just keep on saving and accumulating wealth via increases in their net international asset position.**

Conversely, (5.10a) suggests that countries with a high value for ρ (i.e., low saving countries) are likely to experience current account deficits in general. Furthermore, as long as their subjective discount rate remains above the world rate of interest, they will choose a current account deficit in every future period. The size of such deficits will fall slowly over time if home permanent net income is constant. However, these chronic current account deficits will become worse as permanent net income increases, thereby yielding another empirically testable conclusion from the model. Finally, casual empiricism suggests that the consumption tilting aspect of the intertemporal model is consistent with the fact that low income countries typically are low saving countries with chronic current account deficits.

Furthermore, (5.10a) makes it clear that in the general case where ρ does not equal r, there is no necessary relationship between the sign of the optimum current account and the sign of transitory net income, X_T. For example, a high saving country (i.e., $\rho < r$) will have a tendency to experience persistent current account surpluses. A temporarily negative value for that country's net income, $X_T < 0$, is certain to worsen its optimum current account, but the latter might well remain positive. Similarly, the chronic current account deficits for low saving countries (who have $\rho > r$) are certain to improve if net income rises temporarily, $X_T > 0$. This, however, does not necessarily mean that the current account will become positive when transitory net income is positive.

5.4 THE CAUSES OF CURRENT ACCOUNT IMBALANCES

The next objective is to relate the conclusions obtained from the fundamental equation for the optimum current account with the conclusion in Chapter 3 with regard to the underlying causes of a nonzero current account. Section 5.3 proved that the sign of the current account depends in part on the sign of transitory net income (the consumption smoothing function) and in part on the relationship between the home subjective discount rate and the world's real rate of interest (the consumption tilting function).

On the other hand, Chapter 3 concluded that the sign of the optimum current account depends on international differences in tastes (i.e., intertemporal preferences), factor endowments, and technologies. These generate a comparative advantage for the home country in either present goods or future goods, as manifested in a home **autarky** real rate of interest, r_a, that differs from the real interest rate abroad, r^*.

Figure 5.1 measures the home and foreign real rates of interest on the vertical axis, and indicates the difference between domestic saving and investment horizontally. The solid (Sv – I) curve is relevant initially for the home country. It has a positive slope because a higher real rate of interest reduces investment, and stimulates domestic saving. The value for the real interest rate that yields (Sv – I) = 0 is the autarky rate of interest, and is given by r_a at point A in Figure 5.1.

The autarky real rate of interest will always equal the subjective rate of discount, ρ, if transitory net income is zero. To see this, note first that (Sv – I) = 0 implies commodity market equilibrium for a **closed** economy, and this means that consumption, C, equals actual net income, X. If transitory net income, X_T, is zero, then actual net income equals permanent net income, X. Thus, in a closed economy, $C = X$ when Sv – I = 0 and $X_T = 0$. However, from (5.9b), $C = X$ and $X_T = 0$ means that $\phi = 1$. From (5.9d), this requires that $\rho = r$. But, in a closed economy, r is the autarky rate of interest. Therefore, **the autarky rate of interest equals the subjective rate of discount when transitory net income is zero.**

Figure 5.1 assumes that initially actual net income is at its permanent level, and that the economy is in equilibrium at point A, where the autarky

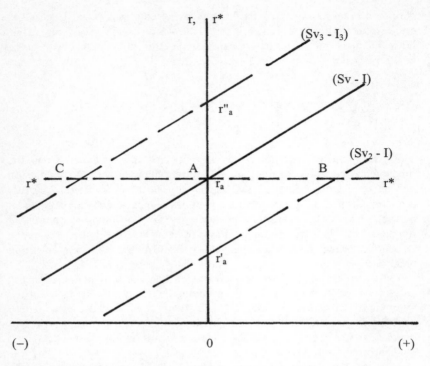

Figure 5.1 Causes of a nonzero optimum current account

real interest rate, r_a, equals the exogenous world rate of interest, r^*. The results of the previous paragraph ensure that in this case the home subjective discount rate also equals the world rate of interest. This, in turn, means that $\phi = 1$, and that the fundamental equation for the optimum current account is given by (5.10b). Thus, the optimum current account is zero initially.

Now let home net income rise temporarily (perhaps via a temporary increase in productivity) thereby yielding a positive transitory net income. The fundamental equation for the optimum current account, (5.10b), tells us that such an event will generate an optimum current account surplus. In Figure 5.1 this occurs because the positive transitory net income stimulates domestic saving and shifts the $(Sv - I)$ curve to the right to $(Sv_2 - I)$. The new autarky rate of interest r'_a lies below the foreign real interest rate. This induces a net capital outflow of AB for the home country, that will be matched by a current account surplus of AB in Figure 5.1. Thus, the 'fundamental equation' approach and the 'interest rate' approach yield the same conclusion.[9]

Figure 5.1 also illustrates how a subjective rate of discount that differs from the real rate of interest can generate a nonzero current account, even though transitory net income is zero. To explain, assume the same initial situation as in the previous case. That is, the home country has: (a) zero transitory net income, (b) a subjective discount rate, ρ, equal to the autarky real rate of interest of r_a at point A, and equal to the foreign real interest rate, r^*, and (c) a zero optimum current account. Then let an exogenous decrease in the home subjective rate of discount stimulate domestic saving and shift the $(Sv - I)$ curve to the right to $(Sv_2 - I)$. The new autarky rate of interest r'_a indicates the new lower value for ρ.

In this situation, the home country experiences a net capital outflow that is matched by a current account surplus of AB in Figure 5.1. This current account surplus will occur in each future period, unless transitory net income temporarily becomes sufficiently negative. In this case, the current account could conceivably turn negative for a brief time. However, when transitory net income returns to zero, the persistent current account surplus will return.

In terms of the fundamental equation for the optimum current account, initially the equality of the subjective discount rate with the real rate of interest means that $\phi = 1$ in (5.10a). An exogenous decrease in the subjective discount rate causes ϕ to fall below unity. From (5.10a) this generates an optimum current account surplus when transitory net income is zero. The decrease in the home subjective rate of discount reduces home consumption, increases home saving, and generates a positive optimum current account, via the consumption tilting function of the current account.[10] Consequently, we again obtain the same conclusion from the 'fundamental equation' and the 'interest rate' approaches, namely that a change in time preferences such that the home country is willing to save at a lower real interest rate will create a current account surplus.

Finally, turn to the effects of a permanent increase in the productivity of new (but not existing) capital via an advance in technology. Assume initially that the subjective discount rate equals the autarky real interest rate and the foreign real interest rate at point A in Figure 5.1. A permanent increase in the productivity of home capital immediately creates a negative transitory net income as defined by (5.3e). This arises for two reasons. First, an increase in the productivity of new capital stimulates domestic investment, which directly reduces current net income.[11] Second, the increase in the productivity of new capital raises permanent net income, **X**, above current net income, X. This, in turn, stimulates current consumption and reduces home saving.

In terms of the fundamental equation for the optimum current account, (5.10b), the negative transitory net income yields an optimum current account deficit. In terms of the analysis of Chapter 3, the increase in investment and decrease in saving described in the previous paragraph both shift the (Sv − I) curve in Figure 5.1 to the left from (Sv − I) to say, (Sv$_3$ − I$_3$). This raises the home autarky real rate of interest above r* to r"$_a$, and induces a net capital inflow of CA that is matched by an equal current account deficit. Thus, again, the 'interest rate' approach and the 'fundamental equation' approach generate the same conclusion.

5.5 THE SAVING VERSUS INVESTMENT PUZZLE

5.5.1 Introduction

Chapter 1 pointed out that the work of Feldstein and Horioka (1980) and Feldstein (1983) stimulated a huge literature that has consistently demonstrated that saving and investment are highly correlated in a positive manner, using both cross-sectional and time series data. This is perplexing because the intertemporal model suggests that saving and investment can be totally uncorrelated if capital moves freely internationally. Recall that this is tied up with the fact that the optimization process occurs in two steps, with the investment decision being completely independent of the saving decision. The Feldstein–Horioka controversy, therefore, casts doubt on the relevance of the intertemporal model.

Also, this topic is important for government macroeconomic policy. If the free movement of capital internationally means that domestic investment can be totally unrelated to home saving (as in the intertemporal model) then government policies to increase economic growth by stimulating domestic saving are useless. On the other hand, if domestic investment is consistently related to domestic saving in a positive manner, then the rate of economic growth might rise in response to government policies to stimulate saving.

Scholars have come up with a long list of possible solutions to the Feldstein–Horioka puzzle. No attempt is made here to review each of these.[12] Rather, the objective is to explain a representative sample of suggested solutions to this puzzle in order to show that the intertemporal approach is not irrelevant simply because of the fact that saving and investment are highly correlated.

5.5.2 A Positive Productivity Shock

One reason why a positive relationship between domestic saving and investment can exist even though capital flows freely internationally is a positive productivity shock in the home country. Such an event also shows how the intertemporal model is consistent with the following stylized facts:[13] (a) investment and the current account are negatively correlated;[14] and (b) investment is more volatile than the current account.

Figure 5.2 assumes that the home autarky rate of interest is determined at point A, where the solid saving and investment curves intersect. Also, by assumption, the world rate of interest, r*, exceeds r_a. If the home country can borrow or lend internationally at an interest rate of r*, then it will experience an excess of domestic saving at point C over domestic investment at point B. Thus, the home country optimally lends internationally (a net capital outflow) that is matched by a current account surplus of BC.

Assume now that home output rises exogenously via an increase in the productivity of existing and new capital, and that there are temporary and permanent components to this increase.[15] The higher productivity for new capital will stimulate domestic investment. In Figure 5.2 the investment curve shifts to the right to the dashed I' curve, and (at an unchanged value for r*) domestic investment rises from 0I at point B to 0I'at point B'. This tends to decrease the current account surplus.

If the temporary component of the increase in productivity is relatively large, then it is possible that current output rises more than permanent output, thereby generating a positive value for transitory net income. In this case, home saving increases, thereby shifting the saving curve in Figure 5.2

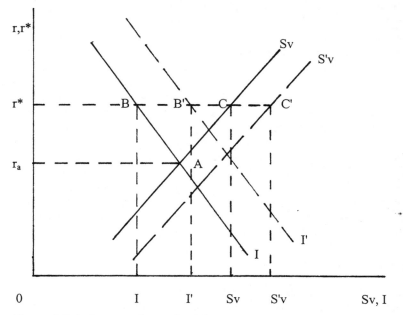

Figure 5.2 An increase in productivity

to the right to the dashed S'$_v$ curve. At the unchanged foreign real interest rate of r*, home saving rises from 0Sv at point C to 0S'v at point C'. This tends to increase the current account surplus. Consequently, both saving and investment increase, as in the Feldstein–Horioka controversy.[16]

The net change in the current account depends on the relative volatility of saving versus investment, and it is well known that investment is more volatile. Thus, in this situation, investment will increase more than saving, which means that the optimum current account will deteriorate. Figure 5.2 illustrates this because the current account surplus decreases from BC to B'C', as in stylized fact (a) above. Furthermore, the higher value for saving tends to dampen the negative effect of the increase in investment on the current account. Thus, investment is more volatile than the current account, as in stylized fact (b) above.

5.5.3 Retained Earnings and Endogenous Fiscal Policy

Gertler and Rogoff (1990) point out that firms typically use retained earnings primarily for investment purposes. Most firms invest much more domestically than they do internationally. Since retained earnings are included as part of private saving within the national income and product accounts of all nations, this implies that there is an automatic positive correlation between this portion of home saving and domestic investment.[17]

Another possible explanation for the high positive correlation between saving and investment deals with the idea of endogenous fiscal policy. Several scholars have hypothesized that fiscal policy might vary in response to movements in the current account balance, and that this fiscal response creates the observed positive correlation.[18] For example, suppose that the home current account deteriorates via an increase in domestic investment. The home government might respond to this current account deficit with a decrease in government expenditure and/or an increase in taxes. Each of these events increases government (and, hence, domestic) saving. Therefore, the endogenous fiscal policy creates a positive relationship between saving and investment. This hypothesis is empirically testable. That is, it should be possible to ascertain if the exogenous component of real world government budgets improves in response to current account deficits. Apparently, however, this has not been done.

5.5.4 The Large Country Case

The saving versus investment puzzle can be explained, at least in part, by the ability of a large home country to alter the world's real rate of interest. To explain, until now our intertemporal model has assumed that the small home country is too small to affect the foreign real interest rate. If, however, variations in home saving or investment are large enough to exert a nontrivial effect on the foreign interest rate, then it is possible for a shock to either S_v or I to cause the other variable to move in the same direction.

Figure 5.3 assumes that solid S_v and I curves are relevant initially. The home country's autarky rate of interest is r_a at point A. By assumption, this exceeds the initial value for the world real rate of interest as given by r^*_1. Consequently, the home country borrows BC internationally (a capital inflow) and runs a current account deficit of equal magnitude. Next assume that domestic investment rises exogenously, so that the investment curve shifts to the right to the I' curve in Figure 5.3. At an unchanged world rate of interest, home saving is unchanged at point B. This means that the funds for the extra domestic investment must be borrowed internationally, thereby yielding a new larger net capital inflow and current account deficit of BC'.

If the home country is sufficiently large, then its increased demand for funds in world financial markets might push the world interest rate upward, as to r^*_2 in Figure 5.3. At this higher interest rate, home saving at point G is larger than initially, and domestic investment at point H remains larger than initially at point C. Therefore, the exogenous increase in domestic investment indirectly induces an increase in home saving, which is consistent with the Feldstein–Horioka puzzle.

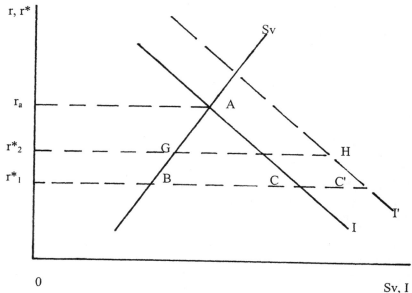

Figure 5.3 The large country case

5.5.5 A Small Capital Importer

The typical intertemporal model assumes that home and foreign bonds are perfect substitutes. However, in reality the bonds of any country are perhaps never **perfect** substitutes for the bonds of other countries. Therefore, a small debtor country is likely to have to pay a progressively higher rate of interest as it borrows more internationally.[19]

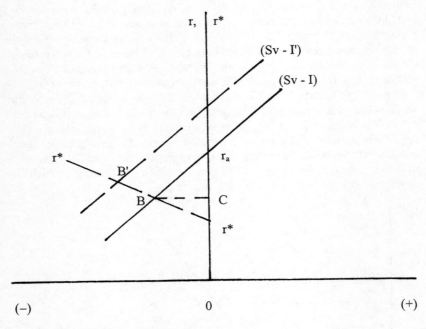

Figure 5.4 A small capital importer

In Figure 5.4 the solid $(S_v - I)$ is initially relevant. The autarky rate of interest, r_a, is found where saving minus investment equals zero. By assumption r_a is higher than the real interest rate abroad, r^*. This implies that it will be optimal for the home country to borrow internationally (a net capital inflow) and run a current account deficit. The world real interest rate is given by the vertical intercept of the r^*r^* line, which indicates the real rate of interest at which the home country can borrow in international capital markets. If home and foreign bonds are not perfect substitutes, then the r^*r^* curve is not a horizontal line as in previous graphs. Rather, it has a negative slope, as in Figure 5.4, because the home country must pay a higher interest rate as it borrows more internationally.

The initial equilibrium is at point B in Figure 5.4, where the home country borrows BC internationally. This gives an initial current account deficit of BC. Then an exogenous increase in domestic investment shifts the optimum current account curve to the left to $(S_v - I')$. The new equilibrium at point B' is at a higher real rate of interest, because the increase in home borrowing makes their bonds more risky. The higher interest rate, in turn, means that home saving will exceed its initial level. Therefore, the exogenous increase in investment indirectly induces an increase in saving, even though the home country is small in world markets.[20]

5.6 SUMMARY

1. When the subjective discount rate, ρ, is assumed to equal the real rate of interest, r, then the consumption function in an infinite horizon model is given by $C = (1-\beta) W = [\rho/(1+\rho)] W = X + (1-\beta)X_T$, where W is wealth, X is permanent net income, and X_T is transitory net income. In this case, $r/(1+r)$ or $(1-\beta)$ is substituted for $\rho/(1+\rho)$. The last equality indicates that (when $\rho = r$) consumption will equal permanent net income if transitory net income is zero.

2. The optimum current account is defined as 'saving minus investment', and when the consumption functions in #1 are relevant this is given by $Sv - I = \beta X_T$. This represents a simplified version of the 'fundamental equation for the optimum current account'.

3. In this case, the optimum current account will be nonzero only when transitory net income is nonzero. This can occur if income, investment, or government spending diverge from their permanent values.

4. The 'fundamental equation' in #2 illustrates the 'consumption smoothing' function of the current account. For example, a temporary increase in net income and output induces a current account surplus (i.e., most of the extra net output is exported) accompanied by a net capital outflow. The latter increases home claims on future foreign output. This allows home consumption to be higher in the future. Therefore, the current account surplus allows consumption to rise in all future periods in response to a temporary increase in net income and output.

5. In the general case where ρ need not equal r, the consumption function in an infinite horizon model can be written as $C(t+n) = \phi(t+n) [r/(1+r)]W$ or $C(t+n) = \phi(t+n) [X + [r/(1+r)]X_T]$

6. The $\phi(t+n)$ term equals unity in the special case where ρ equals r. In this situation, the two versions of the consumption function given in #5 reduce to those in #1.

7. If $\rho > r$, then the world real rate of interest is too low to induce home agents to save. Consequently, $\phi(t+n) > 1$, and consumption will always exceed permanent net income when transitory net income is zero.

8. Alternatively, if $\rho < r$, then $\phi(t+n) < 1$, and consumption is less than permanent net income when transitory net income is zero.

9. The 'fundamental equation for the optimum current account' in the general case (wherein ρ need not equal r) is given by:

$$Sv - I = [1 - r/(1+r)]\phi X_T + (1-\phi)X$$

In this general case, the optimum current account can be nonzero, even when transitory net income is zero. Such nonzero current accounts are of the 'consumption tilting' variety.

10. Countries with a high subjective discount rate (an aversion to saving) will have $\phi > 1$. This means that they will want to have a current account deficit when transitory net income is zero, and perhaps also when it is positive.

11. Countries with a low subjective discount rate (a high propensity to save) will have $\phi < 1$. Consequently, they will want to have a current account surplus when transitory net income is zero, and perhaps also when it is negative.

12. Countries with persistent current account imbalances (as when $\rho \neq r$) are likely to have the absolute value of their current account imbalance rise with increases in the value for their permanent net income.

13. A country's autarky real rate of interest equals its subjective rate of discount when transitory net income is zero.

14. The 'fundamental equation' is consistent with the conclusion in Chapter 3 that the underlying cause of a nonzero net capital flow and offsetting current account is a home autarky real rate of interest that differs from the world real interest rate.

15. Temporary increases in home net income: (a) increase home saving, (b) lower the home autarky interest rate, (c)cause the capital account to deteriorate, and (d) improve the current account. This temporary increase in home net income means that transitory net income is positive in the 'fundamental equation', which then yields a positive optimum current account of the consumption smoothing type.

16. A decrease in the home subjective discount rate reduces the home autarky real rate of interest, which induces a capital outflow and offsetting current account surplus. In terms of the 'fundamental equation', $\rho < r$ yields $\phi < 1$, thereby generating persistent current account surpluses of the consumption tilting variety.

17. An increase in the productivity of home capital raises the home autarky interest rate, and generates a net capital inflow accompanied by a current account deficit. In the 'fundamental equation', the higher productivity of home capital creates a negative transitory net income, which implies a current account deficit of the consumption smoothing variety.

18. The high positive correlation between home saving and domestic investment represents an indictment of the intertemporal approach. This is true, because the latter suggests that investment and saving decisions will be totally independent of each other in an open economy that has no restrictions on the international flow of capital. However, the intertemporal model can be consistent with a high positive correlation between saving and investment for a number of reasons. Some of these are given in #19 through #23 immediately below.

19. Increases in the productivity of home capital that contain a permanent and a temporary component can induce an increase in investment, and an increase in saving.

20. Most retained earnings (which are part of home saving) are used for investment projects domestically.

21. Governments might use tight fiscal policy (which raises home saving) in response to current account deficits that are caused by increases in investment.

22. If the home country is large in world financial markets, then an exogenous variation in home saving (investment) can alter the world real rate of interest and induce a change in investment (saving) in the same direction.

23. If home bonds are imperfect substitutes for world bonds, then the interest rate at which a debtor country can borrow internationally will increase as it borrows more. Thus, an increase in domestic investment prompts more international borrowing and a higher interest rate on such loans. This raises the real rate of interest at home and stimulates home saving.

NOTES

1. Apparently, Sachs (1982) was the first to develop a simple version of this 'fundamental equation'. A more complex version is equation (3.9) in Obstfeld and Rogoff (1995a).
2. The literature calls this equation 'the fundamental equation for the current account'. The word 'optimum' is added here to emphasize that the equation relates only to saving minus investment which can differ from the *ex ante* current account as given by the sum of the trade balance, net interest earnings, and net transfer payments.
3. Baxter and Crucini (1993) also make this assumption.
4. The exogenous level of government spending in each period is omitted from this utility function for simplicity.

5. Cf., for example, Obstfeld and Rogoff (1995a, 1996).
6. See Sargent (1987) for this consumption function.
7. These conclusions are the same as the current conventional wisdom on the subject.
8. See Frenkel and Razin (1992), and Obstfeld and Rogoff (1995a, 1996).
9. The case of a temporary decrease in home net income is left as an exercise for the reader.
10. The case of an increase in the home subjective discount rate is left as an exercise for the reader.
11. This requires that output in the current period rise less than the current period's increase in investment.
12. See, for example, Frankel (1993, ch. 2), Obstfeld (1995), and Obstfeld and Rogoff (1995a, pp.1776 – 80).
13. See Baxter (1995) and Razin (1995) for these and other similar stylized facts.
14. Cf. Sachs (1981).
15. Such an event is consistent with the empirical findings of Backus, Kehoe, and Kydland (1992) that Solow residuals are trend stationary. Davis and Miller (1996) use an intertemporal model to explore the effects on the real exchange rate from of a productivity shock that has permanent and temporary components
16. The key assumption here is that the advance in technology has temporary and permanent components to it. This assumption is also used by Baxter and Crucini (1993) in a model whose simulations replicate the positive correlation between saving and investment.
17. There is a timing problem here. Retained earnings typically accumulate for several time periods, whereas major investment projects occur discontinuously.
18. See, for example, Fieleke (1982), Tobin (1983), and Summers (1986).
19. The author is grateful to Ron Davies for this idea. Also, see Obstfeld and Rogoff (1996, ch. 6) for a scholarly account of risk in international capital markets.
20. Subsections 5.5.3, 5.5.4, and 5.5.5 all deal with reasons why the home real rate of interest might be endogenous. Frankel (1993, ch. 2) points out that if anything creates an inequality between the home and foreign rates of interest, then shocks to domestic saving can alter the home interest rate in a manner that induces a change in domestic investment in the same direction.

6. A commodity market approach to the balance of payments

6.1 INTRODUCTION

Chapter 2 pointed out that one implication of any Walrasian identity is that it is logically impossible for only one market to be out of equilibrium. As a result, in an open economy a nonzero balance of payments (i.e., a nonclearing FX market) must always be accompanied by a disequilibrium in at least one other market. The monetary approach to the balance of payments, MBP, assumes that this nonclearing market is the money market. The Keynesian approach to the balance of payments, KBP, as represented by the open economy IS/LM or Mundell/Fleming model, can be interpreted as assuming that the bond market does not clear.[1]

Chapter 2 pointed out that no one has developed a commodity market approach to the balance of payments, CBP, wherein a disequilibrium in the home commodity market exists in conjunction with a nonzero balance of payments.[2] The objective of this chapter is to take a first step in this direction, by presenting a simple CBP model, and by exploring several policy implications that follow logically from it.

Part of the appeal of the MBP is its simplicity. Real world open economies are perhaps infinitely complex. Hence, any 'one equation theory' represents an extremely naive abstraction with regard to how open economies function. However, if this one equation theory appears to be consistent with the facts, and if it has reasonable micro-foundations, then it can be useful as well as appealing, even though it clearly is too simple.

The CBP model developed here is also a one equation theory that is perhaps naively simple. However, from Chapter 2 we know that it has a reasonable micro-foundation. Economic units can have cash flow imbalances if their actual sales of commodities do not equal what they had planned. In the aggregate such a situation amounts to a commodity market disequilibrium, and this can be associated with a nonzero balance of payments.

It is surprising that a CBP does not exist, because it represents a fixed exchange rate version of the so-called 'equilibrium approach' to the exchange rate of Lucas (1982) and Stockman (1980, 1987). The latter points out that the real exchange rate is the relative price of the home versus foreign commodity.[3] Hence, it seems appropriate to focus on the commodity market when examining the determinants of the real exchange rate. The basic idea of this chapter is that the balance of payments can be nonzero if something (such as sticky commodity prices and a fixed nominal exchange rate) prevents the commodity market from clearing before transactions take place.

Section 6.2 explains: (a) the structure of a CBP model; and (b) the circumstances under which the CBP is likely to be relevant. Section 6.3 develops a very simple version of a CBP. Then section 6.4 explores the relevance of the CBP with respect to: (a) criticisms of the MBP; (b) the appropriate fiscal policy to eliminate a payments deficit; and (c) the need for expenditure reducing policies if a balance of payments deficit occurs when output is at its maximum level. The latter shows that painful 'expenditure reducing' policies are never necessary to correct a payments deficit if the CBP is the relevant theory.

Section 6.5 uses the CBP to investigate the widely accepted idea that tariffs are not a desirable tool for balance of payments adjustment, because they distort relative prices and reduce the level of wellbeing within a small open economy. It is shown that when a balance of payments deficit is associated with an excess supply of the home commodity, then higher tariffs to reduce a payments deficit exert two opposing influences on domestic wellbeing, namely: (a) the well known deadweight loss from a tariff, and (b) a welfare gain from the elimination of commodity market disequilibrium. Consequently, payments adjustment via higher tariffs can conceivably generate a net welfare gain. The chapter ends with a summary in section 6.6.

6.2 THE STRUCTURE AND RELEVANCE OF THE CBP

As in Chapters 3 through 5, we continue to assume that money exists only as a unit of account, and that nontraded goods do not exist. Consequently, the model contains only commodities, and bonds. This means that the open economy Walrasian identity within a period frame-work reduces to (6.1a).

$$X_c + X_A \equiv -BP \qquad (6.1a)$$

$$X_c \equiv Y - (C + I + G) - BT \equiv V_c - BT \qquad (6.1b)$$

$$X_A \equiv V_A - KF \qquad (6.1c)$$

$$V_c + V_A \equiv 0 \qquad (6.1d)$$

By way of review: (a) X_c in (6.1a) and (6.1b) is the *ex ante* total market excess supply of the home commodity; (6.1b) indicates that this equals $V_c =$ (home output minus domestic absorption) minus the *ex ante* balance of trade, BT; (b) X_A in (6.1a) and (6.1c) represents the *ex ante* excess supply of home bonds, as given by V_A [the initial quantity of bonds held by home residents minus total home demand for bonds] minus *ex ante* net capital flows, KF; and (c) in the case where net international transfer payments and interest payments are zero, the home aggregate budget constraint is given by (6.1d).

If money does not exist as a good (as in the standard intertemporal model), and if the home bond market always clears instantaneously, then any nonzero *ex ante* balance of payments will be associated with a nonclearing commodity market.[4] More specifically, a payments **surplus** will be accompanied by an excess **demand** for the home commodity, $X_c <$ 0, and a payments **deficit** goes with an excess **supply** of the home commodity, $X_c > 0$. This is just the opposite of conventional thinking that says that a payments deficit often arises when a booming economy creates an excess demand for commodities, stimulates imports, and creates trade and payments deficits.

The general approach to the balance of payments presented in Chapter 2 suggests that the conventional wisdom in the previous sentence might be tied up with the fact that a booming economy can create an excess supply in the **bond** market. For example, suppose that a strong cyclical upswing stimulates investment (and bond supply) by more than it stimulates saving (and bond demand). If the bond market does not clear quickly, then an excess supply of bonds might exist when transactions occur. In this case, any balance of payments deficit will be associated with this excess supply in the home bond market, which means that the KBP is the relevant theory. **In sum, the broadly accepted idea that a booming economy can generate a balance of payments deficit is consistent with the KBP.**

Perhaps the most likely situation wherein the CBP is relevant is when world demand for home exports changes exogenously. If the home commodity market is initially in equilibrium, then an exogenous decrease in exports can create an excess supply of the home commodity, and a concomitant balance of payments deficit. Conversely, an exogenous increase in world demand for home exports simultaneously generates a payments surplus that is associated with an excess demand for the home commodity.

Also, the CBP will be relevant if home preferences for foreign versus domestic commodities vary. For example, an exogenous shift in home preferences in favor of imports can simultaneously create an excess supply of the home commodity and a balance of payments deficit. Alternatively, if home preferences change away from imports, this can yield an excess demand for the home commodity and a payments surplus.

6.3 A SIMPLE CBP MODEL

The CBP presented here represents a simple infinite horizon intertemporal model, with the complication that home and foreign commodities are not perfect substitutes. However, as Taylor (1995, p. 25) points out, the ideas associated with a commodity market approach to the exchange rate (and, hence, also for the CBP) could be developed with no mention of intertemporal optimization. That is, there is nothing inherently inter-temporal about the fact that the real exchange rate is a relative price that is determined in commodity markets, and/or commodity markets might occasionally be in a state of disequilibrium if the real exchange rate changes slowly. The model is given by:

$$C = (1 - \beta)W \qquad\qquad (6.2a)$$

$$Ex = Ex(Q, C^*) \qquad Ex_1, Ex_2 > 0 \qquad (6.2b)$$

$$Im = QIm(Q, C) \qquad Im_1 < 0 \qquad Im_2 > 0 \qquad (6.2c)$$

$$W = X_T + X/(1 - \beta) \qquad\qquad (6.2d)$$

$$\boldsymbol{X} = \boldsymbol{Y} - \boldsymbol{I} - \boldsymbol{G} \qquad\qquad (6.2e)$$

$$X_T = X - \boldsymbol{X} \qquad\qquad (6.2f)$$

$$X = Y - I - G \qquad\qquad (6.2g)$$

$$\beta = 1/(1+r) \qquad\qquad (6.2h)$$

$$I = I(r) \qquad I' < 0 \qquad\qquad (6.2i)$$

For review, (6.2a) indicates that when the home subjective discount rate equals the real rate of interest, then current period consumption, C, is a positive function of real wealth, W, in units of the home commodity, as defined via (6.2d). For simplicity, the home country's net international asset position is assumed to be zero.

Ex ante exports, (6.2b), and imports, (6.2c), in units of the home commodity are a function of the real exchange rate, Q, in home commodity units per unit of the foreign commodity, and a positive function of total consumption in the relevant country.[5] Expressions (6.2e) through (6.2g) define permanent net income, X, transitory net income, X_T, and, actual net income, X, as in Chapter 5. The discount factor, β, is defined in (6.2h), with the assumption that the subjective discount rate equals the real rate of interest. Investment is a negative function of the real rate of interest in (6.2i), and government expenditure is exogenous and fixed.

All foreign variables are constant, the real exchange rate is initially plus unity, the trade balance is initially zero, and exchange rate expectations are static. Home and foreign bonds are perfect substitutes. Since the home country is small compared to the rest of the world, it follows that the home bond market always clears instantaneously. That is, the net capital flow, KF, automatically equals minus V_A in (6.1c). This, in turn, implies that the home real interest rate always equals the foreign rate.

The *ex ante* excess supply of home commodities, X_c, is given by (6.3a), while the *ex ante* balance of payments, BP, is given by (6.3b). This uses

$$X_c = Y - (1-\beta)W - I(r) - G - Ex(Q,C^*) + QIm[Q, (1-\beta)W] \quad (6.3a)$$

$$BP = Ex(Q, C^*) - QIm(Q, C) - V_A \quad (6.3b)$$

the fact that the home bond market always clears instantaneously, which implies that the V_A term in (6.3b) (which represents the difference between initial home bond holdings and the *ex ante* value of bonds that home agents wish to hold) always equals minus the net capital flow.

The balance of payments curve, BP, in Figure 6.1, has a slope given by (6.4a) below. The terms η^* and η are, respectively, the price elasticity of the foreign demand for home exports and the price elasticity of home demand for imports. This slope is positive on the assumption that the Marshall–Lerner condition holds.

The commodity market excess supply curve is represented by X_c in Figure 6.1. From equation (6.1a) and the assumption that the home bond market is always in equilibrium, it follows that the X_c curve is the mirror image of the BP curve. Consequently, differentiating (6.3a) to obtain the slope of the X_c curve yields (6.4b).

$$dBP/dQ = Ex_1 - Im(\ ) - QIm_1 = \eta^* + \eta - 1 > 0 \quad (6.4a)$$

$$dXc/dQ = -Ex_1 + Im(\ ) + QIm_1 = 1 - \eta^* - \eta < 0 \quad (6.4b)$$

A real depreciation of the exchange rate, $dQ > 0$, improves the trade balance and the balance of payments in (6.4a). Simultaneously, it increases world demand for the home commodity and decreases the excess supply of it (i.e., it creates an excess demand) in (6.4b). The value for the real exchange rate

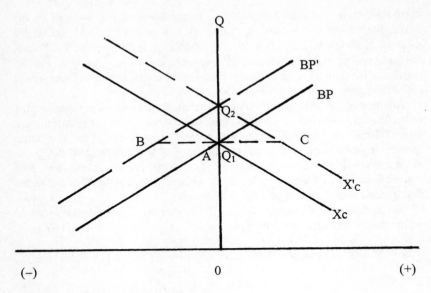

Figure 6.1 A simple CBP model

that generates a zero balance of payments occurs at point A in Figure 6.1, with a real exchange rate of Q_1.

6.4 SOME IMPLICATIONS OF THE CBP

6.4.1 A Counter-Example to the MBP

Rabin and Yeager (1979, 1983) criticize the MBP's assertion that a balance of payments deficit is always tied up with an excess supply of home money by offering several counter-examples. Their reasoning in one of these counter-examples goes something like this. Assume that all markets are initially in equilibrium, with a zero balance of payments. Then let an exogenous decrease in foreign demand for home exports create both a balance of trade and balance of payments deficit. They maintain that a disequilibrium in the home money market cannot possibly be the underlying cause of such a payments deficit, because the negative export shock has no initial impact on the home money market.

Rabin and Yeager's counter-example is illustrated in Figure 6.1. The economy is initially at point A, where the X_c and BP curves intersect. At point A, the real exchange rate is Q_1, the balance of payments is zero, and the home commodity market is in equilibrium. Then foreign preferences shift away from the home commodity. Thus, home exports fall and the trade balance and balance of payments deteriorate. This shifts the BP curve in Figure 6.1 to the left by the distance AB to BP'. Simultaneously, the decrease in exports creates an excess supply of the home commodity. Hence, the X_c curve shifts to the right to X'_c, with the distance AC equal to the distance BA.

If the nominal exchange rate is fixed, then the real exchange rate can rise to its new equilibrium value of Q_2 only via a change in relative price levels. If commodity prices are sticky, then a balance of payments deficit of BA, and a concomitant excess supply of home commodities, will exist. In sum, Rabin and Yeager's counter-example to the MBP is valid, and it is consistent with the commodity market approach to the balance of payments.

6.4.2 Aggregate Demand Policies for Balance of Payments Adjustment

The CBP provides important insights with regard to government policies to eliminate a balance of payments deficit. First, as Chapter 2 pointed out, the obvious payments adjustment policy, in general, is to facilitate market clearing. When the CBP is relevant, then the real exchange rate can move more quickly to its new equilibrium value of Q_2 in Figure 6.1 if the nominal exchange rate is flexible and/or if commodity prices are not sticky. In this case any payments deficit will be relatively short-lived.

Second, the CBP suggests that a widely accepted policy conclusion in the 'income-absorption' approach to the balance of payments is not always correct. This conclusion is that two appropriate government policies to correct a payments deficit are: (a) a tight monetary policy and/or (b) a contractionary fiscal policy. The logic here is tied up with a focus on the trade balance, and how it is affected by variations in aggregate demand. The presumption is that any policy induced decrease in aggregate demand will also reduce home demand for imports. If so, then supposedly the trade balance and balance of payments will improve in response to tight monetary and/or fiscal policy.

In truth, there are situations wherein these policy actions are correct. For example, if a payments deficit is associated with an excess supply of money (as in the MBP), then clearly policy (a) will directly reduce this excess supply and simultaneously reduce the payments deficit. Also, if a payments deficit is associated with an excess supply of bonds (as in the KBP), then the government's purchase of bonds that is an integral part of policy (b) will directly reduce this excess supply and decrease the size of the payments deficit.

However, if a payments deficit is associated with an excess supply in the home commodity market (as in the CBP), then a policy induced decrease in the aggregate demand for the home commodity (via tight monetary and/or fiscal policy) will **exacerbate** the situation. Such an action will increase the excess supply of the home commodity, and worsen the balance of payments deficit. Indeed, when a home payments deficit is associated with an excess supply in the commodity market, then one correct policy with regard to aggregate demand is a bond financed **increase** in government spending.

The obvious question is 'How in the world can an **increase** in government expenditure **reduce** a balance of payments deficit?' The logic underlying this important conclusion is as follows. A bond financed expansionary fiscal policy affects both the commodity market and bond market. More specifically 'income minus absorption' or V_c in (6.1b), decreases via any increase in government expenditure. Also, V_A in (6.1c) increases as a result of the sale of government bonds to finance the fiscal expansion. From (6.1d) it follows that $dV_c + dV_A \equiv 0$, i.e., the initial effect of a bond financed fiscal expansion on the commodity market just offsets the initial effect on the bond market.

The decrease in V_c reduces the total market excess supply of home commodities, X_c in (6.1b). Simultaneously the increase in V_A creates an incipient excess supply of home bonds, $X_A > 0$ in (6.1c). However, by assumption, the home bond market always clears instantaneously via the foreign purchase or sale of whatever quantity of bonds is dictated by the magnitude of V_A. In this case, the positive value for V_A means that foreigners will buy home bonds. This amounts to a home capital inflow, which improves the balance of payments.

Therefore, within the CBP a balance of payments deficit can be eliminated via a bond financed fiscal expansion that induces an improvement in the capital account. All of these examples illustrate a more general conclusion. The underlying 'cause' of a payments deficit can dictate the appropriate policy response.[6] Furthermore, what is desirable in one case can conceivably worsen the situation in another case.

6.4.3 Expenditure Switching Policies

Johnson (1961) pointed out that a payments deficit that exists when output is at its full employment level cannot be eliminated via an expenditure switching policy such as a depreciation of home money or higher import tariffs. His logic was that an expenditure switching policy in favor of the home commodity will simply raise home prices unless the government also engages in some type of (usually painful) expenditure reducing policy.

To explain, a nominal depreciation of home money will (with sticky commodity prices) temporarily reduce the relative price of home goods, i.e., a **real** depreciation. This improves the *ex ante* trade balance and balance of payments. However, unless more home output becomes available for exports and/or to replace imports, the long run effect of the nominal depreciation is simply to increase home prices. Thus, in the long run, the real exchange rate will return to its original value. Consequently, if output is at full employment, then a nominal depreciation also requires a policy that decreases home absorption. Such a policy is often resisted by governments, especially of low income countries, because it reduces consumption levels.

However, suppose that home output is at its full employment level, and then an exogenous decrease in the demand for home exports creates a payments deficit that is tied up with an excess supply of the home commodity. Within a Keynesian type of model, output and income will eventually decrease via the workings of a multiplier effect. However, this decrease in output need not occur. A timely expenditure switching policy is the appropriate action, and the latter does not need to be accompanied by an expenditure reducing policy if the CBP is relevant.

To explain, recall that in Figure 6.1 the dashed BP' and X'_c curves yield a balance of payments deficit of BA at real exchange rate Q_1. This payments deficit exists concomitantly with an excess supply of the home commodity of AC. In this case, an expenditure switching policy such as a depreciation of home money will increase the real exchange rate to Q_2 and return the balance of payments to zero. The switch in demand toward the home good that the real depreciation induces does not increase the relative price of the home commodity in the long run, because the home commodity market is in a state of excess supply when this depreciation takes place.

Also, when the CBP is relevant, then higher import tariffs can improve the *ex ante* trade balance and balance of payments, and not require a reduction in domestic absorption. In Figure 6.1, higher tariffs will decrease imports and shift the BP' curve to the right. Simultaneously, higher tariffs switch home demand away from the foreign commodity. This means that it now takes a lower value for the real exchange rate to clear the home commodity market. Therefore, higher import tariffs shift the X'_c curve in Figure 6.1 down and to the left. An appropriate increase in import tariffs can shift BP' to BP and X'_c to X_c. In this case, the home economy achieves a full macro-equilibrium, with a zero balance of payments, at the existing real exchange rate of Q_1.

6.5 THE WELFARE COST OF PAYMENTS ADJUSTMENT VIA TARIFFS

A widely accepted idea is that import tariffs are an undesirable tool for balance of payments adjustment, because they distort relative prices and thereby induce home agents to buy less than the socially optimum quantity of the imported good. This section reviews this well known idea. It also summarizes the idea that market disequilibrium also has a welfare cost associated with it. Consequently, if a tariff increases home demand for home goods and eliminates a commodity market excess supply, this creates a welfare gain compared to the disequilibrium situation. The end result is the possibility that the net change in domestic wellbeing (from using an import tariff to correct a balance of payments deficit) can conceivably be **positive** if the deficit is associated with an excess supply of commodities. This section briefly explores these ideas in a nonrigorous manner.

By assumption, home prices, P, and foreign prices, P*, are sticky, and the nominal exchange rate, S in units of home money per unit of FX, is fixed. Therefore, the real exchange rate $Q = SP^*/P$ is constant, and PPP holds, i.e., $Q = 1$. The relative price of the foreign commodity that home consumers perceive (including the effect of an ad valorem tariff, τ, on the home price of imports) is represented by Q' in (6.5). It is assumed that $\tau = 0$ initially, which means that initially $Q = Q' = 1$.

$$Q' = (1+\tau)SP^*/P = (1+\tau) Q \qquad (6.5)$$

In this case, Q' replaces Q as an argument in the import demand function, (6.2c). Q' is the 'tariff adjusted relative price of the imported good', as

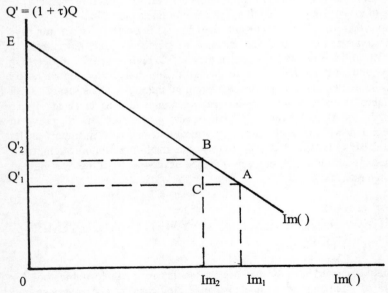

Figure 6.2 The deadweight loss from an import tariff

perceived by home agents. **Note well that any variation in Q' arises here solely via changes in the tariff rate, because Q is fixed in the short run by assumption.** Consequently, variations in Q' have no effect on exports. Figure 6.2 depicts the home demand for imports in units of the foreign commodity, Im( ). Initially, the home country is at point A on its import demand curve, with Q'_1 and Im_1. Total home consumers' surplus from imports is given by the area of the triangle EAQ'_1. This area is in units of the home commodity.

The inverse, 1/Q', is the tariff adjusted relative price of the home commodity', as perceived by home agents. Since home and foreign prices as well as the nominal exchange rate are fixed in the short run, any variation in 1/Q' also arises solely via changes in the tariff rate. Consumption demand for the home commodity in Figure 6.3 is given by total consumption minus the home commodity value of imports, C( ) – Q Im( ). It is a negative function of 1/Q'. As the tariff rate, τ, increases, this reduces the tariff adjusted relative price of the home commodity, i.e., it decreases 1/Q'. Consequently, the desired quantity of home imports falls. The result is an increase in the quantity of the home commodity demanded for consumption by home agents. In Figure 6.3 this is illustrated by the negatively sloped curve, C( ) – Q Im( ).

Domestic output available for home consumption, Z, is defined in (6.6a) as net income, X in (6.2g), minus exports, Ex( ). In Figure 6.3, domestic output available for home consumption is represented by a vertical line, be-

$$Z = X - Ex(\ ) \tag{6.6a}$$

$$Z = C(\ ) - Q\,Im(\ ) \tag{6.6b}$$

cause it is invariant with regard to 1/Q'. The reasons for this are: (a) total home output is fixed in any given period, and (b) exports are a function of the real exchange rate, Q, in (6.2b), and, by assumption, Q is constant here. Thus, variations in 1/Q' (via changes in the tariff rate) have no effect on the quantity of exports.

By assumption, initially the commodity market is in a state of excess supply in Figure 6.3. Initially, we have $1/Q'_1$, and an excess supply equal to the distance bh. The bond market is assumed to be in equilibrium. Consequently, there exists a balance of payments deficit of bh. Total consumers' surplus associated with the home commodity is given by the area of the triangle fbj in Figure 6.3. Total sellers' surplus associated with sales of the home commodity to home consumers is given by the area of the rectangle $0jbZ_1$ in Figure 6.3.[7]

Commodity market equilibrium occurs when home consumption demand for the home commodity equals home output minus the quantity of exports.

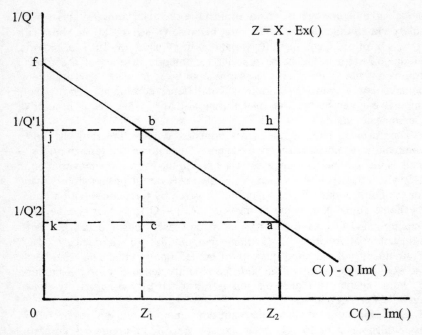

Figure 6.3 The welfare gain from clearing the commodity market

This occurs at point a in Figure 6.3. The economy could move from its initial state of excess supply to this equilibrium point simply via a change in the real exchange rate, Q. However, if the nominal exchange rate is fixed, and if sticky commodity prices mean that it takes time for commodity prices to adjust, then the excess supply of commodities (and the concomitant payments deficit) might persist for some time. The payments deficit, however, can be eliminated quickly via a higher import tariff. If the tariff rate is increased sufficiently, then the tariff adjusted relative price of the home good in Figure 6.3 can fall from $1/Q'_1$ to $1/Q'_2$, thereby yielding commodity market equilibrium at point a, and, hence, a zero balance of payments.

The move to point a increases total consumers' surplus in Figure 6.3 by the area of the quadrilateral kjba. Meanwhile, total sellers' surplus associated with sales to home consumers goes from $0jbZ_1$ to $0kaZ_2$. The combined result is an increase in the sum of consumers' plus sellers' surpluses by the area of the quadrilateral Z_1baZ_2 in Figure 6.3. This is measured in units of the foreign commodity.

This increase in home wellbeing from eliminating the excess supply of the home commodity tends to be offset (at least in part) by the decrease in wellbeing associated with the traditional deadweight loss from an import tariff. In Figure 6.2, the higher tariff rate increases the relative price of the imported good as perceived by home agents from Q'_1 to Q'_2. This reduces the quantity of imports to Im_2, and decreases total consumers' surplus associated with imports by the area of the quadrilateral $Q'_2BAQ'_1$. However, a portion of this decrease goes to the government in the form of tariff revenue, namely $Q'_2BCQ'_1$.

Thus, in Figure 6.2, the higher tariff generates a deadweight loss (in home commodity units) equal to the area of the triangle BAC, which is in units of the **home** commodity. Note, however, that the welfare gain in Figure 6.3 from eliminating the disequilibrium in the commodity market is measured in units of the **foreign** commodity. Consequently, in order to ascertain the overall net gain or loss from the tariff, everything would have to be measured in units of the same commodity. Also, a rigorous investigation of the welfare net gain or loss from eliminating a payments deficit via higher import tariffs would have to take account of the duration of the tariff versus what would have been the duration of the commodity market disequilibrium if the government did nothing.

To explain, import tariffs rarely last for only one time interval. Consequently, the true deadweight loss from the tariff is the present value of the deadweight loss in the current and all future periods. This present value must be calculated over a time horizon equal to the life of the tariff. Similarly, the true welfare gain from eliminating the commodity market disequilibrium is the present value of the gain in the current and all future periods. The latter depends on how long the market disequilibrium would persist if the government did nothing to eliminate it.

The important point is that the net welfare gain or loss from balance of payments adjustment via import tariffs appears to be uncertain. Traditional thinking on the welfare loss from payments adjustment via higher import tariffs implicitly assumes that all commodity markets are always in equilibrium. Hence, it misses the gain from eliminating the market disequilibrium that can be associated with a nonzero balance of payments.

6.6   SUMMARY

1. We know from Chapter 2 that a nonzero balance of payments must always be associated with a disequilibrium in a market in addition to the FX market. The MBP assumes that the money market does not clear, whereas the KBP assumes that the bond market does not clear initially.

2. No one has developed a commodity market approach to the balance of payments, CBP. This is surprising because the CBP represents a fixed

exchange rate version of the equilibrium approach to the determination of the exchange rate.

3. The CBP is relevant if a balance of payments deficit is associated with an excess **supply** in the home commodity market. This is just the opposite of the widely held conclusion that payments deficits arise when home commodity demand is too high.

4. The CBP is most likely to be relevant if the nominal exchange rate is fixed, commodity prices are sticky, and a country experiences an exogenous shock to its exports. It may also be relevant if an exogenous shock to imports occurs.

5. If a payments deficit is associated with an excess supply of the home commodity, then painful expenditure reducing policies are not needed, even if home output is at its maximum level. Expenditure switching policies are sufficient

6. A payments deficit that is associated with an excess supply in the home commodity market can be eliminated via a bond financed **increase** in government spending. The higher level of government spending eliminates the excess supply of commodities. Also, the sale of bonds to finance the increase in government expenditure induces a capital inflow, which eliminates the payments deficit.

7. This is the opposite of the conventional idea that tight monetary and/or fiscal policies are always needed to eliminate a balance of payments deficit. The latter actions, however, appear to be proper if a payments deficit is associated with an excess supply of money, as in the MBP, or an excess supply of bonds, as in the KBP. In general, it seems as though the appropriate government policy depends on which market is out of equilibrium.

8. If a payments deficit is associated with an excess supply of the home commodity, then adjustment via higher import tariffs has two types of welfare effects. Domestic wellbeing falls as a result of a decrease in consumers' surplus that is caused by the higher (after the tariff) price for imports; this represents the traditional 'deadweight loss' from a tariff. Also, domestic wellbeing increases when the excess supply of the home commodity is eliminated. The net effect of balance of payments adjustment via import tariffs on domestic wellbeing appears to be uncertain. It depends, in part, on how long a new tariff will exist, versus the length of time it would take the commodity market to clear if the government did nothing.

9. The widely accepted conclusion that payments adjustment via higher tariffs is always undesirable implicitly assumes that the commodity market is always in equilibrium.

NOTES

1. Recall that an exception to this deals with those versions of the Mundell/Fleming model that specify money market equilibrium in a manner that embodies the MBP.
2. The CBP was anticipated by Rabin (1979) who proved that the balance of payments will equal the excess demand or supply of commodities under certain circumstances. However, he did not develop this important conclusion.
3. There appears to be a lack of consistency in the literature concerning the definition of the real exchange rate. Many scholars define it to be the relative price of the home versus foreign commodity. This is also the terms of trade in a model wherein each country produces only one commodity. On the other hand, if each country produces an indentical traded good and different non-traded goods, then the real exchange rate is usually defined as the relative price of the home nontraded good in terms of the trade good. Such an approach, however, suggests that there are two real exchange rates, since there also exists the relative price of the foreign nontraded good in terms of the traded good. Finally, the real exchange rate can be defined as the rate at which a basket of goods consumed at home (which includes imports) trades for goods consumed abroad (which includes home exports).
4. If money exists as a good, then the relevant open economy Walrasian identity becomes: $Xc + X_A + X_M \equiv -BP$ In this case, the CBP is relevant if both the money and the bond market clear but the commodity market does not.
5. In an open economy intertemporal model, Davis and Miller (1996) rigorously derive import and export functions that are consistent with those used here.
6. The word 'cause' appears within quotation marks, because a balance of payments deficit or surplus is not caused by a nonclearing market. Rather, the open economy Walrasian identity tells us only that a payments imbalance must be **associated with** a nonclearing market other than the FX market.
7. Several important points are in order. First, since home net output, $Y - I - G$, is fixed exogenously here, it follows that home firms will be willing to sell this output at any price. Thus, the total sellers' surplus from selling to home consumers equals the quantity sold multiplied by its relative price. The second point is that the analysis ignores any sellers' surplus associated with government purchases of the home commodity. Also, it ignores any sellers' surplus tied up with the sale of the home commodity for exports or investment. Finally, the analysis ignores any consideration of the welfare effects of intertemporal trade. Thus, the conclusions reached in the text must be considered only as suggestive until future work can rigorously drop these simplifying assumptions.

7. A loanable funds theory of the exchange rate

7.1 INTRODUCTION[1]

From Chapter 2 we know that the Walrasian identity for a three good, open economy period model, is given by

$$X_c + X_A + X_m \equiv - X_{FX} \qquad (7.1)$$

where each X_i represents the total market excess supply of good i. Thus, a disequilibrium in any market (including the FX market) must be accompanied by an offsetting excess supply or demand in at least one other market. In Chapter 6, the nominal exchange rate was fixed and commodity prices were sticky, which meant that the real exchange rate did not move quickly to clear the commodity market. By assumption, therefore, any disequilibrium in the commodity market was associated with a nonzero balance of payments, thereby yielding a commodity market approach to the balance of payments.

The sticky price 'exchange rate overshooting' model of Dornbusch (1976), Frenkel and Rodriguez (1982), and others, also assumes that the commodity market does not clear instantaneously. However, these models assume that a flexible nominal exchange rate constantly clears the FX market. Therefore, the disequilibrium in the commodity market must be accompanied by another nonclearing market other than the FX market. The sticky-price monetary model of the exchange rate (sticky-price MER) of Dornbusch and Frenkel and Rodriguez assumes that the interest rate is always determined via equilibrium in the money market. Hence, if the FX and money markets always clear, then from (7.1) the sticky-price MER implicitly assumes that the bond market is the other market that is out of equilibrium when the commodity market does not clear.[2]

It is well known that the loanable funds and liquidity preference theories generate the same equilibrium interest rate if all markets are in equilibrium.[3] However, in disequilibrium this is not true.[4] The apparent consensus is that in a disequilibrium situation the interest rate generated by bond market equilibrium (the loanable funds theory) is not identical to the interest rate generated by the money market (the liquidity preference theory) unless the money market is altered in one of two ways. These alterations are: (a) money demand must depend on planned transactions, rather than on income, or (b) money demand includes all spillovers from any nonclearing markets.[5] Without at least one of these complications the loanable funds and liquidity preference theories are not equivalent, except when all markets clear.

This chapter explains the importance of these ideas for exchange rate theory. More specifically, since the loanable funds theory generates a different interest rate in disequilibrium (following monetary or fiscal shocks) than the interest rate generated by a monetary model, it follows that the dynamics of the exchange rate depend on which market determines the interest rate. The ideas here were developed by Bhandari (1981), Karacaoglu (1985), Chen *et al.* (1988b), and Miller (1995). They are referred to here as the 'sticky-price loanable funds theory of the exchange rate', or sticky-price LFER.

This new theory provides an explanation for puzzle #10, i.e., the change (during the 1970s) from negative to positive in the three month response of the U.S. nominal interest rate to a monetary shock.[6] In addition, the model is consistent with two other sets of interesting empirical findings, namely: (a) Sachs' (1983) conclusion that with relatively high frequency data there is a short run **negative** relationship between the current account and changes in the value of the home currency in smaller OECD countries, but a **positive** relationship in larger OECD countries; and (b) Fair's (1982) empirical conclusion that in many cases a US fiscal expansion initially causes an appreciation of the dollar, but ultimately a depreciation.

At the purely theoretical level, it is proven below that two conclusions in the 'exchange rate overshooting' literature are not correct if the interest rate is determined in disequilibrium via a loanable funds theory. The first incorrect conclusion is that fiscal shocks cannot cause exchange rate overshooting. The second incorrect conclusion is that a monetary shock is certain to cause overshooting if the interest elasticity of international capital flows approaches infinity.

Section 7.2 develops the long run monetary approach to the exchange rate, MER, and the long run loanable funds approach, LFER. It also reproduces the standard conclusions of these models with regard to the long run effects of a monetary or fiscal shock on prices, interest rates, and the exchange rate. Then section 7.3 reviews the well known dynamics of the interest rate and the exchange rate within the sticky-price MER as a result of a fiscal or a monetary shock. Next, section 7.4 investigates the dynamics of the interest rate and exchange rate within the sticky-price LFER following a fiscal shock. This is followed in section 7.5 by a careful investigation of the dynamics of the interest rate and exchange rate from a monetary shock within the sticky-price LFER. The chapter ends with a summary in section 7.6.

7.2 THE LONG RUN MONETARY AND LOANABLE FUNDS MODELS

Equations (7.2a) through (7.2d) specify the equilibrium conditions in total differential form that relate to the long run MER and LFER. All variables are in logs, which means that the parameters are elasticities, all of which are defined to be positive. Equation (7.2a) specifies commodity market equilibrium. Output does not appear because it is constant at its natural rate. The equation says that any net change in the aggregate demand for the home commodity must be zero. This depends on changes in the trade balance, where the latter is a positive function of changes in the real exchange rate, $dp^* - dp + ds$, where p^* is the foreign price level, p is home prices, and s is the nominal exchange rate in units of home money per unit of FX. The elasticity of the trade balance with regard to the real exchange rate is given by the parameter δ. Also, the demand for the home commodity increases with a decrease in the home interest rate, $di < 0$, and/or any exogenous increase in home government purchases, $dg > 0$.

$$\delta(dp^* - dp + ds) - \sigma di + dg \;=\; 0 \tag{7.2a}$$

$$\delta(dp^* - dp + ds) + k[(di - di^*) - \theta\{dE[s] - ds\}] = 0 \tag{7.2b}$$

$$dm - dp + \lambda di = 0 \tag{7.2c}$$

$$(da + a_1 dp - a_2 di) - k[(di - di^*) - \theta\{dE[s] - ds\}] = 0 \tag{7.2d}$$

$$dE[s] = ds \tag{7.2e}$$

$$\sigma, \; \delta, \; k, \; \lambda, \; a_1, a_2 > 0 \tag{7.2f}$$

Equation (7.2b) specifies balance of payments or FX market equilibrium in total differential form. Changes in the current account, which (for simplicity) is just the trade balance here, are given by $\delta(dp^* - dp + ds)$. To keep the balance of payments zero, any variation in the trade balance must be offset by changes in the net capital flow, $k[(di - di^*) - \theta\{dE[s] - ds\}]$. The **level** of the net capital flow is assumed to depend on divergences from uncovered interest parity, as given by the home minus foreign interest rate differential, $i - i^*$, plus the expected value of any percentage change in the spot rate, $E[s] - s$.

Money market equilibrium is given by (7.2c), which says that any percentage change in the nominal money supply, dm, must equal the percentage change in nominal money demand. The latter is given by the percentage change in home prices plus the effect on money demand from any variation in the home rate of interest. Finally, bond market equilibrium is given by (7.2d), which uses the Walrasian identity (7.1) to deduce that the excess supply of bonds must equal minus the sum of the excess supplies in the FX, commodity, and money markets.[7] The da term represents any exogenous change in bond supply. From (7.1), the values for the parameters da, a_1, and a_2 are determined by the constraints given by (7.3a) through (7.3c).[8]

$$\sigma - a_2 + \lambda \equiv 0 \qquad (7.3a)$$

$$a_1 - 1 \equiv 0 \qquad (7.3b)$$

$$-dg + da + dm \equiv 0 \qquad (7.3c)$$

The long run MER model consists of (7.2a), (7.2b), and (7.2c), with the added condition that the value for the exchange rate (and any changes in it) equals its expected value, as in (7.2e). On the other hand, the long run LFER model replaces the money market equilibrium condition, (7.2c), with bond market equilibrium, (7.2d). The well known solutions to these models are identical and are given by (7.4a) through (7.4c).

The three expressions in (7.4a) indicate that money is neutral in the long run. Variations in it have a proportional effect on the nominal exchange rate (which means that the real exchange rate is unaffected) and on the price level. Thus, it has no permanent effect on the interest rate. The solutions in (7.4b) say that a positive fiscal shock, $dg > 0$, increases home prices and the interest rate in the long run. Notice that the home interest rate can change in the long run, even though the foreign interest rate is constant. This implies that the model allows for **permanent** deviations from uncovered interest parity, UIP.

$$(ds/dm)_{LR} = 1 \qquad (dp/dm)_{LR} = 1 \qquad (di/dm)_{LR} = 0 \qquad (7.4a)$$

$$(dp/dg)_{LR} = 1/\delta(k + \sigma) > 0 \qquad (di/dg)_{LR} = 1/(k + \sigma) > 0 \qquad (7.4b)$$

$$(ds/dg)_{LR} - (\delta\lambda - k)/\delta(k + \sigma) \gtrless 0 \qquad (7.4c)$$

The higher level of home prices worsens the current account, while the increase in the home interest rate improves the capital account. Consequently, the net effect of a positive fiscal shock on the incipient balance of payments, and, hence, on the nominal exchange rate, is uncertain in (7.4c).

7.3 THE STICKY-PRICE MER

7.3.1 The CmCm and AmAm Curves

This section reviews the well known dynamics of the interest rate and exchange rate within the sticky-price MER in response to a fiscal shock and then a monetary shock. In the short run, commodity prices are fixed but the exchange rate and interest rate move quickly to clear the money market and FX market, i.e, these asset markets are always in equilibrium. This means that the commodity market (and, within a period framework, the bond market) can be out of equilibrium in the short run.

Then, in the long run, prices adjust to equilibrate the commodity market. In the interval during which prices are adjusting, the interest rate and exchange rate move to keep the two asset markets (money and FX) in equilibrium. Consequently, the **short run** sticky-price MER model consists of the balance of payments and money market equilibrium equations, (7.2b) and (7.2c), with the added assumption that exchange rate expectations are rational, which means that the long run solution for ds is substituted for $dE[s]$.

The MER is illustrated in Figures 7.1a and 7.1b. The CmCm curves indicate the combinations of the home price level and nominal exchange rate that simultaneously yield money market and commodity market equilibrium. In total differential form, CmCm is given by (7.5a) below. The CmCm curve has a positive slope for the following reasons: (a) An increase in the home price level deteriorates the home trade balance and creates an excess supply of the home commodity. (b) Also, the increase in home prices reduces the home real money supply, which raises the home interest rate, and, hence, reduces domestic investment; this contributes to an even larger excess supply of the home commodity. Therefore, (c), in order to eliminate the excess supply of the home commodity, a depreciation of home money, $ds > 0$, is needed to stimulate the trade balance. The CmCm curve shifts down and to the right with an increase in government spending or the money supply, because these shocks require a higher price level and/or an

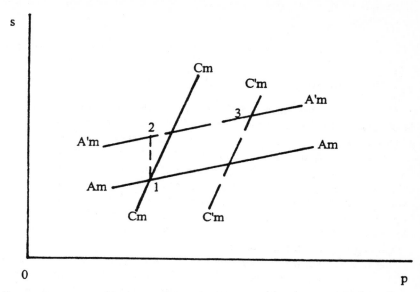

Figure 7.1a Fiscal shocks within the sticky-price MER: undershooting

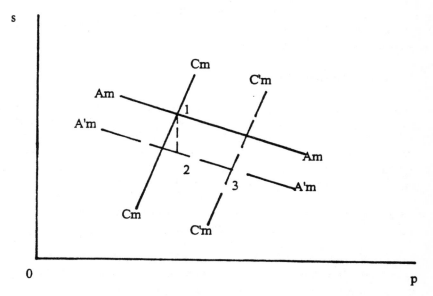

Figure 7.1b Fiscal shocks within the sticky-price MER: undershooting

appreciation of home money in order to maintain commodity market equilibrium.

$$ds = (1 + \sigma/\lambda\delta)dp - (1/\delta)dg - (\sigma/\lambda\delta)dm \qquad (7.5a)$$

$$ds = [(\delta - k/\lambda)/(\delta + k\theta)]dp + [1/(k + k\theta)]\{(k/\lambda)dm + k\theta\, dE[s]\} \quad (7.5b)$$

The AmAm curves in Figures 7.1a and 7.1b depict combinations of the home price level and nominal exchange rate that simultaneously generate money market and balance of payments (or FX market) equilibrium. They are given by equation (7.5b), which indicates that the slope of AmAm depends on the sign of $\delta - k/\lambda$. These terms relate to how a higher home price level affects the incipient balance of payments. The δ term is tied up with the fact that higher home prices deteriorate the trade balance. On the other hand, the k/λ term relates to the fact that higher home prices increase the home interest rate (via a decrease in the home real money supply), which improves the capital account.

On the one hand, if the δ term dominates the k/λ term in (7.5b), then the incipient balance of payments **deteriorates** with higher home prices, and a depreciation of home money, $ds > 0$, is needed to obtain a zero balance of payments. In this case, the AmAm curve has a positive slope as in Figure 7.1a.[9] On the other hand, if the k/λ term dominates the δ term, then the incipient balance of payments **improves** with higher home prices. This, in turn, necessitates a home currency appreciation, $ds < 0$, and yields a negatively sloped AmAm curve, as in Figure 7.1b.

7.3.2 A Fiscal Expansion

Within the sticky-price MER, the short run and long run effects on the exchange rate from a bond financed increase in home government purchases are illustrated in Figures 7.1a and 7.1b. The main idea is that the economy always moves instantaneously to its asset market equilibrium curve, AmAm, via variations in the interest rate and nominal exchange rate. In the short run, it need not be on its commodity market equilibrium locus, CmCm, because commodity prices are sticky. Then, in the long run, commodity prices adjust and the economy moves along its AmAm curve to the point where AmAm and CmCm intersect.

From (7.5a) an increase in government expenditure shifts the CmCm curve to the right as to C'mC'm in both graphs. Also, from (7.5b) the fiscal expansion affects the asset market equilibrium curve, AmAm, via its effect on the change in the long run equilibrium exchange rate. The logic here is as follows. In Figure 7.1a, the shift to the right in the CmCm curve, and the positive slope for the AmAm curve, mean that in the long run the spot rate must increase. The assumption of rational expectations implies that agents correctly anticipate this long run increase in the exchange rate. Consequently, asset markets will clear only at a higher value for the exchange rate. This implies that the asset market equilibrium locus shifts upward, as to A'mA'm in Figure 7.1a, with a fiscal expansion.

The assumptions of sticky prices and of continuous asset market clearing mean that the economy moves in the short run in Figure 7.1a from point 1 to point 2. Home money depreciates. Then, in the long run, home prices rise and the economy moves up and to the right along the A'mA'm curve to point 3. Consequently, in Figure 7.1a home money depreciates in the short run, and depreciates even more in the long run. That is, exchange rate **under**shooting occurs in the short run.

In Figure 7.1b, the rightward shift in the CmCm curve (from the increase in government spending) along with the negatively sloped AmAm curve means that home money must **appreciate** in the long run, i.e., $ds < 0$. When agents anticipate this, it follows from (7.5b) that the asset market equilibrium locus shifts downward, as to A'mA'm in Figure 7.1b. Hence, in the short run with the price level fixed, the economy jumps down from point 1 to point 2 as home money appreciates. Then in the long run, as the price level rises, home money appreciates even more as the economy moves along A'mA'm to point 3. Again, there is exchange rate **under**shooting in the short run. This reproduces the well known conclusion that **fiscal policy cannot cause exchange rate overshooting within the sticky-price MER.**[10]

The dynamics of the interest rate within the sticky-price MER are extremely simple. Since the increase in government spending is financed via the sale of bonds, the money market is not affected initially. Thus, within the sticky-price MER, short run equilibrium occurs at an unchanged interest rate in the MER. Then, as the home price level rises in the long run, the real money supply falls, and this increases the home interest rate.

7.3.3 A Monetary Expansion

The dynamics of the exchange rate in response to a monetary shock (within the sticky-price MER) are illustrated in Figures 7.2a and 7.2b. From (7.5a), a positive monetary shock shifts the CmCm curve down and to the right in both graphs. Also, from (7.5b), a positive monetary shock shifts the AmAm curve upward in both graphs.[11] With sticky prices, but with continuous asset market equilibrium, a positive monetary shock prompts the exchange rate to jump upward in the short run from point 1 to point 2 in both graphs. The intuition is as follows. A positive shock to the nominal money supply, with

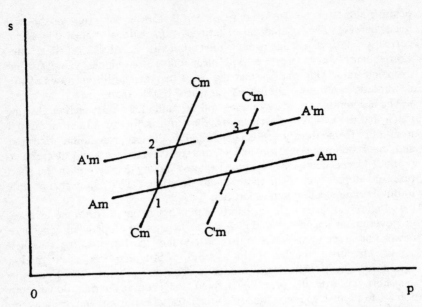

Figure 7.2a Monetary shocks within the sticky-price MER: undershooting

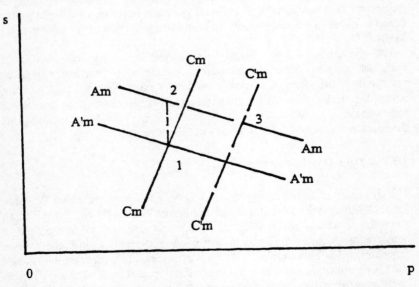

Figure 7.2b Monetary shocks within the sticky-price MER: overshooting

the price level constant serves to increase the real money supply and reduce the home interest rate. The latter deteriorates the capital account, which means that home money must depreciate in order to improve the trade balance and maintain FX market equilibrium.

In the long run, the monetary expansion increases the price level proportionately via (7.4a). In Figure 7.2a, the positive slope for the A'mA'm curve means that the incipient balance of payments deteriorates with an increase in the price level. Consequently, in order to maintain a zero balance of payments (and FX market equilibrium), home money depreciates more in the long run in Figure 7.2a, as the economy moves from point 2 to point 3. Therefore, in this case, a monetary shock causes exchange rate undershooting.[12]

On the other hand, exchange rate **over**shooting takes place in Figure 7.2b. The negatively sloped A'mA'm curve means that the incipient balance of payments improves as home prices increase. Therefore, home money appreciates as the economy moves in the long run from point 2 to point 3 in Figure 7.2b, i.e., the exchange rate initially overshoots its long run equilibrium value. The reason for this is that the gradual increase in the price level in the long run improves the balance of payments, and this necessitates a home currency appreciation in order to keep the balance of payments zero.

The logic in the previous two paragraphs was first pointed out by Chen *et al.* (1988a). **That is, exchange rate overshooting does not depend on the existence of uncovered interest parity, UIP.** Recall that the model here does not require UIP ever to hold.[13] Overshooting occurs simply because the AmAm curve has a negative slope, and this is true because a higher home price level improves the incipient balance of payments. Within the monetary model, this is certain to occur as the interest elasticity of international capital flows, k in (7.2b), (7.2d), and (7.5b), approaches infinity.[14]

An infinite value for this elasticity means that the capital account improves tremendously as the home interest rate rises in response to a higher home price level. This is certain to dominate any deterioration in the trade balance as home prices rise. Hence, the incipient balance of payments is certain to improve with higher home prices, thereby yielding a negatively sloped AmAm curve. In sum, **exchange rate overshooting always occurs (within the sticky-price MER) in response to a monetary shock if the interest elasticity of capital flows approaches infinity.**

In sum, the standard version of the sticky-price MER never generates exchange rate overshooting in response to a bond financed fiscal shock. It, however, yields either exchange rate undershooting or overshooting in response to a monetary shock, regardless of whether UIP holds.

7.4 THE STICKY-PRICE LFER

7.4.1 The Sticky-Price LFER versus the Sticky-Price MER

The sticky-price LFER model is illustrated in Figures 7.3a and 7.3b. In both graphs the $C_L C_L$ curve depicts the combinations of the price level and nominal exchange rate that yield bond market and commodity market equilibrium. Algebraically, this is given by (7.6a). As in the sticky-price MER, the $C_L C_L$ curve has a positive slope.[15] The $C_L C_L$ curve shifts up and to the left with an exogenous increase in bond supply, da > 0, or an expected depreciation of home money, $dE[s] > 0$.[16]

On the other hand, an increase in government purchases shifts the $C_L C_L$ curve down and to the right in both Figure 7.3a and 7.3b. The higher demand for the home commodity creates an excess demand for it. This raises the home price level and/or appreciates home money. The net effect of a bond financed fiscal expansion, i.e., $da = dg > 0$, is to shift the $C_L C_L$ curve down and to the right, provided that there is incomplete crowding out of domestic investment by the higher level of government spending. This will be true if the interest elasticity of investment, σ, is less than unity.

$$ds=[\delta(a_2+k) + \sigma a_1]/\Omega_o]dp+[\sigma/\Omega_o](da+k\theta\,dE[s]) - [(a_2+k)/\Omega_o]dg \quad (7.6a)$$

$$ds=\{[\delta - k/(a_2+k)] /\Omega_1\}dp - \{[k/(a_2+k)]/\Omega_1\}da +$$

$$\{k\theta[1 - k/(a_2+k)]/\Omega_1\}dE[s] \qquad (7.6b)$$

$$\Omega_o = [\delta(a_2+k) + k\theta\sigma] > 0 \qquad (7.6c)$$

$$\Omega_1 = [\delta(a_2 + k) + a_2 k\theta]/(a_2 + k) > 0 \qquad (7.6d)$$

The $A_L A_L$ curves in Figures 7.3a and 7.3b illustrate simultaneous equilibrium in the bond market and FX market. (Ignore the AmAm curves for now.) This is given by equation (7.6b). The slope of $A_L A_L$ depends on $[\delta - k/(a_2 + k)]$ which can be positive or negative. The logic here is similar to that associated with the slope of AmAm, the asset market equilibrium curve in the sticky price MER. That is, the slope of $A_L A_L$ depends on whether an increase in the home price level improves or worsens the incipient balance of payments.

If δ dominates $k/(a_2 + k)$, then a higher home price level worsens the trade balance and current account more than it improves the capital account. The latter occurs because the higher home price level raises the interest rate.

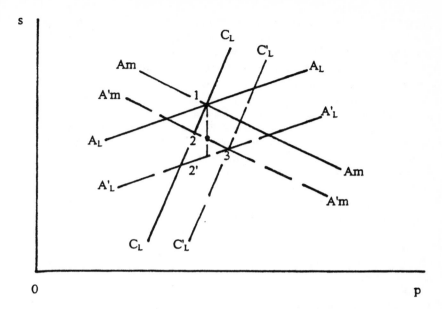

Figure 7.3a Fiscal shocks within the sticky-price LFER: overshooting

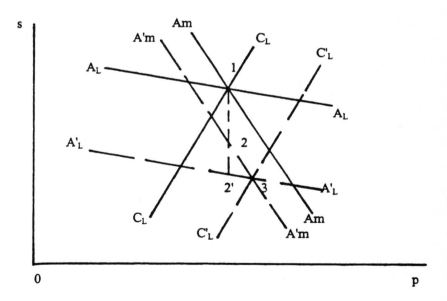

Figure 7.3b Fiscal shocks within the sticky-price LFER: undershooting

Hence, the incipient balance of payments deteriorates as the home price level rises, and we need a depreciation of home money, $ds > 0$, to keep the FX market (and the balance of payments) in equilibrium. Consequently, in this case the A_LA_L curve has a positive slope as in Figure 7.3a.[17]

On the other hand, if the $k/(a_2 + k)$ term dominates the δ term, then the A_LA_L curve has a negative slope, as in Figure 7.3b. In this case, a higher domestic price level improves the capital account (via the concomitant increase in the home interest rate) more than it deteriorates the current account. Therefore, the resulting improvement in the incipient balance of payments requires an appreciation of home money, $ds < 0$, in order to keep the balance of payments zero.

From (7.6b) the A_LA_L curve shifts vertically downward (which is a shift to the right in Figure 7.3a, but a shift to the left in Figure 7.3b) with an exogenous increase in bond supply, $da > 0$. This occurs if a fiscal expansion is bond financed, or if a decrease in the money supply occurs via open market sales of bonds. Equation (7.6b) also tells us that the A_LA_L curve shifts vertically upward when agents expect the nominal exchange rate to depreciate in the future, $dE[s] > 0$.

7.4.2 The Sticky-Price MER versus the Sticky-Price LFER

Recall that the dynamics of the exchange rate within the sticky-price MER depend on the slope of the AmAm curve, the asset market equilibrium locus. It is shown below that the same is true within the sticky-price LFER. However, the sticky-price LFER and sticky-price MER models generate different dynamics for the exchange rate, because the slope of the A_LA_L curve is algebraically larger than the slope of the AmAm curve.[18] This is true because a higher price level increases the home interest rate less within the LFER model than it does within the MER.

To see this, note from the money market equilibrium equation, (7.2c), that the effect on the interest rate from a change in the price level, di/dp, is given by $1/\lambda$. On the other hand, within the LFER, the effect on the interest rate from a change in the price level comes from the bond market equilibrium equation (7.2d), and this is given by $1/(a_2 + k)$. Using the constraints on the parameters given by (7.3a) and (7.3b), it follows that:

$$1/(a_2 + k) = 1/(\lambda + \sigma + k) < 1/\lambda \qquad (7.7)$$

Since a higher price level increases the interest rate less within the LFER, it follows that any given increase in home prices improves the capital account less within the LFER. The negative effect of any given increase in home prices on the current account is the same in both models. Hence, the incipient balance of payments will be less positive or more negative (as home prices rise) within the LFER, than it will be within the MER. Therefore, the exchange rate must change by different amounts (in response to variations in the price level) within the two models. This, in turn, means that the slopes of the asset market curves (and the dynamics of the exchange rate) differ between the two models.

Since the slope of the A_LA_L curve is algebraically larger than the slope of the AmAm curve, it follows that: (a) if A_LA_L and AmAm both have positive slopes, than A_LA_L is steeper; (b) if both curves have negative slopes, then A_LA_L is flatter, as in Figure 7.3b; and (c) it is possible for A_LA_L to be positively sloped, while AmAm is negatively sloped, as in Figure 7.3a. We will see momentarily that all of this leads to very interesting differences in the dynamic response of the exchange rate to monetary or fiscal shocks.

7.4.3 Interest Rate and Exchange Rate Dynamics from a Fiscal Shock

Recall that in the sticky-price MER, a bond financed fiscal expansion has no immediate effect on the interest rate. Then, as the price level rises in the long run, the real money supply falls, and this gradually increases the home interest rate.   On the other hand, the dynamics of the interest rate in response to a bond financed fiscal expansion within the sticky-price LFER are much more interesting. In the short run, the interest rate rises because of the sale of government bonds, $da > 0$ in (7.2d). From (7.4b), the interest rate rises also in the long run. The dynamics of the interest rate depend on the difference between the short run and long run effects, as given by

$$(di/dg)_{SR} - (di/dg)_{LR} \; \overset{>}{\underset{<}{-}} \; 0 \quad as \; -[k\theta(1-\delta) + \delta] \; \overset{>}{\underset{<}{-}} \; 0 \qquad (7.8)$$

The $-[k\theta(1-\delta) + \delta]$ term is certain to be negative if $\delta < 1$. In this case the short run increase in the interest rate is less than the long run increase. However, this expression can conceivably be positive if $\delta > 1$, and this implies that **interest rate overshooting** is possible within the sticky-price LFER if the price elasticity of the trade balance exceeds unity.

In this case, Miller (1995) proves that the incipient balance of payments is certain to deteriorate as the home price level increases in the long run. This means that the nominal exchange rate must depreciate, $ds > 0$, slowly over time as the home price level rises. From (7.2b) an increase in the spot rate (with the change in the expected long run spot rate constant) induces an improvement in the capital account. This, in turn, exerts a downward effect on the home rate of interest. Therefore, a bond financed fiscal expansion initially increases the interest rate, and it is possible that it overshoots its long run increase.

Turn now to the dynamics of the exchange rate. Recall that exchange rate overshooting never occurs in response to a bond financed change in government spending within the traditional version of the sticky-price MER. This is not true within the sticky-price LFER. The short run effect of a bond financed fiscal expansion on the exchange rate within the sticky-price LFER model, $(ds/dg)_{SR}$, is given by

$$(ds/dg)_{SR} = [-k/(a_2 + k)/\Omega_1 + [\{k\theta[1 - k/(a_2 + k)]/\Omega_1\}dE[s]/dg] \quad (7.9a)$$

The first term on the rhs of (7.9a) is negative, while the second term could be positive or negative, depending on the sign of $dE[s]/dg$ via (7.4c). Thus, the exchange rate could conceivably appreciate or depreciate initially.

The dynamics of the exchange rate depend on the relationship between the short run change in the exchange rate given by (7.9a), and the long run change in the exchange rate, $(ds/dg)_{LR}$, given by (7.4c). Subtracting the latter from the former yields:

$$(ds/dg)_{SR} - (ds/dg)_{LR} \gtrless 0 \quad as \quad -[\delta - k/(a_2 + k)] \gtrless 0 \quad (7.9b)$$

Recall, from equation (7.6b), that the sign of $[\delta - k/(a_2 + k)]$ determines the slope of the $A_L A_L$ curve. Assume that this slope is positive, as in Figure 7.3a, and that the AmAm curve has a negative slope. In this case, a bond financed fiscal expansion shifts both asset market equilibrium loci downward from the solid curves to the dashed curves. With the price level initially constant, this appreciates home money in the short run, i.e., $(ds/dg)_{SR} < 0$. In Figure 7.3a, the economy moves from point 1 to point 2 in a sticky-price MER, but from point 1 to point 2' in the sticky-price LFER. Note well that home money appreciates more in the short run within the LFER model than within the MER model.

In the long run, domestic prices rise, and in both models the economy moves along its asset market equilibrium locus in Figure 7.3a toward point 3. Point 3 represents a long run appreciation of home money compared to point 1. Thus, $(ds/dg)_{LR} < 0$ in (7.9b). In the sticky-price MER, the exchange rate continues to appreciate as the price level rises and the economy moves along A'mA'm from point 2 to point 3, i.e., undershooting occurs.

Both the short run and long run changes in the exchange rate are negative on the left side of (7.9b). Furthermore, when the $A_L A_L$ curve has a positive slope, then the second condition in (7.9b) is negative. This means that the long run appreciation, when moving to point 3 in Figure 7.3a, must be less than the short run appreciation. Consequently, in this case, exchange rate **overshooting** occurs in response to a bond financed fiscal expansion within the sticky-price LFER as the economy moves from point 1 to point 2' in the short run, and then eventually to point 3.

Why can the exchange rate initially overshoot its long run equilibrium (in response to a fiscal shock) within the sticky-price LFER model but not within the monetary model? The answer is tied up with the fact that within the sticky-price MER, any short run exchange rate variation (from a fiscal shock) arises solely via the effect of exchange rate expectations on the asset market. The latter depends totally on the slope of the AmAm curve, which, in turn, depends on how a higher home price level affects the incipient balance of payments.

Note that within the sticky-price MER there is no short run change in the interest rate from a bond financed fiscal expansion. This is true because the money market determines the interest rate, and an increase in government spending accompanied by the sale of government bonds does not have a direct impact on money supply or money demand. Hence, in the sticky-price MER, there is no short run interest rate effect (from a bond financed fiscal expansion) on the exchange rate. Thus, the short run change in the exchange rate will always be in the same direction that it moves when prices rise in the long run. Consequently, exchange rate undershooting always occurs.

On the other hand, the sticky-price LFER's assumption that the bond market always determines the interest rate means that a bond financed fiscal expansion immediately increases the home interest rate. This induces a capital inflow, which means that home money must **instantaneously** appreciate for two reasons, namely: (a) the expectation of a long run appreciation, as in the MER, and (b) the need to decrease the value for the current account in order to offset the capital inflow induced by the higher home interest rate. Reason (b) means that it is possible for the short run change in the exchange rate to be in the opposite direction from the movement in the exchange rate as the economy moves along its A_LA_L curve when prices rise in the long run. Consequently, within the sticky-price LFER, exchange rate overshooting can occur in the short run in response to a fiscal shock.

The dynamics of the exchange rate in Figure 7.3a illustrate Fair's (1982) empirical finding that the US dollar often appreciates initially in response to a US fiscal expansion (as in moving from point 1 to point 2'), but then the dollar depreciates later (as in moving from point 2' to point 3). Note, also, that if the current account is zero initially, then the appreciation of home money in moving from point 1 to point 2' in Figure 7.3a will create a current account deficit. This implies that the home current account will be negative as home money depreciates, when moving from point 2' to point 3 in Figure 7.3a.

This negative relationship between the current account and the exchange rate is what Sachs (1983) found to be true for smaller OECD countries. It can occur within the sticky-price LFER model only if the $A_L A_L$ curve has a positive slope, and this arises if the incipient home balance of payments deteriorates as the home price level rises. The latter, in turn, is more likely if the trade balance price elasticity, δ, is larger, and/or if capital flows respond less vigorously to interest rate variations.

It is well known that trade elasticities rise as the time perspective increases. Consequently, the sticky-price LFER model predicts that lower frequency data are more likely to exhibit a negative relationship between the current account and the change in the exchange rate. This is what recent empirical studies have found.[19]

On the other hand, Sachs (1983) found a **positive** relationship between the current account and variations in the exchange rate within larger OECD countries. Such a situation is illustrated in Figure 7.3b, where the economy begins at point 1 and then a bond financed positive fiscal shock occurs. As before, the $C_L C_L$ curve shifts down and to the right to $C'_L C'_L$, and both asset market loci (the $A_L A_L$ and the AmAm curves) shift downward. The exchange rate jumps downward (a home appreciation) to point 2 in the MER and to point 2' in the LFER.

In this case, undershooting occurs in both models, because the exchange rate continues to appreciate as the economy moves to point 3 in the long run. Consequently, the current account deficit that arises when home money initially appreciates in the short run exists as home money appreciates more in the long run as the economy moves from point 2' to point 3 in Figure 7.3b. This positive relationship between the current account and the exchange rate arises when the $A_L A_L$ curve has a negative slope, and this is more likely as the interest elasticity of capital flows increases, as should be true in more advanced economies.

7.4.4 A Monetary Shock Within the Sticky-Price LFER

This section first shows that a monetary expansion within the sticky-price LFER model can conceivably generate exchange rate undershooting or overshooting for reasons that are similar to those within the sticky-price MER. Then it proves that following a positive monetary shock: (a) it is possible for exchange rate **undershooting** to occur, even if the interest elasticity of capital flows is infinite, and (b) the home interest rate can initially **rise**, as in puzzle #10.

Within the sticky-price LFER, the short run effect of a monetary expansion via open market operations, $da = -dm < 0$, is given by (7.10a). This comes from solving the asset market equilibrium equation, (7.6b), for ds/dm, with the rational expectations assumption that the expected change in the exchange rate equals the actual long run change in the exchange rate, $(ds/dm)_{LR} = +1$.

$$(ds/dm)_{SR} = [k(1 + \theta a_2)/(a_2 + k)] / \Omega_0 > 0 \qquad (7.10a)$$

This is qualitatively the same result as in the sticky-price MER, namely a monetary expansion causes the exchange rate to depreciate initially. In Figures 7.4a and 7.4b, an increase in the money supply via the purchase of bonds shifts the $C_L C_L$ curve to the right, and shifts the $A_L A_L$ curve upward. With sticky commodity prices, the exchange rate jumps upward in the short run from point 1 to point 2 in each graph.

To determine the conditions under which exchange rate undershooting or overshooting occur here, subtract the long run change in the exchange rate, $(ds/dm)_{LR} = +1$ from (7.10a), to obtain:

$$(ds/dm)_{SR} - (ds/dm)_{LR} \overset{>}{\underset{<}{-}} 0 \text{ as } -[\delta - k/(a_2 + k)] \overset{>}{\underset{<}{-}} 0 \qquad (7.10b)$$

Consequently, the dynamics of the exchange rate depend on the slope of the asset market equilibrium locus, just as in the sticky-price MER. If the $A_L A_L$ curve has a positive slope as in Figure 7.4a, then exchange rate **undershooting** occurs, because home money depreciates initially, and then it depreciates more in the long run as the economy moves from point 2 to point 3. However, if the $A_L A_L$ curve has a negative slope, as in Figure 7.4b, then exchange rate overshooting occurs in the short run. The initial depreciation of home money is followed in the long run by a gradual appreciation as the economy moves from point 2 to point 3. The logic here is similar to that within the sticky-price MER.

Recall that exchange rate overshooting is assured within the sticky-price MER as the interest elasticity of capital flows, k, approaches infinity. This is not true within the sticky-price LFER, as can be seen by taking the limit of the term within the square brackets on the rhs of (7.10b) as k approaches infinity. The sign of this term determines the slope of the $A_L A_L$ curve.

$$\lim_{k \to \infty} [\delta - k/(a_2 + k)] = \delta - 1 \qquad (7.10c)$$

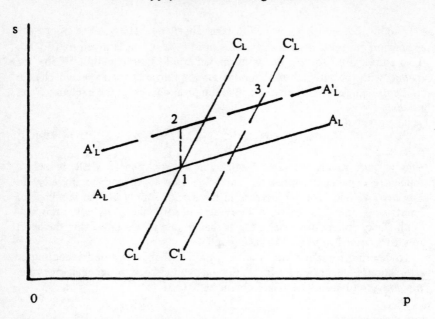

Figure 7.4a Monetary shocks within the sticky-price LFER: undershooting

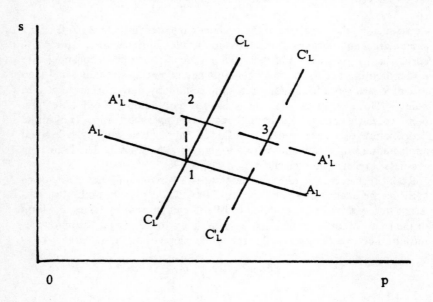

Figure 7.4b Monetary shocks within the sticky-price LFER: overshooting

Consequently, the A_LA_L curve will always have a positive slope, as in Figure 7.4a, if the price elasticity of the trade balance exceeds unity. In this case, exchange rate **undershooting** always occurs. In other words, if the trade balance is sufficiently price elastic, than a monetary shock cannot cause exchange rate overshooting within the sticky-price LFER, even if the interest elasticity of capital flows approaches infinity.

The reason for this difference between the LFER and MER sticky-price models is the assumption that within the MER (wherein the bond market can be out of equilibrium in the short run) the change in the net capital flow is determined completely via the change in the magnitude of the *ex ante* net capital flow. This is given by the $k[(di - di^*) - \theta\{dE[s] - ds\}]$ term in (7.2b). Clearly, for any nonzero interest rate differential, this becomes infinite as the interest elasticity of net capital flows, k, approaches infinity.

In this case, a higher home price level is certain to improve the balance of payments when it increases the home interest rate. Consequently, home money will have to appreciate, ds < 0, with higher prices in order to keep the balance of payments zero. Graphically, in this case, the asset market equilibrium locus within the sticky-price MER is certain to have a negative slope. This, in turn, ensures 'overshooting'.

Within the sticky-price LFER model, the *ex ante* value for the change in net capital flows is also determined by $k[(di - di^*) - \theta\{dE[s]ds\}]$. **However, even if this is infinite, the actual change in the net capital flow will be only what is needed to clear the home bond market.** Bond market equilibrium, in turn, requires the net capital flow to equal the difference between the initial holdings of bonds by home residents and their planned stock demand for bonds at the end of the time period.

This is represented by the V_A term in Chapter 2, equation (2.3d). Consequently, even if the interest elasticity of capital flows is infinite, the actual net capital flow will simply equal V_A. If the bond market had been in equilibrium before the monetary shock, then the change in the net capital flow will equal dV_A, even if the change in the *ex ante* capital flow is infinite.

The idea here is similar to the well known case of a small country whose commodity is a perfect substitute for the world's commodity, as in the intertemporal open economy model of Chapter 3. In such a situation, the home country perceives an infinitely elastic world demand for or supply of this commodity, i.e., the world will automatically buy or sell as much of this commodity as the home country desires. However, the home trade balance does not become infinitely large or small. It simply equals the difference between total home supply and total home demand for the traded commodity, V_c in Chapter 2, equation (2.3d). Since macro-model builders have tended to ignore the bond market, they apparently have not realized that an infinite interest elasticity for capital flows does **not** mean that the net capital flow becomes infinite when the home interest rate varies.

In this case, the balance of payments is not certain to improve when the net capital flow improves via the increase in the domestic interest rate that occurs when home prices rise. It depends on how much the higher price level affects V_A, versus how it worsens the trade balance and current account, i.e., it depends on the magnitude of δ. When the latter exceeds unity, then the deterioration in the trade balance dominates, and overshooting cannot occur.

Finally, consider the dynamics of the interest rate within the sticky-price LFER following a home monetary expansion. We know that in the sticky-price MER, a positive monetary shock initially increases the real money supply, and thereby reduces the home interest rate in the short run. Then, as the home price level rises in the long run, the real money supply falls to its initial value, and concomitantly the interest rate rises to its original value.

As pointed out above, Stokes and Neuberger (1979) as well as Melvin (1983) found that the short run response of the US interest rate to a monetary shock was negative during the 1970s, i.e., puzzle #10. Within the sticky-price LFER, the short run response of the interest rate to an open market increase in the money supply, $(di/dm)_{SR}$ comes from the bond market equilibrium equation, (7.2d), with $da = -dm$, $dE[s]/dm = 1$, and ds/dm as given by (7.10a) This response is

$$(di/dm)_{SR} = -[k\theta(1-\delta) + \delta]/\Omega_2 \qquad (7.11a)$$

$$\Omega_2 = a_2(\delta + k\theta) + k\delta > 0 \qquad (7.11b)$$

From (7.11a), the home interest rate can conceivably rise in the short run if $\delta > 1$, which (we know) ensures that exchange rate undershooting occurs in response to a monetary shock. In this case, agents correctly expect home money to depreciate as the home price level increases. This induces a capital outflow, which, in turn, means that a **higher** domestic interest rate is needed in order to keep the home bond market in equilibrium, as in puzzle #10.[20]

7.5 SUMMARY

1. It is well known that the liquidity preference and loanable funds theories generate the same value for the equilibrium interest rate if all markets are in equilibrium. However, in a disequilibrium situation, the

two theories yield different values for the interest rate, unless special circumstances exist.

2. Since the loanable funds theory yields a different interest rate than the liquidity preference theory when all markets do not clear, and since the exchange rate depends on the interest rate, it follows that the dynamics of the exchange rate will differ, depending on which market determines the rate of interest.

3. The sticky-price monetary model of the exchange rate, sticky-price MER, assumes that the commodity market does not clear in the short run, and that the interest rate is always determined in the money market.

4. Within an open economy period model, this implies that the sticky-price MER implicitly assumes that the bond market is the other nonclearing market when sticky commodity prices prevent an instantaneous clearing of the commodity market.

5. The well known conclusions of the standard sticky-price MER are as follows: (a) A bond financed fiscal shock can never cause exchange rate overshooting; also, there is no effect on the interest rate in the short run, but the interest rate rises in the long run in response to a positive fiscal shock. (b) A positive monetary shock via open market operations initially reduces the home rate of interest; then in the long run as the price level increases, the rate of interest returns to its initial value. (c) A monetary shock can conceivably cause exchange rate undershooting or overshooting, depending on how the incipient balance of payments changes as the home price level rises. (d) Exchange rate overshooting from a monetary shock is certain if the interest elasticity of international capital flows is infinite.

6. The UIP condition is not needed for a monetary shock to generate exchange rate overshooting within the sticky-price MER. All that is needed is for the incipient balance of payments to improve as the home price level increases.

7. Within the sticky-price LFER model, a bond financed fiscal expansion can conceivably cause interest rate overshooting if the trade balance deteriorates strongly as home prices rise. Also, a bond financed fiscal expansion can generate exchange rate overshooting in the short run. Initially, home money appreciates, but then it can conceivably depreciate as the home price level rises in the long run. This occurs if the incipient balance of payments improves as the home price level increases.

8. The dynamics of the exchange rate in #7 are consistent with what Fair (1982) found for the US dollar with regard to many currencies. In general, the magnitude of the price elasticity of the trade balance, δ, influences the relationship between the sign of the current account and

the change in the exchange rate following a bond financed fiscal expansion. It is possible for home money to appreciate or depreciate when the home current account is negative.

9. A monetary shock within the sticky-price LFER model can cause exchange rate undershooting or overshooting, for reasons that are similar to those within the sticky-price MER.

10. If the price elasticity of the trade balance is sufficiently high, then a monetary shock cannot cause 'overshooting' within the sticky-price LFER, even if the interest elasticity of capital flows is infinite.

11. Within the sticky-price LFER, a positive monetary shock can conceivably cause the interest rate to increase initially, as in puzzle #10. This happens if agents correctly expect home money to depreciate in the future (as the inflationary effects of the monetary expansion are felt), and if these expectations exert a sufficiently strong influence on net capital flows.

APPENDIX: THE SLOPE OF A_LA_L VERSUS THE SLOPE OF A_MA_M

1. The expression for each slope can be written as follows:
   a. AmAm slope $= (\delta\lambda - k)/\lambda(k\theta + \delta)$
   b. A_LA_L slope $= [\delta - k/(a_2 + k)]/\Omega_1$

2. The slope of A_LA_L will exceed the slope of AmAm if 1b exceeds 1a. Begin by writing this inequality. Then substitute for Ω_1 from (7.6d)), cross multiply, expand each expression, cancel terms, and substitute $a_2 = \sigma + \lambda$ from (7.3a). This yields: $\lambda\delta k^2\theta > -\delta k^2 - \sigma k^2\theta - k\delta\sigma$, which always holds.

NOTES

1. This chapter depends heavily on Miller (1995).
2. This statement is true in a period framework, or in a stock/flow model, as is implicit in the Frenkel and Rodriguez (1982) model, wherein the current account or trade balance is added to the net capital flow in order to determine the *ex ante* balance of payments. However, the Dornbusch (1976) model is an asset market model, wherein stock-adjustment capital flows completely determine the balance of payments, because the volume of current account transactions and the pure flow component of capital flows are assumed to be miniscule in size compared to the stock-adjustment capital flow. Dornbusch does not consider what a nonclearing commodity market implies with regard to disequilibrium in other 'flow' markets. Nevertheless, from equation (2.5a) above, a pure flow three good open economy Walrasian identity is of the form: $FXc + FX_A + FX_M \equiv - FBP$, where FX_i represents the pure flow excess supply of good i, and where

FBP is the flow balance of payments. Clearly, if the commodity market is out of equilibrium, i.e., $FXc \neq 0$, then at least one other flow market must also not clear.

3. See, for example, Patinkin (1958) and Hicks (1986).
4. See Chang (1976), Ferguson and Hart (1980), Smith (1980), Tsiang (1980), Visser (1986), McGregor (1988), and Miller (1992).
5. Cf. Miller (1992).
6. Cf. Stokes and Newberger (1979) and Melvin (1983).
7. Karacaoglu (1985) and Chen *et al.* (1988b) also derive the bond market equilibrium equation in this manner.
8. Miller (1995) proves in Appendix A that, since all variables are in logs, these constraints hold only if commodity, bond, and money units are chosen such that the initial value for each good's quantity is unity.
9. In this case, the model will be stable only if the CmCm curve is steeper than the AmAm curve. If so, then in each disequilibrium zone a vector combination of the changes in the price level (which always moves the system toward the CmCm curve) and changes in the exchange rate (which always moves the system toward the AmAm curve) can take the system toward equilibrium.
10. A bond financed home fiscal expansion represents one example of an exogenous shift in world preferences toward the home commodity. Flood and Taylor (1995, p. 266) assert that the latter type of real shock, in general, never causes exchange rate overshooting within the sticky-price monetary model. However, Levin (1986) develops a sticky-price MER model wherein a fiscal shock can generate exchange rate overshooting.
11. The higher money supply reduces the home interest rate and worsens the capital account. Thus, it takes a lower home price level or depreciation of home money in order to obtain FX market equilibrium. Also, the AmAm curve shifts in response to a monetary expansion via the effect of this on the expected long run depreciation of home money, as determined in (7.4a).
12. This possibility was first pointed out by Frankel and Rodriguez (1982).
13. In Dornbusch's (1976) original version of the 'exchange rate overshooting' model, UIP holds at all times. Hence, many international economics textbooks **incorrectly** state that exchange rate overshooting is necessarily tied up with UIP.
14. Cf. Frenkel and Rodriguez (1982). Footnote 2 pointed out that in Dornbusch's (1976) original version of the sticky-price MER, the incipient balance of payments is determined completely via stock adjustment capital flows. In this case, the AmAm curve is certain to have a negative slope and overshooting always occurs in response to a monetary shock.
15. The reasons for this are identical to the reasons within the sticky-price MER.
16. An exogenous increase in bond supply raises the home interest rate in (7.2d). This reduces domestic investment, which, in turn, means that the commodity market will clear only if home money depreciates (to stimulate the trade balance) or if home prices fall. Also, If home money is expected to depreciate, $dE[s] > 0$, then funds will flow out of the home country, which, in turn, means that the demand for home bonds falls. This raises the domestic interest rate, and reduces domestic investment.
17. As in the sticky-price MER, if both the C_LC_L curve and the asset market equilibrium curve, A_LA_L, have a positive slope, then the model will be stable only if the C_LC_L curve is steeper.
18. The proof is given in the Appendix to this chapter.
19. See Balvers and Bergstrand (1997), Clark and MacDonald (1999), and the references to this topic in Rogoff (1996).
20. Engel and Frankel (1984) suggest that this puzzle was caused by agents reacting to monetary growth rates that temporarily diverged from the Fed's announced target. However, the Fed did not begin to make such announcements officially until 1979.

8. A modern foreign exchange market theory: I

8.1 INTRODUCTION

Chapters 8 and 9 develop a partial equilibrium short run FX market approach to the exchange rate. Even though the FX market theory of the exchange rate has continued to be used in essentially all textbooks,[1] it fell into disfavor in scholarly circles in the late 1960s and early 1970s. One important weakness of the traditional FX market theory was its very casual treatment of international capital flows. Traditionally, the demand and supply for FX from export and import activities were rigorously derived, but the effect of capital flows on the demand and supply for FX was typically added on in an *ad hoc* manner.[2]

In addition, since the bulk of FX market transactions appears to be tied up with capital flows rather than trade flows, it seemed reasonable to model the price of FX (i.e., the exchange rate) in a manner similar to what is used for other financial markets.[3] The asset market theories of the exchange rate include alternative versions of the monetary approach and portfolio balance models of the exchange rate.

Unfortunately, as pointed out in Chapter 1, asset market models of the exchange rate have performed so poorly empirically that scholars have essentially given up trying to use them to model exchange rates in the short run and medium run. Also, as pointed out in Chapter 1, a new avenue for research has been the development of an institutional approach to the subject, which goes by the name, the 'micro-foundations of the FX market'.[4] The model developed below is in the same spirit as the 'micro-foundations' literature, because it focuses on the FX market.

Pippenger (1998) argues cogently in favor of a return to a FX market flow approach to exchange rate theory.[5] He points out that asset market models imply that nonsterilized FX market intervention by a central bank should exert a permanent effect on the exchange rate. The logic comes from the capital asset pricing model, CAPM. In order to induce investors to hold more of any asset, its expected rate of return must increase permanently via a decrease in the asset's current price (assuming an unchanged expected future price). Thus, according to the CAPM, if the monetary authorities sell

FX, then the exchange rate (the home currency price of FX) should decrease permanently.

However, the consensus from many empirical studies, including Pippenger's (1998), is that (in the absence of expectations effects) nonsterilized FX intervention exerts only a temporary effect on the exchange rate.[6] This is consistent with a FX market flow approach to the exchange rate. In the latter, FX market intervention shifts either the FX demand or supply curve. Such a shift alters the exchange rate, but only in the period during which the intervention occurs. If there is no intervention in the next time period, then the FX market demand and supply curves will return to their previous positions, thereby yielding an exchange rate equal to its previous value.

This chapter attempts to incorporate international capital flows in a rigorous manner into a simple FX market theory of the exchange rate. Even though the model is highly stylized, it is consistent with at least eight of the puzzling stylized facts given in Chapter 1. Section 8.2 reviews and extends what was said in Chapter 1 about these puzzles. Section 8.3 develops the model, and explains how this modern FX market theory exhibits many properties of asset market models of the exchange rate. Section 8.4 shows that the model generates discontinuous jumps from one value of the spot rate to another. In the process, it offers an explanation for puzzles #1, #2, and part of #9. A perspective on this FX market model is offered in section 8.5. The chapter ends with a summary in section 8.6.

8.2 PUZZLING STYLIZED FACTS AGAIN

8.2.1 Puzzles #1 and #2: Volatile Exchange Rates and Discontinuous Jumps

The well known relative volatility of the exchange rate (in comparison to most of the fundamentals that are thought to influence it) is tied up in part with the fact that the spot rate occasionally experiences discontinuous jumps. These jumps have been modeled successfully via the use of jump diffusion models.[7] Such models can replicate real world time series data for the spot rate, especially for the currencies of the European Monetary Union during the last part of the 20th century. Research along these lines, however, has not provided a theory as to why the random jumps occur.

One possibility is that exogenous shocks to the FX market occasionally experience large variations, and that these induce the jumps in the spot rate. Such an explanation, however, is not very satisfying because it simply shifts the puzzle down one level, i.e., now we need a theory as to why exogenous shocks experience discontinuous jumps. Another possible explanation for

Puzzle #2 is tied up with uncovered interest parity, UIP. The latter suggests that the spot rate will jump instantaneously in response to a variation in the interest rate differential. However, Eichenbaum and Evans (1995) present evidence that this does not occur. They find that the movement in the spot rate in response to an exogenous monetary shock in the US takes place very slowly, over many months.   Thus, the discontinuous jumps remain unexplained. Their existence suggests the possibility that the underlying model contains multiple equilibria, which is a key element in the FX market developed below.

8.2.2 Puzzle #9: Fundamentals in the Short Run versus the Long Run

As Chapter 1 pointed out, it is well documented that empirical models of the exchange rate based on fundamentals cannot predict short run variations in the exchange rate any better than a random walk model.[8] In addition, empirical exchange rate models typically have unstable coefficients (when moving from one time interval to another) and often have coefficients with the wrong sign. This amounts to Obstfeld and Rogoff"s (2000) 'exchange rate disconnect puzzle'.

However, there is evidence that fundamentals are useful in explaining movements in the exchange rate over relatively long time intervals, i.e., when using yearly or lower frequency data. For example, Mark (1995) finds that income and prices are useful in explaining exchange rates over two to three year time intervals, within the context of a monetary model of the exchange rate. Along the same lines, evidence that fundamentals are important in the long run has been presented by Flood and Taylor (1996) with regard to PPP, and by Chinn and Meese (1995) who use various models to show that the exchange rate is related in the long run to money, income, interest rates, and inflation rates. Similarly, the long run empirical models of Stein (1994), Williamson (1994), Isard and Faruquee (1998) and Clark and MacDonald (1999) appear to fit the data quite well, at least within sample. However, no one has attempted to construct a theory wherein the fundamentals exert very little or no effect on the exchange rate in the short run, but a predictable effect in the long run. The FX market model below does this.

8.2.3 Puzzle #3: Short Run Drifts and Long Swings

Casual empiricism suggests that short run drifts in the exchange rate occur frequently. This is supported by the fact that profits could have been earned via short term speculation. Furthermore, Eichenbaum and Evans (1995) have documented that the dollar's value moves consistently in the same direction for several years in response to exogenous shocks to US monetary policy. Finally, the spectacular rise in the value of the dollar during the first half of the 1980s suggests that under certain conditions a short term trend can develop into a long swing.[9]

Endogenous trends in the spot rate have been generated rigorously in a model by Frankel and Froot (1986). They begin with the assumption that FX market participants determine their exchange rate expectations via a combination of the forecast of chartists and the forecast of fundamentalists. Then, for simplicity, they assume that chartists always forecast a zero change in the spot rate; that is, chartists always have static expectations with regard to the level of the exchange rate. Also, they assume that the fundamental forecast is determined simply via a regressive expectations function. With these assumptions they show that their model can generate an endogenous persistent movement in the exchange rate away from its fundamental value.

However, Frankel and Rose (1995) point out that no one has developed a theory of endogenous short term trends or long swings that allows fundamentals to win in the long run, i.e., a model wherein the fundamentals eventually exert an influence that ends any long term trend. The FX market model developed below uses the results of Frankel and Froot (1986) by showing how regressive long term expectations can generate endogenous short term drifts or trends in the spot rate that can (under certain conditions) develop into a long swing. Furthermore, it allows fundamentals to win in the long run by having a long swing in the spot rate affect the current account in a manner that progressively increases the probablility that the long swing will end.

8.2.4 Puzzle #4: The Forward Discount Bias

The forward discount (or premium) bias, FDB, has become more complicated by some recent empirical results. We first carefully review the FDB and the most prominent attempts to explain it. Then we turn to the more recent evidence that suggests that: (a) the extent of the FDB is extremely variable over time, and (b) the FDB might exist only for high to medium frequency data.

In order to understand the FDB, assume that UIP, adjusted for a risk premium, μ, always holds in an *ex ante* sense, as in (8.1a), where: (a) $(i - i^*)$ is the home minus foreign interest rate differential, (b) $s(t)$ is the log of the current spot rate in home money units per unit of FX, (c) $E[\ \ ]$ is the expected value operator, and $E[s(t+n)]$ is the expected value for the spot rate 'n' periods into the future.

If covered interest parity, CIP, always holds,[10] then the home minus foreign interest rate differential in (8.1a) can be replaced by the forward discount or premium, $[f(t+n) - s(t)]$ as in (8.1b), where $f(t+n)$ is the log of the forward rate in period $(t+n)$.[11]

$$E[ds(t+n)] - [i - i^*] + \mu \tag{8.1a}$$

$$E[ds(t+n)] = [f(t+n) - s(t)] + \mu \tag{8.1b}$$

Since reliable time series data on exchange rate expectations are not readily available, tests of (8.1a) and (8.1b) substitute the actual future change in the log of the spot rate, $ds(t+n)$, for the expected future change. A large number of empirical studies, using many bilateral exchange rates between the currencies of the advanced countries over various time intervals, have estimated α and β in

$$ds(t+n) = \alpha + \beta[i - i^*] \tag{8.2a}$$

$$ds(t+n) = \alpha + \beta[(f(t+n) - s(t)] \tag{8.2b}$$

The simultaneous existence of UIP and CIP suggests that $\beta = 1$ and that $\alpha = \lambda$ in both equations. However, Froot and Thaler (1990) report that the mean value for estimates of β in scores of regression equations is -0.88. This implies one or more of the following: (a) UIP does not hold, implying that financial markets are not efficient;[12] (b) the constant term in (8.2a) and (8.2b) is not really constant, and it covaries with changes in the interest rate differential; or (c) there is a problem with substituting the actual future change in the log of the spot rate, $ds(t+n)$, for the expected change, $E[ds(t+n)]$, i.e., exchange rate expectations errors exist.

Froot and Thaler (1990) have entertained the idea in (a) that financial markets might not be efficient, but most economists are reluctant to consider this. Consequently, in order to explain the surprising empirical finding of a negative β, economists have hypothesized either that: (a) the risk premium, μ, is variable in an appropriate manner; and/or (b) exchange rate expectations errors, ε, exist, where

$$\varepsilon = E[ds(t+n)] - ds(t+n) \tag{8.3}$$

Solving (8.3) for $E[ds(t+n)]$, and substituting this solution into (8.1a) and (8.1b) yields

$$ds(t+n) = [i - i^*] + (\mu - \varepsilon) \tag{8.4a}$$

$$ds(t+n) = [f(t+n) - s(t)] + (\mu - \varepsilon) \tag{8.4b}$$

Equation (8.4a) tells us that if risk adjusted UIP holds, then a negative relationship between the interest rate differential and the future change in the spot rate, as implied by the estimated negative values for β in (8.2a), means that an **increase** in the interest rate differential must be accompanied by an even larger **decrease** in $(\mu - \varepsilon)$. If μ decreases with an increase in the interest rate differential, this implies that a relatively higher home interest rate is associated with an increase in the perceived risk associated with holding home financial assets. This is consistent with the CAPM, and it prompted economists in the 1980s and early 1990s to hypothesize that the forward discount bias was caused by a variable risk premium.

As pointed out above, the CAPM suggests that an asset's risk premium should rise with: (a) increases in the relative supply of that asset, and (b) increases in the covariance between the rate of return on this asset and the average rate of return on the entire portfolio of risky assets. Unfortunately, calculations using the CAPM have shown that the forward discount bias cannot be explained by a risk premium that varies appropriately unless totally unreasonable values for the parameters in investor's utility functions are assumed.[13]

Also, Frankel and Froot (1989) break down the contribution of variations in μ versus their estimates of variations in ε in determining the FDB. They conclude that variations in the risk premium are trivial compared to variations in the prediction errors. Consequently, economists have discarded the hypothesis that the FDB is caused by a variable risk premium.[14]

Since the FDB exists almost universally, economists deduced that if it is caused by prediction errors, then we need a reason why such errors are persistent and are of the same sign for extended periods of time. Two reasons have been suggested, namely: (a) the existence of a peso problem, and (b) gradual learning about a general shift in the nature of monetary policy.[15] The peso problem refers to the possibility that agents correctly expect the spot rate to move in a certain direction, but this movement does not occur for some time.[16] For example, if the home currency is pegged, but PPP calculations suggest that the home currency is substantially overvalued, then it might be reasonable to anticipate that the peg will fall and home money will depreciate eventually. However, it might take many time periods (perhaps years) before the peg collapses. In this case, $E[ds(t+n)]$ will not equal the actual $ds(t+n)$ for a prolonged period of time, implying that ε will be persistently nonzero and of the same sign.

Reason (b) for persistent prediction errors is illustrated by a situation where: (a) the monetary authorities have allowed a high growth rate for the money supply and a high inflation rate, that have been accompanied by regular depreciations of home money; and (b) they announce that the monetary growth rate will be reduced in the future. If the central bank has not followed through on such announcements in the past, then agents might rationally expect a high monetary growth rate and regular home money depreciations to continue. This means that if the tighter monetary policy really does occur, then $E[ds(t+n)]$ will not equal the actual $ds(t+n)$ for as long as it takes agents to become convinced that the general nature of monetary policy has indeed changed. Again, exchange rate prediction errors will be persistent and of the same sign.

There is a problem with the literature on reasons why exchange rate prediction errors might be persistent and of the same sign for extended time intervals, namely it does not go far enough in explaining the forward discount bias. That is, persistent exchange rate expectations errors are not enough to yield a negative β. From equation (8.4a), the future spot rate will fall when the interest rate differential increases only if the prediction error is **positively** correlated with and **more volatile** than $[i - i^*]$. Lewis (1995) points this out, and explains why gradual learning about a regime shift can move the prediction error in the proper direction, but she does not explore the relative volatility issue. Apparently, no one has attempted to explore this important issue empirically.

The two complications associated with the FDB that were mentioned at the beginning of this subsection relate to empirical findings with regard to the size of the β coefficient in (8.2a) and (8.2b). Empirical studies by Flood and Taylor (1995) and Meredith and Chinn (1998) have discovered that estimates of the β coefficient rise in algebraic value as the duration of one time interval increases. Furthermore, when five year moving averages for the data are utilized, estimates of β become insignificantly different from plus unity, i.e., **the FDB no longer exists.** This implies that the forward discount bias might be simply a high frequency phenomenon. Chapter 9 below shows that our FX market model also yields an implied value for β that increases algebraically as the duration of one time interval rises.

Baillie and Bollerslev (2000) use monthly DM per \$ data from March, 1973 through November 1995, and obtain an estimated value for β of -2.23 over the entire sample. The value for β is then estimated 208 different times via the use of five year rolling regressions of monthly data. The estimated value for β is negative in most cases, but it varies tremendously, with a minimum value of -13.00, and a maximum value of 3.52. The clear implication is that the degree of the FDB is not constant over time. Consequently, any explanation for the FDB must be able to generate this result. Chapter 9 derives a theoretical expression for β and shows how it will vary with key parameters in the model. Of particular interest is the conclusion that the algebraic value for β falls during periods when FX market speculation is perceived to be more risky. This, of course, is empirically testable.

8.2.5 Puzzle #5: Volatility Clusters and Heteroskedasticity

Baillie and Bollerslev (1989), Hsieh (1991) and Hogan and Melvin (1994) show that frequency distributions for changes in the log of the spot rate exhibit heteroskedasticity when using very high frequency (daily or weekly) data, but not for lower frequency data. This appears to occur, at least in part, because of the existence of occasional clusters of volatility.

The only explanation that has been offered for this stylized fact is that exogenous shocks to the FX market might also exhibit this same pattern of tranquility and volatility. Although this is conceivable, it is not very satisfying. Chapter 9 shows how profit taking by FX market speculators can create occasional periods of exchange rate volatility and, hence, heteroskedastic frequency distributions for changes in the exchange rate.

8.2.6 Puzzle #6: Leptokurtic Frequency Distributions

Booth and Glassman (1987), Akgiray *et al.* (1988), and Hsieh (1988) find that the frequency distributions for changes in the log of the spot rate are leptokurtic for high frequency data, up to and including monthly data. That is, the frequency distributions have higher peaks and longer tails than in a normal distribution. This means that there are relatively more small and more large variations in the spot rate, but fewer medium size variations than in a normal distribution. However, the distributions do not exhibit leptokurtosis for annual data and for most quarterly data.

Jorion (1988) and Nieuwland *et al.* (1991) point out that the leptokurtosis puzzle might arise because of: (a) discontinuous jumps in the spot rate, as in puzzle #2, or (b) time varying parameters within a model that would yield a normal distribution if all parameters were constant. It seems reasonable that discontinuous jumps (that show up in high frequency data) might cancel each other and, therefore, not appear in low frequency data. This would yield normal distributions for exchange rate variations with low frequency data, just as Jorion (1988) and Nieuwland *et al.* (1991) have suggested. However, as pointed out above, no theory exists as to the underlying cause(s) of discontinuous jumps.

On the other hand, explanation (b) appears to be at odds with the decrease in the degree of leptokurtosis as the relevant time interval increases. One would expect more variation in a model's parameters in going from one long time interval to another, than in going from one brief time interval to another. In this case, the degree of leptokukrtosis would increase as the frequency of the data decreased.

The position taken here is that the existence of leptokurtosis for high frequency data but not for low frequency data is a consequence of anything that causes the spot rate to be more volatile in the short run than in the long run. Two such causes are: (a) occasional discontinuous jumps in the spot rate, puzzle #2, and (b) short run drifts or trends in the spot rate, puzzle #3, that tend to be reversed over longer time periods. Thus, any model that is consistent with puzzle #2 and puzzle #3 will provide a possible explanation for puzzle #6.

8.2.7 Puzzle #8: Extrapolative versus Recursive Exchange Rate Expectations

Chapter 1 pointed out that surveys of FX market dealers by Allen and Taylor (1990), Cheung *et al.* (2000), Lui and Mole (1998), MacDonald and Marsh (1996), and Cheung and Chinn (2001) show that agents use of a combination of fundamentals and technical analysis (often charts) when formulating exchange rate expectations. Short run expectations give very little or no weight to fundamentals, and are often extrapolative in nature. That is, agents believe that the most recent changes in the spot rate will continue in the short run as in (8.6a) below, where $s^e(t+1)$ is the expected spot rate in the next period, and $s(t-1)$ is the most recently observed value for the spot rate.

$$s^e(t+1) - s(t-1) = \varphi\,[\,s(t-1) - s(t-2)]\qquad \varphi > 0 \qquad (8.6a)$$

$$s^e(t+n) - s(t-1) = \psi(t+n)\,[s*(t+n) - s(t-1)]\quad 0 < \psi(t+n) \le 1 \quad (8.6b)$$

$$s^e(t+n) = \psi(t+n)\,s*(t+n) + [1 - \psi(t+n)]s(t-1) \qquad (8.6c)$$

$$\psi(t+n) = \theta \sum_{k=0}^{n-1}(1-\theta)^k \quad 1 - \psi(t+n) = (1-\theta)^n \quad \lim_{n\to\infty} \psi(t+n) = 1 \quad (8.6d)$$

On the other hand, the surveys of FX market dealers tell us that the long run forecast of most agents is recursive. This is represented by (8.6b) which implies that agents expect the spot rate to move in the long run by some percentage, $\psi(t+n)$, of the difference between the long run fundamental value for the spot rate, denoted by $s*(t+n)$, and the most recently observed value for the spot rate $s(t-1)$. The $\psi(t+n)$ term represents the anticipated speed of movement of the spot rate over a long time interval, 'n', toward its fundamental value.

Notice from (8.6c), which is simply a rearranged version of (8.6b), that the recursive forecast, $s^e(t+n)$, is a weighted average of the long run fundamental value and the most recently observed value for the spot rate. The surveys indicate that progressively more weight is given to fundamentals, i.e., $\psi(t+n)$ rises, as the time horizon of the exchange rate forecast increases. This is formalized by (8.6d), if $0 < \theta < 1$.

It is no puzzle as to why exchange rate expectations are extrapolative in the short run but recursive in the long run. The simple answer is 'these expectations work and they can be used profitably!' The puzzle is 'why do they work?' Are the expectations simply self-fulfilling? That is, does the spot rate drift away from its fundamental value in the short run and return to its fundamental value in the long run simply because speculators bet that it will? Alternatively, is there some unknown dynamic process that makes this happen? The model developed below suggests a mechanism by which this dynamic process occurs.

8.2.8 Puzzle #7: Profit Making Speculation

Dooley and Shafer (1984), Sweeney (1986), Gencay (1999) and Dewachter (2001) all show that FX market speculation that employs simple technical rules could have generated profits during the flexible exchange rate era. Furthermore, Leahy (1995) and Neely (1998) find that during the flexible exchange rate era, it would have been profitable for speculators simultaneously to bet: (a) in the short run **against** the FX market activities of the US government, and (b) in the long run **with** the FX market activities of the US government.

FX market intervention by the Fed and US Treasury has tended to 'lean against the wind'. For example, they have bought FX when the spot rate was thought to be below its long run equilibrium value. In this case, short term speculators could have profited by betting that FX would continue to depreciate in the short run. That is, the short run speculators could have earned a profit by **selling** FX, and repurchasing it a short time later. Simultaneously, the evidence shows that, in the case wherein the Fed and Treasury were selling FX, long term speculators could have profited by **buying** FX and holding it for an extended period.

This puzzle appears to be simply a reflection of puzzles #3 and #9. LeBaron (1999) finds that the greatest profits from short term FX market speculation arise when speculation occurs one day **before** the Fed intervenes. Hence, Neely and Weller (2001, p.969) conclude that, 'the profitability of technical trading rules is a consequence of strong and persistent trends in exchange rates, which intervention is intended to reverse.' On the other hand, if the exchange rate tends in the long run to move toward a value consistent with the fundamentals, then additional profits can be obtained by betting on the fundamentals in the long run. In this case it also pays to bet with the FX market activities of the Fed if the time horizon is the long run.

8.3 THE MODEL

There have been attempts to explain almost all of the puzzling stylized facts given above. However, typically each explanation uses a different model.[17] Also, there are multiple explanations for some of the puzzles. For example, McCallum (1994), Gourinchas and Tornell (1996) and Mark and Wu (1998) develop models that can generate the forward discount bias, but each for a different reason.[18] Consequently, readers who are skeptical of a FX market flow theory of the exchange rate should keep the principle of Occam's Razor in mind, because this model offers explanations for **many** puzzles.[19]

8.3.1   Key Assumptions

First, the model contains exporters and importers, as well as agents who engage in long term direct foreign investment. Their activities determine the 'fundamental balance of payments'. In addition, the model contains short term and long terms speculators. Second, long term exchange rate expectations, with a time horizon of, 'n' periods, are regressive, while short term expectations, with a one period time horizon, are extrapolative, i.e., they exhibit bandwagon effects. These expectations are given by (8.6a) and (8.6b).

Third, long term speculators include two types of agents: (a) uncovered interest arbitragers whose objective is to earn a high rate of return, primarily via interest earnings; they do not focus on making a profit from exchange rate variations; however, since they accept a nonzero FX position, they are, technically, FX market speculators; and (b) agents whose primary objective is to profit from exchange rate variations in the long run; they are FX market speculators in the everyday sense of the term. In reality, the time perspectives of the many LT-speculators will differ, but for simplicity it is assumed that the relevant time horizon is 'n' periods for all such agents.

Fourth, LT-speculators are risk averse and require a nontrivial risk premium, μ, in order to take a long term position in FX. One might think that μ is represented by the bid–ask spread. However, the latter might be a good proxy for the risk that FX market makers assume when they take a position in FX over a very brief (a few minutes to a few hours) time interval. The absolute value for μ will be much larger than the bid–ask spread, because it measures the risk premium associated with taking a **long term** position in FX. In reality, μ is undoubtedly endogenous and variable over different states of the world.[20] In particular, it is likely that μ will increase during periods of exchange rate volatility. However, for simplicity, our rigorous analysis assumes that μ is exogenous. We conjecture, later, as to the consequences of allowing μ to become endogenous.

Fifth, UIP adjusted for risk holds in an *ex ante* sense for LT-speculators. Sixth, the exogenous interest rate differential is highly persistent, but it decays gradually and approaches zero as time approaches infinity. This assumption is supported by the work of Baillie and Bollerslev (1994), Bekaert and Hodrick (1992), and Bekaert (1995) who find empirically that the forward discount or premium is highly persistent, but that it decays over time. Since there is much evidence in support of CIP, this implies that the time series properties of the interest rate differential are undoubtedly similar to those of the forward discount or premium.

Seventh, the Marshall–Lerner, M–L, condition does not hold in the short run. Thus, the trade balance and current account **improve** initially when home money **appreciates**. However, the M–L condition is satisfied in the long run, implying that an **appreciation** of home money eventually **worsens** the trade balance and current account.[21]

8.3.2 Long Term Speculators and the Γ Curve

LT-speculators buy FX when it becomes sufficiently cheap and sell it when it becomes sufficiently dear. This implies the following activities:

Regime 1: Sell FX if: $s(t) \geq s^e(t+n) + \mu - ID(t)$ (8.7a)

Regime 2: Buy FX if: $s(t) \leq s^e(t+n) - \mu - ID(t)$ (8.7b)

$ID(t)$ is the exogenous home minus foreign interest rate differential, where the time dimension of the interest rates is identical to the time horizon of LT-speculators.

The activities of LT-speculators are illustrated by the discontinuous Γ curve in Figure 8.1 that represents their demand for FX (if $\Gamma > 0$) or supply of FX (if $\Gamma < 0$). They supply FX when the spot rate has a relatively high value such as s1 in regime 1, and demand FX when the spot rate has a relatively low value such as s2 in regime 2. By assumption the Γ curve becomes perfectly elastic once the threshold values for the spot rate have been reached.

If LT-speculators had heterogeneous exchange rate expectations as found by MacDonald and Marsh (1996) and Cheung and Chinn (2001), then the discontinuous Γ curve would have a negative slope. A negative slope would also exist if the risk premium required to hold FX increases with the magnitude of long term speculative activities. A negatively sloped Γ curve would be more realistic, but would greatly complicate the analysis. Hence, we formally assume a discontinuous, but perfectly elastic Γ curve. The effects on the model from relaxing the simplifying assumption of a perfectly elastic Γ curve are explored in Chapter 9.

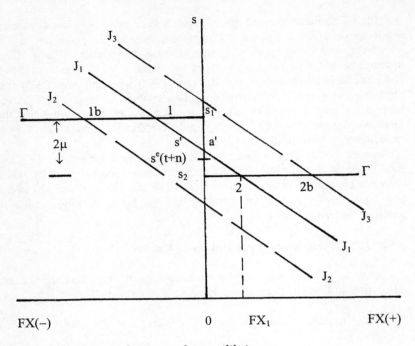

Figure 8.1 Foreign exchange market equilibrium

From (8.7a) and (8.7b), if the interest rate differential is zero, then the Γ curve is symmetric around $s^e(t+n)$, the value for the spot rate that is expected to prevail at the end of the time horizon of LT-speculators. In this case, they will buy FX (actually they will buy FX and use it to purchase foreign bonds that are denominated in FX) if the most recent spot rate lies $\mu\%$ below the value that is expected to prevail at the end of their time horizon.[22] Conversely, they will sell FX (and buy home bonds) if the most recent value for the spot rate lies $\mu\%$ above its expected long term value.[23]

The Γ curve shifts upward or downward by the magnitude of any change in $s^e(t+n)$. Furthermore, the Γ curve shifts downward, and is no longer symmetric around $s^e(t+n)$, if the interest rate increases in favor of the home country. To explain, (a) if home agents require an expected FX appreciation of $\mu\%$ in order to buy FX when the interest rate differential is zero, then (b) if $ID(t) > 0$, they will not buy FX unless the expected appreciation is somewhat larger, because they will lose interest income if they hold foreign bonds rather than home bonds. In this case, the spot rate at which speculative FX purchases occur must decrease by the magnitude of ID. Similarly, a negative interest rate differential shifts the Γ curve upward by the absolute value of ID.

8.3.3 The Fundamental Balance of Payments and the J-Curve

The fundamental balance of payments consists of the current account plus net direct foreign investment flows, and is determined by the first five terms in the J-function below. The last two terms in the J-function refer to the net FX activities of short term speculators, $(Cs - Cd)$, and profit taking activities by LT-speculators, $\Omega(t)$.

$$J(t) = Z_0 + v(t) + j_1 s(t) + j_2 s(t-k) + j_3 ID(t) + (Cs - Cd) + \Omega(t) \quad (8.8a)$$

$$j_1 = \eta' + \eta^{*'} - 1 < 0 \qquad j_2 = \eta + \eta^* - 1 > 0 \qquad j_1 + j_2 > 0 \quad (8.8b)$$

$$j_3 > 0 \qquad v \sim N(0, \sigma^2_v) \quad (8.8c)$$

The terms $Z_0 + v(t)$ in (8.8a) represent the value for an unspecified set of exogenous fundamentals that affect the fundamental balance of payments. They exhibit normally distributed random shocks with permanent, Z_0, and temporary, $v(t)$, components. Agents can distinguish between these temporary and permanent shocks, and have static expectations with regard to the permanent component. The η and η^* parameters are, respectively, the home and foreign **long run** price elasticity of demand for the other country's goods, while η' and $\eta^{*'}$ are the corresponding **short run** price elasticities of demand.

The conditions in (8.8b) reflect the assumption that the M–L condition is not satisfied in the short run, $\eta' + \eta^{*'} - 1 < 0$, but it is satisfied in the long run, $\eta + \eta^* - 1 > 0$. This means that in the short run the fundamental balance of payments in (8.8a) is a **negative** function of the log of the **current** spot rate, s(t). Consequently, an appreciation of home money, ds < 0, initially **improves** the trade balance and fundamental balance of payments, thereby moving the FX market down and to the right along a negatively sloped J-curve in Figure 8.1.

However, an appreciation of home money exerts a lagged negative effect on the trade balance and fundamental balance of payments. In reality, this lagged effect is distributed over many periods. For simplicity, it is assumed that this lagged effect occurs entirely k periods after the appreciation. This gives a positive relationship between the fundamental balance of payments and the lagged value for the log of the spot rate, $s(t - k)$, i.e., $j_2 > 0$. A home currency appreciation in period $(t - k)$ worsens the trade balance and shifts the J-curve to the left in period t.[24]

In addition, (8.8a) indicates that the fundamental balance of payments is a positive function of the interest rate differential, $ID(t)$. This assumes that any fluctuation in $ID(t)$ is always associated with a similar variation in the relative rate of return on home capital goods. Consequently, an increase in *ID(t)* induces an improvement in net direct foreign investment flows.[25]

Lyons (1998) reports that in reality the half-life of FX dealers' speculative positions is approximately ten minutes. The model here attempts to take this into account by assuming that one time period is very brief, and that short term speculators, or chartists, chase short term trends, and hold a speculative position in FX for only one period at a time. Consequently, the value for the interest rate differential is not relevant in their decision making.[26]

When short term speculators or chartists first enter the FX market, then either the *Cd* term (if they demand FX) or the *Cs* term (if they supply FX) in (8.8a) is positive while the other term is zero. After that both terms are positive because: (a) short term speculators wipe out all of their speculative position from the previous period, and (b) there are always some short term speculators who reenter the market in order to bet that an established trend will continue. Net FX sales (purchases) by chartists shift the J-curve to the right (left).[27]

The fundamental exchange rate for period *t+n*, *s*(t+n)*, is the value for the spot rate that yields a zero fundamental balance of payments in that period. To obtain an expression for this, solve (8.8a) for *s*(t+n)* with the assumptions that: (a) the spot rate is constant at its fundamental value, i.e., $s(t) = s(t-k) = s^*(t+n)$, and (b) there is no short term speculative activities and no profit taking by LT-speculators, i.e., $(Cs - Cd) = \Omega(t) = 0$. This yields

$$s^*(t+n) = Z_0/(j_1+j_2) - j_3 \, ID/(j_1+j_2) = aZ_0 + bID(t+n) \qquad (8.9)$$

$$a > 0, \ b < 0$$

Note that even though it is assumed that the interest rate differential approaches zero in the very long run, the interest rate differential in period *t+n* need not be zero because '*n*' is less than infinity.

8.3.4 Foreign Exchange Market Equilibrium

FX market equilibrium occurs when the fundamental balance of payments is offset by the sum of all speculative FX market activities. In Figure 8.1 this is equivalent to having the excess supply of FX as given by the J( ) function be matched by the excess demand for FX by LT-speculators. Figure 8.1 shows that if the J_1 curve is relevant, then the model generates an unstable equilibrium for the spot rate at point a' that is bounded by two stable equilibria. The exchange rate s' associated with the unstable equilibrium at point a' is not in general equal to the value for the fundamental exchange rate, $s^*(t+n)$, given by (8.9). This is true because temporary random shocks to the fundamental balance of payments, and short term speculative activities shift the J-curve and change s', but do not alter s*.

With the J_1 curve in Figure 8.1, one stable equilibrium occurs at point 1 in regime 1, with a spot rate of s1. In regime 1, LT-speculators sell FX in an amount equal to the net demand for FX associated with the J-curve. Another stable equilibrium exists at point 2 in regime 2, with a spot rate of s2. In regime 2, LT-speculators buy FX in an amount equal to the net sales of FX associated with the J-curve.

The dynamics of the exchange rate are governed by the following.

$$s(t) = s1(t) \qquad if \qquad J[s2(t)] < 0 \qquad (8.10a)$$

$$s(t) = s2(t) \qquad if \qquad J[s1(t)] \geq 0 \qquad (8.10b)$$

$$s(t) = s(t-1) \qquad if \qquad J[s1(t)] < 0 \ \ and \ \ J[s2(t)] > 0 \qquad (8.10c)$$

Condition (8.10a) says that the exchange rate will equal s1 if no equilibrium exists in regime 2, as will be true if the value for the J-function is negative when the exchange rate equals s2, i.e., $J[s2(t)] < 0$. On the other hand, condition (8.10b) states that the exchange rate will equal s2 if no equilibrium exists in regime 1, i.e., if $J[s1(t)] \geq 0$. Finally, (8.10c) implies that for any given position of the Γ curve: (a) the market will remain in the same regime, with the same value for the spot rate as in the previous period provided that, (b) each regime contains a potential equilibrium point; i.e. if $J[s1(t)] < 0$ and $J[s2(t)] > 0$.

Recall that one reason why the traditional FX market model was discarded in scholarly work was because it focused on trade flows, and consequently it generated a volume of FX market transactions that was much smaller than what is observed in reality.[28] The FX model developed here attempts to remedy this deficiency. The total volume of FX transactions at an equilibrium position such as point 2 in Figure 8.1 can greatly exceed the quantity FX_1 at point 2. This is true for several reasons.

First, the J-curve reflects the **net** trade balance and **net** long term direct foreign investment activities. Obviously, the value for gross transactions can greatly exceed their net value. Also, if such transactions are subject to a FX market transactions multiplier, as described in section 1.3.15 above, then the volume of gross transactions rises even more. Moreover, and most importantly, the J-curve reflects the **net** FX market activities of short run speculators. As pointed out above, by assumption, these agents remain in the market for only one period at a time. Consequently, they are constantly entering and leaving the market, which implies that their gross FX market activities can be huge compared to their net value.

8.3.5 Similarities to Asset Market Models

This FX market model has many properties exhibited by asset market models. First, temporary variations in the current account shift the J-curve but do not affect the exchange rate, provided that the FX market remains in the same regime. Second, a permanent change in the current account via a variation in the permanent component of fundamentals, dZ_0 in (8.9), alters the current spot rate via its effect on long term expectations, $s^e(t+n)$, and shifts the Γ curve upward or downward. Such a variation in the spot rate is given by

$$ds(t) = ds^e(t+n) = \psi a\, dZ_0\,(t) \qquad (8.11a)$$

Third, from the first two properties, as well as (8.7a) or (8.7b) and (8.10a) and (8.10b), it follows that the short run dynamics of the exchange rate are dominated by shifts in the Γ curve. These arise via changes in exchange rate expectations and/or in the interest rate differential. Consequently, the short run dynamics of the spot rate are dominated by the same factors that drive the exchange rate within asset market models.

Fourth, from (8.7a) and (8.7b), long run *ex ante* UIP adjusted for risk holds at all times, as in most asset market models. Finally, from (8.9), (8.6b), and either (8.7a) or (8.7b), it follows that a monetary shock that alters the interest rate differential but does not cause a regime switch will cause the spot rate to change instantaneously by:

$$ds(t) = [\psi b ID' - 1]\, dID(t) \qquad (8.11b)$$

where $ID' = \delta E[ID(t+n)]/\delta ID(t) > 0$. The ID' term is positive because a current period increase in the interest rate differential will not decay completely to zero over the time horizon of LT-speculators.

An increase in the interest rate differential, *ceteris paribus*, shifts the Γ curve downward by an equal magnitude, and decreases the spot rate by this amount if the FX market remains in the same regime. This is given by the $- dID(t)$ term in (8.11b). Also, a higher current period interest rate differential implies a slightly higher expected value for the interest rate differential 'n' periods later. This exerts a negative effect on $s^*(t+n)$, which, from (8.6c) reduces the expected future spot rate, $s^e(t+n)$. The latter shifts the Γ curve downward farther, and reduces the current spot rate more, as indicated by the $[\psi b ID']dID(t)$ term in (8.11b). Thus, an increase in the interest rate differential in favor of home assets appreciates home money instantaneously by more than the variation in the interest rate differential. This is consistent with the dynamics of the exchange rate in many asset market models.

8.4 DISCONTINUOUS JUMPS IN THE SPOT RATE AND PUZZLES #1, #2, and #9

An important difference between this FX market model and either the traditional FX market models or a typical asset market model is that the market can jump discontinuously from one stable equilibrium to another. This is a consequence of the assumption that the M–L condition does not hold in the short run, and, hence, multiple equilibria exist.[29]

For example, assume that the market is initially at point 2 in Figure 8.1, where the J_1 curve intersects the regime 2 portion of the Γ curve. If the J-curve shifts to the left to J_2, then an equilibrium no longer exists in regime 2. Thus, the market jumps up to point 1b in regime 1 via an instantaneous depreciation of home money by the magnitude 2μ. If, in future periods, the J-curve shifts to J_3, then an equilibrium no longer exists in regime 1. Consequently, the market will jump discontinuously down to regime 2 to a point such as 2b. The switching between alternative stable equilibria provides an explanation for puzzle #2, discontinuous jumps in the spot rate. Regime switching also helps to explain the volatility of exchange rates relative to the volatility of the fundamentals that are thought to affect them, as in puzzle #1.

Furthermore, the existence of regime switching means that the model generates **hysteresis**, because it remains in an existing regime even if the events that induced an earlier switch to that regime are completely reversed. For example, let the market initially be in regime 2 at point 2 in Figure 8.1. Then assume that a temporary variation in the fundamentals shifts the J-curve from J_1 to J_2, which means that an equilibrium no longer exists in regime 2. Thus, the FX market switches from regime 2 to regime 1, and moves to point 1b. Since the variation in the fundamentals is temporary, the J-curve returns to its original position, J_1, in the next period. However, the market will not switch back to regime 2, because an equilibrium continues to exist in regime 1.

The significance of this hysteresis is that the market can generate both s1 and s2 for a fixed position of the J-curve, and, hence for a fixed set of values for the fundamentals. Consequently, in the short run, there need not be a stable relationship between the exchange rate and the fundamentals, as in the 'exchange rate disconnect puzzle'.[30] This, in turn, suggests that empirical exchange rate models will predict better if the estimation technique allows for time varying parameters. The works of Wolff (1987) and Schinasi and Swamy (1989) support this conclusion.

8.5 A PERSPECTIVE

One possible criticism of the model developed here is that there is scant evidence that much long term FX market speculation takes place in reality. This is because agents whose main objective is to profit from exchange rate variations appear to have a very brief time perspective. On the other hand, the volume of gross and net long term portfolio capital flows appears to be substantial. These include purchases and sales by individuals and institutions of stocks, bonds, etc., as well as the movement of funds into and out of banks, including long term bank loans.

To the extent that nonzero FX positions arising from such activities are not covered in the forward market, they represent long term FX market speculation. Finally, the volume of FX market activities arising from such activities can be significantly higher than the value of these investments if the latter create a FX multiplier via the 'hot potato' phenomenon, as described in Chapter 1.

Another possible criticism of this FX market model is the assumption that the M–L condition does not hold in the short run, but that it holds in the long run. These assumptions are consistent with a plethora of empirical studies on international trade, and with the well known phenomenon called the J-curve. On the other hand, Rose and Yellen (1989) and Rose (1991) challenge the idea that the J-curve phenomenon exists, or that the exchange rate has any influence at all on the balance of trade.[31]

A final criticism is the simplifying assumption that the discontinuous Γ curve is perfectly elastic once the spot rate has reached the value where it is profitable for LT-speculators to buy or sell FX. This property of the model arises via the assumptions that: (a) regressive exchange rate expectations are homogeneous; and (b) the risk premium on FX does not need to increase in order to induce LT-speculators to increase their FX position. Even though similar assumptions appear (often implicitly) in many asset market models of the exchange rate, section 9.7 explores how these simplifying assumptions affect the model.

8.6 SUMMARY

1. Even though the FX market approach to the determination of the exchange rate has continued to be used in textbooks, it has been discarded in scholarly circles since the early 1970s.

2. One reason for this is the unrigorous manner in which the traditional FX market model handles capital flows. Another reason is the desire to model the price of FX in a manner similar to that used for other assets, thereby leading to asset market models of the exchange rate.

3. Asset market models of the exchange rate have performed so poorly empirically, that the profession has essentially given up using them to explain short term to medium term movements in the exchange rate.

4. This has prompted economists to: (a) study the institutional details of the FX market, because this is where the exchange rate is determined; and (b) argue that a FX market flow model is consistent with the empirical finding that unsterilized FX market intervention has only a temporary effect on the exchange rate.

5. The FX market theory of the exchange rate developed here integrates capital flows more rigorously than in the traditional FX market model. The objective of this modern FX market theory of the exchange rate is to provide one model that is consistent with many puzzling stylized facts. This is in contrast to the fact that we now have one or more different theories to explain each of the puzzles.

6. The key assumptions in this FX market model are: (a) The M–L condition does not hold in the short run, but it holds in the long run. (b) LT-speculators, require a nontrivial risk premium, μ, in order to take a nonzero position in FX; they have recursive exchange rate expectations, and buy FX when it becomes sufficiently cheap, or sell FX when it becomes sufficiently dear. (c) Short term speculators take a FX position for one period at a time; they have extrapolative expectations, which induces them to bet that any existing short term drift or trend in the spot rate will continue.

7. The fundamental balance of payments consists of the current account plus net direct foreign invest flows. The fundamental exchange rate, s*, is the value for the spot rate that yields a zero fundamental balance of payments.

8. The J-curve depicts how the fundamental balance of payments plus (short term speculative activities and profit taking by LT-speculators) varies with the exchange rate. Its negative slope implies that an appreciation of home money, $ds < 0$, initially **improves** the trade balance, because the M–L condition does not hold in the short run. Eventually, however, the M–L condition holds, and, thus, a home currency appreciation worsens the trade balance and shifts the J-curve to the left in the long run.

9. Short run equilibrium in the FX market occurs when the fundamental balance of payments equals minus the FX market activities of all speculators. Graphically, this occurs where the J-curve intersects the discontinuous Γ curve. The model generates an unstable equilibrium

that is bounded by two stable equilibria: (a) one at a high value for FX in regime 1; (b) another at a low value for FX in regime 2

10. The volume of FX market transactions generated by this model can greatly exceed the value of trade flows, primarily because the model assumes that short term speculators remain in the market for only one period at a time.

11. This FX market flow model has many properties exhibited by asset market models, namely: (a) temporary variations in the trade balance (and other components of the fundamental balance of payments) have no effect on the exchange rate, provided that the FX market remains in the same regime; (b) permanent variations in the trade balance (and other components of the fundamental balance of payments) alter the exchange rate via their effect on exchange rate expectations; (c) exchange rate fluctuations are dominated by variations in the interest rate differential and by changes in exchange rate expectations; (d) long term uncovered interest parity always holds in an *ex ante* sense; (e) a change in the interest rate differential induces an immediate variation in the spot rate by a larger percentage.

12. The existence of an unstable equilibrium that is bounded by two stable equilibria means that the spot rate can jump discontinuously from one value to another, as the FX market switches regimes. This is consistent with puzzle #2, and it helps to explain the volatile nature of exchange rates, puzzle #1.

13. Multiple equilibria imply that the market can generate two values for the spot rate with a fixed set of fundamentals. This means that there will be no stable relationship between the exchange rate and fundamentals in the short run, i.e, puzzle #9.

NOTES

1. Krugman and Obstfeld (1996) represents an exception to this practice.
2. This is not true for Tsiang (1958), who began the integration of speculative capital flows into the FX market model. Tsiang, however, focused on how speculation would affect the stability of the FX market, and did not explore the ramifications of his work more broadly.
3. Recall, however, that Chapter 1 pointed out that the huge volume of FX market transactions arises in part via: (a) the use of the dollar as an intermediate currency, (b) the 'hot potato' phenomenon, and (c) the continuous rolling over of speculative FX positions by FX market dealers. None of these necessarily involves international capital flows, because they can occur via transactions between residents of the same country.
4. Cf., for example, Flood (1991) and Frankel *et al.* (1995).
5. Mark and Wu (1998) use a FX market model that utilizes an overlapping generations model.
6. See Henderson (1984) and Obstfeld (1990).
7. See, for example, Akgiray and Booth (1998), Ball and Roma (1993), Jorion (1988) and Malz(1996).
8. Meese and Rogoff (1983a and 1983b).

9. See Engel and Hamilton (1900).
10. Taylor (1995) points out that CIP holds at all times (within the limits given by transactions costs) if careful attention is paid to the timing of data for the forward rate, the spot rate, and interest rates.
11. Equation (8.1a) can be rewritten as $i^* + E[ds(t+1)] = i + \mu$. If $\mu > 0$, then the expected rate of return for a home agent placing funds abroad, $i^* + E[ds(t+1)]$, exceeds the rate of return for a home agent investing funds at home, i. Thus, a positive value for μ implies that the foreign financial asset is riskier. The same logic can be used to deduce that $\mu < 0$ if the home asset is riskier.
12. If UIP does not hold, then higher risk adjusted profits can be earned either at home or abroad, but agents do not act to take advantage of these excess profits to an extent that is sufficient to eliminate them. For example, if a higher risk adjusted rate of return is expected abroad, then market efficiency requires that funds flow abroad in such a magnitude that these excess profits are eliminated. This could occur either via a decrease in the foreign interest rate, and increase in the home interest rate, or an over appreciation of foreign money. The latter implies that foreign money will depreciate in the future, thereby reducing the expected rate of return from investing abroad.
13. The coefficient of relative risk aversion has to be unrealistically high.
14. See Engel (1996) for an excellent survey of this literature.
15. See Krasker (1980) for the original paper on the peso problem. Lewis (1989) explores the effects of gradual learning about a shift in monetary policy.
16. Kaminsky (1993) examines the peso problem for the dollar/pound exchange rate.
17. Recall from Chapter 1 that an exception to this is Obstfeld and Rogoff (2000). However, their list of puzzles contains only four of the puzzles considered in this book.
18. Meredith and Chinn (1998) explain the FDB by using McCallum's model.
19. Occam's Razor is defined in *The American Heritage Dictionary*, 2nd. College ed., 1985, Boston: Houghton Mifflin, p.860 as: 'A rule in science and philosophy stating that the simplest of two or more competing theories is preferable.'
20. Bollerslev and Melvin (1994) find empirical evidence that the bid–ask spread rises with exchange rate volatility. This should increase the risk premium, μ, here
21. Devereux (2000) shows theoretically, that the effect of a devaluation on the current account (in an intertemporal model) depends on the traditional M–L condition if export and import prices are set in the producer's currency.
22. LT-speculators include both home agents who buy FX, and foreign agents who borrow home money and use it to buy FX.
23. The activities in this case include home agents borrowing FX abroad, and selling it in order to invest at home.
24. Chen (2000) uses the assumption that the M–L condition does not hold in the short run in an open economy intertemporal model. He shows that this generates endogenous cyclical fluctuations for the exchange rate.
25. No conclusion reached below would change if the J-function did not contain the interest rate differential.
26. Flood and Rose (1996) point out that in reality interest is neither owed nor paid if an open position in FX is maintained for only one day.
27. The profit taking FX activities of LT-speculators will be discussed in Chapter 9.
28. Visser (2000, p.27) points out that, ironically, the simplest portfolio balance models (which were developed to replace the FX market approach) generate a **zero** volume of FX market transactions, because the exchange rate adjusts until home agents are happy with their initial holdings of foreign bonds.
29. This instability does not require firms to instantaneously pass-through exchange rate variations. If all trade is invoiced in the currency of the exporter, then the FX value of exports will fall instantaneously (and the FX value of imports will remain unchanged initially) if the home currency depreciates. Thus, a home currency depreciation will immediately worsen the FX value of the trade balance and fundamental balance of payments, even if there is a **zero** pass-through.

30. Furthermore, Chapter 9 shows that the model can generate endogenous drifts or swings away from the fundamental exchange rate, thereby implying that any given set of fundamentals can be associated with an **infinite** number of values for the spot rate in the short to medium run.
31. Their conclusions come primarily from regression equations that explain very little of the variation in the trade balance, and that contain essentially no statistically significant variables. However, note that they find some evidence that is consistent with a J-curve when the **levels** of variables (rather than their first differences) are used.

9. A modern foreign exchange market theory: II

9.1 INTRODUCTION

This chapter shows how the FX market model developed in the previous chapter is consistent with the last seven puzzling stylized facts listed in section 8.2. Section 9.2 carefully explains why the model can generate endogenous short term drifts in the exchange rate that can conceivably develop into a long swing, puzzle #3. Also, it shows how a long swing sows the seeds of its own demise by altering the current account in a manner that progressively increases the probability that the swing will end. In other words, the model provides a way for fundamentals to win in the long run, as in puzzle #9.

Section 9.3 proves that the modern FX market model is consistent with the FDB, puzzle #4. This is done by deriving an expression for the β coefficient that has been estimated in the FDB literature. This expression indicates that β: (a) is likely to be negative if the duration of one time interval is very brief; (b) will not be constant over time and will be algebraically smaller during turbulent periods; and (c) becomes algebraically larger as the duration of one time interval grows. Section 9.4 explores the heteroskedastic nature of frequency distributions for changes in the spot rate that arises when high frequency data are used, but not when low frequency data are used, i.e., puzzle #5. Several alternative explanations are reviewed, including the existence of volatility clusters. It is then explained how the FX market model can generate volatility clusters via the profit taking activities of LT-speculators.

Section 9.5 uses the results of section 9.4 to explain why the model is consistent with the fact that frequency distributions for exchange rate variations are leptokurtic when using very high frequency data, but are normal for lower frequency data. Section 9.6 explores the rationality of extrapolative short run expectations, but recursive long run expectations, puzzle #8. It uses the results to show that the model is consistent with the fact that it has been profitable simultaneously to bet against the FX activities of the Fed in the short run, and bet with their FX activities in the long run, puzzle #7. Section 9.7 explores the effects of relaxing some key assumptions in the model. Finally, section 9.8 contains a summary, including a list of the model's empirically testable conclusions.

9.2 SHORT TERM DRIFTS AND LONG SWINGS: PUZZLES #3 and #9

9.2.1 Introduction and Review

The main idea here comes from Frankel and Froot (1986), as in section 8.2.3 above. Within our FX market model, regressive expectations by LT-speculators create an inherent tendency for the exchange rate to drift slowly away from its fundamental value in response to an exogenous shock. These endogenous drifts occur even though no destabilizing speculation takes place. It is explained why, in general, such a drift is likely to be short-lived. However, under certain circumstances (especially a nonzero interest rate differential whose absolute value is large and growing) it becomes possible for the short term drift to develop into a long swing. Finally, it is shown that any long swing will affect the current account in a manner that progressively increases the probabilility that the long swing will end.

By way of review, FX market equilibrium occurs in Figure 9.1 where the (+) or (−) excess supply of FX as given by the J-curve is matched by the (−)

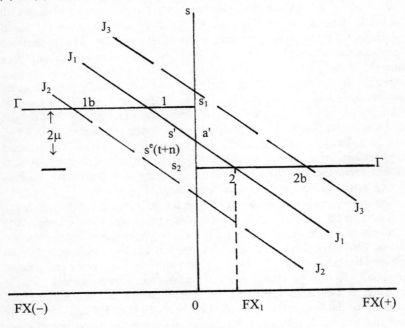

Figure 9.1 The modern foreign exchange market model

or (+) excess demand for FX by LT-speculators, as represented by the discontinuous Γ curve. From an alternative perspective, in equilibrium the excess demand for FX from the fundamental balance of payments equals the excess supply of FX from all activities of long term and short term speculators.[1] Figure 9.1 illustrates that if the J_1 curve is relevant, then the model generates an unstable equilibrium for the spot rate at point a' that is bounded by two stable equilibria. With the J_1 curve, the stable equilibria occur at point 1 in regime 1 (where LT-speculators sell FX) and at point 2 in regime 2 (where LT-speculators buy FX).

It would not be very interesting to build a model wherein the spot rate experiences short term drifts or long term swings away from its fundamental value if this occurs because of destabilizing speculation. What we seek is a reason why such movements in the spot rate might occur independently of destabilizing speculation. If such a reason exists, this will provide a rationale for agents to speculate against the fundamentals, but we will not be guilty of 'assuming' the conclusion. Consequently, this section initially assumes that there is **no** short term speculation. Then, later, we allow short term destabilizing speculation to occur.

The procedure is to assume that an exogenous shock to the interest rate differential induces a regime switch in the FX market. Then the endogenous nature of short-term drifts in the exchange rate is explored. This includes an investigation of the conditions under which an existing short term drift is more likely to develop into a long swing. Finally, we learn why a long swing is apt to end endogenously in the long run.

9.2.2 Endogenous Drifts Away from the Fundamental Exchange Rate

Figure 9.2 assumes that initially in period t: (a) the home minus foreign interest rate differential is zero, (b) the fundamental value for the spot rate, s^*, lies between s_1 and s_2, and (c) the market is in regime 1, at point 1. Then let the interest rate differential increase exogenously in period t by $dID(t) = ID(t) > 0$. This affects the FX market in that period in two ways, namely: (a) it improves the fundamental balance of payments, which shifts the J-curve to the right to J_2; and (b) it lowers the value for the spot rate at which LT-speculators begin to buy FX, thereby shifting the Γ curve downward to Γ' in Figure 9.2.

Since an equilibrium no longer exists in regime 1, the FX market jumps discontinuously from regime 1 to regime 2, and moves from point 1 to point 2. The magnitude of this instantaneous appreciation of home money is represented by

$$\Delta s_0 = -2\mu + \psi b E[ID(t+n)] - ID(t) < 0 \qquad (9.1)$$

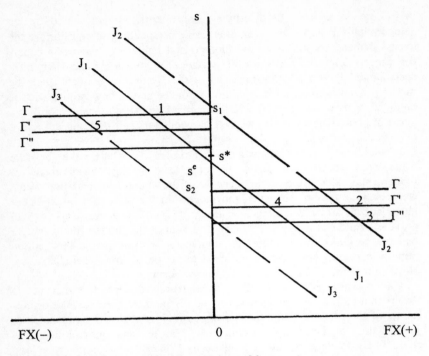

Figure 9.2 Endogenous short term drifts and long swings

The -2μ term relates to the jump downward from regime 1 to regime 2, for any given position of the Γ curve. Also, (9.1) reflects the fact that the Γ curve shifts downward because: (a) the interest rate differential is now positive instead of zero, which means that the Γ curve is no longer symmetric around $s^e(t+n)$; and (b) the expected value for the exchange rate that will prevail at the end of the time horizon of LT-speculators, $s^e(t+n)$, decreases slightly.[2]

Expression (8.6c) shows that the regressive expectations of LT-speculators imply that the value for the spot rate that they expect to exist at the end of their time horizon, $s^e(t+n)$, is a weighted average of the fundamental rate and the most recently observed value for the spot rate. Therefore, the instantaneous appreciation of home money in period t by $\Delta s_0 < 0$ in (9.1) means that in period t+1 the regressive expectations value for the future period $(t+n)$ spot rate falls by $(1-\psi)\Delta s_0$.

This reduction in $s^e(t+n)$ prompts a decrease in the value for the spot rate at which LT-speculators buy FX. Thus, the Γ' curve in Figure 9.2 shifts downward in period t+1 to a position such as Γ''. If the market remains in regime 2, then the exchange rate in period t +1 decreases endogenously by

$(1 - \psi) \Delta s_0$, as in moving from point 2 to point 3. Furthermore, if the interest rate differential and s* remain constant for k periods, and if the market remains in regime 2, then in any period (t+k) we have

$$ds(t+k) = \Delta s_0 (1 - \psi)^k \qquad (9.2a)$$

$$s(t+k) = s_1(t-1) + \Delta s_0 \sum_{n=0}^{k} (1-\psi)^n \qquad (9.2b)$$

$$\lim_{k \to \infty} s(t+k) = s(t-1) + \Delta s_0/\psi \qquad (9.2c)$$

Under these conditions the spot rate will appreciate endogenously in each period as it approaches the limit given by (9.2c), where $s(t-1)$ is the value for the spot rate before the interest rate differential changed, and Δs_0 is the value for the initial jump down from regime 1 to regime 2. From (9.2a) and (9.2c), the drift in the exchange rate will be faster and larger if: (a) the initial change in the spot rate, Δs_0, is larger in absolute value, or (b) the time horizon of LT-speculators is shorter, thereby reducing the value for ψ. The latter implies that short term drifts in the exchange rate will be more pronounced as LT-speculators become relatively myopic.

Note well that, in this situation, LT-speculators ostensibly are acting in a **stabilizing** manner because they are **buying** FX when the spot rate lies below its fundamental value. Since short term speculators are inactive here by assumption, it follows that continuous appreciations of home money away from its fundamental value do not require destabilizing speculation. The key idea is that an initial fall in the spot rate progressively decreases the value of the exchange rate at which stabilizing speculation begins. This, in turn, is a consequence of regressive expectations.

9.2.3 The Duration of Endogenous Movements Away from the Fundamental Rate

Any existing short term drift can end abruptly via a switch from regime 2 to regime 1 if an equilibrium no longer exists in regime 2. Three possible reasons for this are: (a) the positive interest rate differential decreases, and this shifts the Γ curve upward; (b) a negative shock to the fundamental balance of payments shifts the J-curve sufficiently to the left; and/or (c) exchange rate expectations change via an increase in the value for the fundamental exchange rate, thereby shifting the Γ curve upward. Since most drifts in the exchange rate appear to be relatively brief, it is likely that one or more of these events occurs regularly.

Note, however, that with the fundamental exchange rate, s*, and the interest rate differential constant, a switch upward from regime 2 to regime 1 via a negative shock to the J-curve is a necessary but not sufficient condition for a negative drift in the spot rate within regime 2 to end. If the spot rate has been drifting downward in regime 2 for $k-1$ periods, and then it switches up to regime 1 in period $t+k$, the change in the spot rate that occurs is given by

$$ds(t+k) = 2\mu + (1-\psi)^k \Delta s_0 \qquad (9.2d)$$

where $\Delta s_0 < 0$ is the value for the initial jump down to regime 2. Thus, for a sufficiently large absolute value for Δs_0, and/or a small value for k (i.e., the endogenous drift has not existed very long) a downward drift in the spot rate can conceivably continue in spite of a switch from regime 2 to regime 1. However, this becomes progressively less likely as the age of the short term drift increases and $(1-\psi)^k$ approaches zero. This suggests that, *ceteris paribus*, destabilizing short term speculation is more likely to be profitable if short term speculators 'get in' early and 'get out' fast.

An existing downward drift in the spot rate in regime 2, referred to here as R2, is more likely to continue if the conditional probability of the market remaining in regime 2, $Pr[R2/R2]$, increases. The effect on this probability from a variation in the interest rate differential is given by

$$\delta Pr[R2/R2]/\delta ID(t) = V'\{j_3 + j_1(\psi bID'-1) \sum_{n=0}^{k}(1-\psi)^n\} > 0 \qquad (9.3)$$

$V\{\ \}$ represents the cumulative frequency distribution for the normally distributed temporary shock term $v(t)$ in the J-function, (8.8a). Consequently, we have $V' > 0$. Furthermore, $j_3 > 0$ in (8.8c), while $j_1 < 0$ in (8.8b), and $\lambda(\psi bID'-1) < 0$ in (8.11b), because $b < 0$. Therefore, it follows from (9.3a) that an increase in the interest rate differential raises the conditional probability of the market remaining in regime 2. Hence, an existing downward drift (a persistent appreciation of home money) within regime 2 is more likely to continue if there is a large interest rate differential in favor of the home country. This is consistent with what Froot and Thaler (1990) point out concerning the real world relationship between interest rate differentials and short term trends in the exchange rate.

Figure 9.3 illustrates this important conclusion. Assume that the market is in regime 2 at point d. Thus, the magnitude of a negative shock to the J-curve required to induce a switch to regime 1 is given by the distance cd. However, an increase in the interest rate differential: (a) shifts the J-curve to the right, as to J', thereby requiring a negative shock to the J-curve of ce in

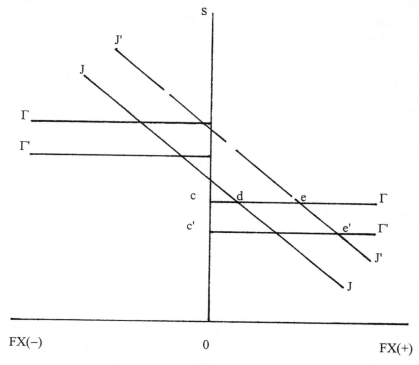

Figure 9.3 The probability that a drift will continue

order to induce a regime shift; and (b) shifts the Γ curve downward, as to Γ', which increases the size of a negative shock required to induce a regime switch even more to c'e'.

Section 9.6 explores the rationality of the model and proves, among other things, that under the right circumstances it can be Muth rational to bet that an existing short term drift in the spot rate away from its fundamental value will continue for at least one more period. This conclusion holds even if no destabilizing speculation takes place. Under such circumstances it becomes rational for short term speculators to bet that the short term drift away from the fundamental exchange rate will continue. Thus, they will sell FX, thereby yielding $Cs - Cd > 0$ in the J-function. (8.8a). This shifts the J-curve to the right, and raises the conditional probability of remaining in regime 2 by

$$\delta Pr[R2\,/R2]/\delta(Cs - Cd) \;=\; V' > 0 \qquad\qquad (9.3b)$$

In Figure 9.3, a shift to the right in the J-curve (as a result of speculative sales of FX by short term speculators) increases the size of a negative shock to the fundamental balance of payments that is needed to induce a switch up to regime 1. Therefore, even though destabilizing speculation is not needed to generate a movement away from the fundamental exchange rate, it increases the probability that such a short term drift will continue, which is just as one would expect.

The combination of a large positive interest rate differential (that perhaps increases over time) and of short term destabilizing speculation raises the probability that a short term drift in the spot rate can turn into a long swing. On the other hand, if short term speculators get almost completely out of the FX market (because they believe that a short term drift is about to end), then the J-curve shifts to the left. This makes is more likely that a regime switch will occur, and, hence, make the expectations self-fulfilling.

9.2.4 Why the Fundamentals Can Win in the Long Run

If a positive interest rate differential decays slowly over time (as empirical evidence suggests[3]) then any endogenous downward drift in the spot rate within regime 2 can end even if a switch to regime 1 does not occur. To see this, assume that the interest rate differential decays by $\pi\%$ each period. This exerts an upward pressure on the Γ curve in period $t+k$ by the amount given by $\pi(1-\pi)^{k-1}\Delta ID_0$, where $\Delta ID_0 > 0$ is the initial shock to the interest rate differential that started the endogenous drift. This works against the ongoing endogenous tendency for the Γ curve to drift downward, as given by $(1-\psi)^k \Delta s_0$. Therefore, the Γ curve can reverse its direction of movement and begin to drift upward, while remaining in regime 2 if

$$\pi(1-\pi)^{k-1}\Delta ID_0 + (1-\psi)^k\Delta s_0 > 0 \qquad (9.4)$$

In sum, the model suggests that: (a) exogenous shocks to the interest rate differential initiate and help to maintain persistent drifts in the spot rate, and (b) slowly decaying interest rate differentials help to end any endogenous drift, both by increasing the probability of a regime switch and by offsetting the endogenous downward drift directly. These conclusions mean that the model is consistent with the 'delayed overshooting' found by Eichenbaum and Evans (1995). As pointed out previously, their empirical work suggests that an exogenous negative monetary shock in the US is followed by a persistent appreciation of the dollar for many months. Then the dollar begins to depreciate. Within the context of our FX market model, this suggests that it might take many months for the interest rate differential to decay sufficiently to reverse the endogenous drift in the spot rate.

However, our FX market model implies that any long swing in the exchange rate can end endogenously, even if the interest rate differential does not decay. The reason for this is that the Marshall–Lerner condition is satisfied in the long run, and this ensures that the long swing will alter the trade balance in a manner that progressively increases the conditional probability of a 'bubble bursting' regime switch.[4]

To explain, equation (8.8a) tells us that an appreciation of home money, $ds < 0$, in any period will deteriorate the trade balance 'k' periods later, and shift the J-curve to the left. Hence, if the spot rate has been drifting downward from period t until period $t+k$, then the shift in the J-curve in period $t+k$ (in response to the endogenous appreciation in period 't') is given by:

$$\Delta J(t+k) \; = \; j_2 \, ds(t+k) = j_2 (1 - \psi)^k \Delta s_0 \tag{9.5a}$$

Recall that $j_2 = \eta + \eta^* - 1 > 0$, as defined in (8.8b), gives the lagged long run response of the trade balance and fundamental balance of payments to an exchange rate variation. Since Δs_0 is negative, (9.5a) implies that any long term downward swing in the spot rate eventually shifts the J-curve progressively farther to the left in each period. This horizontal shift to the left in the J-curve, as given by (9.5a), amounts to a shift **downward** in the J-curve by

$$Downward \; Shift \; in \; J\text{-}curve = -(j_2/j_1)(1 - \psi)^k \Delta s_0 \tag{9.5b}$$

where $j_1 = \eta' + \eta^{*'} - 1 < 0$, as defined in (8.8b), is the short run response of the trade balance and fundamental balance of payments to an exchange rate variation.

Expression (9.5b) can be used to obtain a sufficient condition for the model to generate progressive decreases over time in the probability of remaining in regime 2. This requires the downward shift in the J-curve given by (9.5b) to dominate the endogenous downward drift in the Γ curve in the same period. (In this case, the new short run equilibrium will lie closer to the vertical axis, implying that it now takes a smaller random shift to the left in the J-curve to induce a switch upward to regime 1.) The latter is given by $(1 - \psi)^k \Delta s_0$. Therefore, the condition is[5]

$$j_2 > -j_1 (1 - \psi)^k \tag{9.5c}$$

where k is the time interval in (8.8a) needed for an exchange rate variation to exert its lagged effect on the trade balance. If the duration of one time interval in the model is extremely brief, such as one day or one week, then short run trade elasticities will be essentially zero. In this case, (8.8b) indicates that $j_1 \approx -1$, and (9.5c) reduces to simply

$$j_2 > (1 - \psi)^k \tag{9.5d}$$

If the weight given to fundamentals in determining the recursive expectations of LT-speculators, ψ, is greater than zero, then the rhs of (9.5d) is less than unity and gradually approaches zero over time. Also, j_2 is the sum of the long run trade elasticities minus unity. A large number of empirical studies suggests that j_2 is almost always greater than plus unity.[6] At any rate, this is certain to be greater than zero when the M–L condition is satisfied in the long run. Thus, it is certain that eventually a long swing will progressively reduce the conditional probability of remaining in regime 2. This, in turn, implies that a switch from regime 2 to regime 1 (which can end the long swing) becomes progressively more likely. In sum, the model provides a mechanism by which a long swing in the exchange rate can end endogenously.[7]

An empirically testable implication of this conclusion deals with the duration of real world long swings in the exchange rate. The key reason why a long swing can end endogenously (even when the interest rate differential does not decay) is that a prolonged trend in the spot rate alters the trade balance and current account. **Consequently, this implies that, all other things equal, countries with lower long run trade elasticities will have greater durations for any long swings in the value for their currency**. An example might be developing countries whose exports are primary products.

9.3   THE FORWARD DISCOUNT BIAS: PUZZLE #4

This section proves that our modern FX market model is consistent with the forward discount bias, FDB. The extent of the FDB suggested by empirical work requires the model to generate a **negative** relationship between the interest rate differential and the change in the spot rate in the next period, i.e., a negative β coefficient in equation (8.2a). Furthermore, in order to be consistent with the more recent evidence on the FDB, the model should be able to generate a β coefficient that: (a) varies over time, and (b) becomes algebraically larger as the duration of one time interval increases.

The plan is to use the model to obtain an expression for the rational expectations, RE, value for the change in the spot rate one period forward, and then determine how this is affected by an exogenous change in the interest rate differential. Begin by assuming initially that the market has been drifting downward in regime 2 for k periods, from period t to period $t+k$, following a shock to the spot rate in period t of $\Delta s_0 < 0$.

If the interest rate differential is assumed to be constant, then the RE value for the change in the spot rate in the next period, $(t+k+1)$, is given by

$$E[ds(t+k+1)] = Pr[R2 /R2](1 - \psi)^{k+1}\Delta s_0 +$$

$$[2\mu + (1 - \psi)^{k+1}\Delta s_0]\{1 - Pr[R2 /R2]\} \qquad (9.6a)$$

The first term on the rhs of (9.6a) is the magnitude of the endogenous downward drift in period $t+k+1$ if the market remains in regime 2, multiplied by the conditional probability of this occurring. The latter depends in part on the value for $ID(t)$. The second term on the rhs of (9.6a) is the magnitude of the upward jump in the spot rate if the market switches from regime 2 to regime 1 in the next period, multiplied by the conditional probability of this event.

Now assume, instead, that the interest rate differential increases in period $t+k$ by the magnitude $dID(t+k) > 0$, and that this differential decays by $\pi\%$ in each future period. The RE value for the change in the spot rate in period $t+k+1$ becomes

$$E[ds(t+k+1)] = Pr[R2 /R2](1 - \psi)^{k+} \Delta s_0 +$$

$$[2\mu + (1 - \psi)^{k+1} \Delta s_0]\{1 - Pr[R2 /R2]\} +$$

$$[\psi bID'-1]dID(t+k)(1 - \psi) - [\psi bID'-1]\pi dID(t+k) \quad (9.6b)$$

This differs from (9.6a) in three ways, namely: (a) the addition of the $[\psi bID' - 1] dID(t+k) (1 - \psi)$ term, which relates to the fact that the increase in the interest rate differential in period $(t+k)$ instantaneously causes the spot rate to fall by $[\psi bID' - 1] dID(t+k)$. This, in turn, begins another infinite series of drifts in the spot rate, and the value for this drift in period $t+k+1$ is $[\psi bID'- 1] dID(t+k) (1-\psi)$; (b) the addition of the last term on the rhs, $- [\psi bID'- 1] \pi dID(t+k)$, which relates to the instantaneous effect on the spot rate in period $t+k+1$ from the decay in the interest rate differential during that period;[8] and (c) the fact that $Pr[R2 /R2]$ must now be evaluated using the interest rate differential that exists in period $t+k+1$; since the differential has increased, this conditional probability of remaining in regime 2 will be higher.

The effect of the increase in the interest rate differential on the RE value for the change in the future spot rate, $dE[ds(t+k+1)]/dID(t+k)$, is the model's equivalent to the β coefficient in empirical work on the FDB, as in (8.2a). This is found by subtracting (9.6a) from (9.6b) to obtain:

$$\beta = -2\mu\{dPr[R2\,/R2]/dID(t+k)\} + [\psi\,bID'-1](1-\psi-\pi) \qquad (9.6c)$$

We know that $b < 0$ in (8.9), $ID' > 0$ from the discussion immediately below (8.11b), and $dPr[R2\,/R2]/dID(t+k) > 0$ from (9.3a). Hence, it follows that a sufficient (but not necessary) condition for the model to generate a negative value for β is $(\psi + \pi) < 1.0$. (Recall that ψ is the weight given to fundamentals when LT-speculators determined their recursive exchange rate expectations, and π is the rate of decay in the interest rate differential.) This condition is more likely if: (a) LT-speculators give a relatively small weight to fundamentals in formulating their regressive exchange rate expectations; and/or (b) the rate of decay in the interest rate differential, π, is low. Note, however, that a negative β is possible in (9.6c) even if we have $(\psi + \pi) > 1.0$, because the term $-2\mu\{dPr[R2\,/R2]/dID(t+k)\}$ is negative. In sum, under reasonable conditions, the model is consistent with the empirically observed negative value for β.

In reality both the risk premium, μ, and the effect of an interest rate variation on the conditional probability of remaining in regime 2, $dPr[R2\,/R2]/dID(t+k)$, are apt to vary over time.[9] Thus, the model can generate a β that is not constant, as has been observed empirically. An empirically testable conclusion deals with the size of β during tranquil versus turbulent periods. **If the risk premium, μ, rises when the exchange rate has been more volatile, then (9.6c) suggests that the β coefficient will be algebraically smaller during those periods.**

Finally, the model is consistent with the fact that estimates of β become progressively algebraically larger as lower frequency data are used. Recall that survey evidence suggests the weight given to fundamentals, ψ, increases as the time horizon increases. If the latter is quite long, then ψ might approach plus unity. Furthermore, as pointed out above, empirical evidence suggests that interest rate differentials are highly persistent, but decay slowly over time.

This rate of decay in the interest rate differential, π, will also increase and approach plus unity as the duration of one time interval grows progressively longer. In sum, both π and ψ will approach plus unity for extremely low frequency data. If so then $(1-\psi-\pi) \approx -1$, and $[\psi bID' - 1](1-\psi-\pi) >$ $+1$ in (9.6c). Also, $dPr[R2\,/R2]/dID(t+k)$ in (9.6c) is less than unity. If the product of this term and 2μ term in (9.6c) is less than unity, then the model will generate a positive β when the relevant time interval is sufficiently long. At any rate, the model is certain to have a β coefficient that grows algebraically larger as the duration of one time interval increases.

9.4 HETEROSKEDASTICITY AND VOLATILITY CLUSTERS: PUZZLE #5

There are several reasons why our FX market model is consistent with heteroskedastic frequency distributions for changes in the log of the spot rate that exist for high frequency data but not for low frequency data. Assume, for example, that one time interval in the model equals one week, and that we examine five years' worth of weekly data for changes in the spot rate. If regime switching occurs randomly, then in some five year periods there might be relatively few weeks during which a regime switch occurs.

On the other hand, in other five year periods the number of regime switches might be larger (or smaller). This would mean that the frequency distributions for variations in the spot rate would exhibit heteroskedasticity when moving from one five year sample period of weekly data to another. However, if lower frequency data (say quarterly) are used, then some of the discontinuous jumps in the spot rate are likely to cancel. In this case, the degree of heteroskedasticity will decrease when moving from one five year sample of quarterly data to another.

The same conclusions hold even if the number of regime switches is identical in each five year interval. This can happen if the magnitude of the risk premium (which affects the size of the discontinuous jumps in the spot rate when regime switching occurs) varies over time. In this case, the magnitude of the jump in the exchange rate (when a regime switch takes place) will vary over time. This can generate heteroskedasticity when moving from one sample period to another. However, as before, if we examine lower frequency (say, quarterly) data over the same five year intervals, then many of the weekly regime switches might be reversed. In such a case, the degree of heteroskedasticity between five year intervals would shrink.

The same logic applies with regard to short term drifts in the exchange rate. For example, assume that all five year intervals have the same number of short term drifts, but that the average magnitude of these drifts changes randomly over time. If high frequency data are used, we will observe different degrees of exchange rate volatility in moving from one five year sample period to another. However, if low frequency data are used, then the average magnitude of short term drifts within each time period makes less difference, because the drifts will tend to cancel each other.

The existence of volatility clusters that occur from time to time is related to the 'regime switching' explanation given above for heteroskedasticity. The FX model developed here suggests that volatility clusters can arise when regime switching prompts investors to engage in profit taking. In order to see this, recall that the $\Omega(t)$ term in the J-function, (8.8a), reflects profit taking activities by LT-speculators. Even though the primary focus of many LT-speculators is not be to profit from FX market speculation, it seems reasonable that some profit taking will occur if the spot rate jumps in the direction which LT-speculators have expected, i.e., toward $s^e(t+n)$.

Therefore, assume that any regime switch elicits profit taking by LT-speculators that creates either FX sales, $\Omega(t) > 0$ in (8.8a), or FX purchases, $\Omega(t) < 0$. Furthermore, let these profit taking actions represent a nontrivial portion, ω, of the cumulative FX position of LT-speculators. The latter is given by the cumulative value for the J- function from all previous periods.

If: (a) the cumulative value for $J(\ )$ is zero in period t, (b) $R(i)$ ... $(i = 1, 2)$ represents the regime in which the market has been operating recently, and (c) $R(t+h)$ indicates the regime that is relevant in period $t+h$. Then

$$\Omega(t+h) = 0 \quad if \quad R(t+h) = R(i) \tag{9.7a}$$

$$\Omega(t+h) = \omega \sum_{n=0}^{h} J(t+n) \quad if \quad R(t+h) \neq R_i \tag{9.7b}$$

Condition (9.7a) says that no profit taking occurs if the FX market remains in the same regime in which it has been functioning recently. On the other hand, condition (9.7b) states that profit taking **sales** of FX, $\Omega(t+h) > 0$, will take place if a regime switch occurs and if LT-speculators have a net positive position in FX. Such sales shift the J-curve to the right.

Assume that LT-speculators begin (in period t) with a zero net FX position, and that the market remains in regime 2 (where LT-speculators are **buying** FX) for h periods. In period $t+h$ they will have accumulated a net positive position in FX. Such a situation is assumed to exist in Figure 9.2 at point 4, where J_1 intersects the Γ' curve. Then let a permanent negative shock to the fundamentals shift the J-curve from J_1 to the left to J_3. This induces a jump to regime 1, with an instantaneous home depreciation, and a new equilibrium at point 5 in Figure 9.2.

From (9.7b) this means that LT-speculators will take profits by selling FX, thereby **temporarily** shifting the J-curve to the right. If this shift is sufficiently large, it can immediately induce a switch back to regime 2. For example, if J_3 shifts to J_2, then the market will end up in period $t+h+1$ in a position such as point 2. Thus, if profit taking is sufficiently large, then one regime switch can be followed by a reversal of this switch in the next period, thereby initiating a volatility cluster.

If profit taking induces the market to end up at point 2 in Figure 9.2 in period $t+h+1$, then the volume of profit taking in that period is given by the horizontal distance between the J_3 and J_2 curves. Since the market has returned to regime 2, profit taking sales of FX will be essentially zero in the next period, $t+h+2$. Consequently, if the fundamentals have not changed between period $t+h+1$ and period $t+h+2$, then the J-curve will return to J_3 in period $t+h+2$. This will induce another regime switch, and the spot rate instantaneously jumps upward again. Thus, the volatility cluster is prolonged, and it will end when a regime switch does not elicit enough profit taking to induce another switch.

In sum, heteroskedastic frequency distributions for changes in exchange rates can arise for several reasons, and one of these is via volatility clusters associated with profit taking in the FX market. These abrupt jumps in the spot rate are likely to show up in very high frequency data, but will tend to cancel in low frequency data. Such clusters are more likely to occur as the cumulative FX position of LT-speculators increases. Consequently, the model generates another potentially empirically testable conclusion, namely that volatility clusters are more likely as the time spent in one regime increases.

9.5   LEPTOKURTOSIS: PUZZLE #6

The reasoning in section 9.4 applies also to the fact that frequency distributions for exchange rate variations are leptokurtic for daily, weekly, and sometimes monthly data, but they approximate a normal distribution for quarterly or lower frequency data.[10] Regime switching and short term drifts in the spot rate will yield a larger than normal frequency for large changes in the spot rate when high frequency data are examined. However, as the duration of one time interval increases, the regime switches and short term drifts will tend to cancel, thereby reducing the frequency of large changes in the spot rate.[11]

9.6   RATIONALITY AND PUZZLES #4, #7, #8, AND #9

This section explores the rationality of recursive long term exchange rate expectations, and of extrapolative short term exchange rate expectations, as suggested by surveys of FX market dealers. This is done by using the model to determine the RE value for the future change in the spot rate: first, in the long run, and, then, in the short run. The results are used to explain why it has been profitable simultaneously to bet in the short run **against** the FX activities of the Fed, but to bet **with** these activities in the long run, provided that the Fed's FX market activities always tended to 'lean against the wind'. This section also shows how the model generates an exchange rate prediction error that is consistent with the FDB.

9.6.1 Long Run Rationality

The RE value for the spot rate at the end of the time horizon of LT-speculators is found by taking a weighted average of the values for: (a) the RE value for the spot rate in regime 1 in period $(t+n)$, and (b) the RE value for the spot rate in regime 2 in period $(t+n)$, with the weights determined by the probabilities (as determined by the model) of the market being in each regime.

Represent the probability that the market will be in regime 2 in period $t+n$ by $Pr(t+n)$. Consequently, the RE value for the spot rate in period $t+n$ is

$$E[s(t+n)] = E[s1(t+n)][1-Pr(t+n)] + E[s2(t+n)] Pr(t+n) \qquad (9.8)$$

The RE value for $s2(t+n)$ is given by $s^e(t+n)$ minus the sum of the expected value for the interest rate differential in period $t+n$, $E[ID(t+n)]$, and the expected value for the risk premium, $E[\mu]$ as in (9.9a) below.[12] Inserting (9.9a) into (9.8) and noting that $E[s1(t+n)] = E[s2(t+n)] + 2E[\mu]$, gives (9.9b).

$$E[s2(t+n)] = s^e(t+n) - E[ID(t+n)] - E[\mu] \qquad (9.9a)$$

$$E[s(t+n)] = s^e(t+n) - E[ID(t+n)] + \{1 - 2Pr(t+n)\}E[\mu] \qquad (9.9b)$$

Substituting for $s^e(t+n)$ from (8.6c) and substracting $s(t-1)$ from both sides of (9.9b) yields

$$E[s(t+n)] - s(t-1) = \psi(t+n)[s^*(t+n) - s(t-1)] -$$

$$E[ID(t+n)] + \{1-2Pr(t+n\}E[\mu] \qquad (9.10)$$

Thus, the RE value for the change in the exchange rate over the time horizon of LT-speculators has two components to it. The first component, $\psi(t+n)[s^*(t+n) - s(t-1)]$, is the regressive forecast in (8.6b). The second component represents the RE value for the 'regressive forecast error'.

$$\varepsilon(t+n) = -E[ID(t+n)] + \{1 - 2Pr(t+n)\}E[\mu] \qquad (9.11a)$$

Recall from Chapter 8 that a zero interest rate differential gives a Γ curve that is symmetric around $s^e(t+n)$. In such a case the unconditional probability of being in either regime is 0.50. Thus, $Pr(t+n) = 0.50$ when the expected interest rate differential for period t+n is zero. In this case, $\varepsilon(t+n)$ will be zero.

On the other hand, if the interest rate differential is positive, then the Γ curve is no longer symmetric around, $s^e(t+n)$, and $Pr(t+n) > 0.5$. From (9.11a), in this case the RE forecast error will be negative. That is, the regressive forecast for the change in the exchange rate (over the time horizon of LT-speculators) will be algebraically larger than its RE value. Conversely, the regressive forecast will be algebraically smaller than the RE forecast when the expected interest rate differential is negative. In general, therefore, the regressive expectations forecast will rarely equal its RE value.

The regressive forecast error will vary with the expected value of the interest rate differential at the end of the time horizon of LT-speculators. This, in turn, depends on the state of the world, 'w', at the time when regressive expectations are formulated. Algebraically,

$$\varepsilon(t+n)_w = \{- E[ID(t+n)] + [1 - 2Pr(t+n)]E[\mu]\}_w \qquad (9.11b)$$

where there is an infinite number of possible states of the world; that is, $w = 1 \ldots \infty$. The regressive forecast will be **unbiased** if the regressive forecast errors sum to zero.

$$\lim_{n \to \infty} \sum_{w=1}^{n} \varepsilon(t+n)_w = 0 \qquad (9.11c)$$

As pointed out above, $Pr(t+n) = 0.50$ when $E[ID(t+n)] = 0$. Thus, it follows from (9.11b) that condition (9.11c) will be satisfied if the **mean** value for the expected interest rate differential is zero over all possible states of the world. Under this seemingly reasonable condition, regressive expectations are Muth rational in the very long run. That is, even though they are usually incorrect, the recursive forecast errors tend to cancel in the very long run. This is similar to the conclusion in Dornbusch (1976) that regressive expectations are Muth rational within the context of his 'sticky-price monetary model' if the interest rate differential gradually decays to zero in the long run.

Therefore, the model generates an RE value for the exchange rate that, in general, moves toward its fundamental value over the time horizon of LT-speculators, as in puzzle #9. Thus, it is rational to bet in the long run **with** the FX market activities of the US government, if the interventions always 'lean against the wind', as in puzzle #7.

9.6.2 The Forward Discount Bias Again

Section 8.2.4 explained that the existence of persistent exchange rate prediction errors that have the same sign is not sufficient to generate a FDB.

From (8.2a), a β that is less than plus unity requires the prediction error to be negatively correlated with the interest rate differential. Furthermore, a **negative** β requires that the prediction error be negatively correlated with the interest rate differential, and be more volatile than the differential. Differentiating the expression for the 'regressive forecast error', (9.11a), with respect to the current period's interest rate differential yields

$$d\varepsilon(t+n)/dID(t) = -dE[ID(t+n)]/dID(t) - 2E[\mu]dPr(t+n)/dID(t) \quad (9.12)$$

Recall that $Pr(t+n)$ is the probability of the market operating in regime 2 in period $t+n$, and that this increases as the interest rate differential rises.[13] If 'n' is very large, then the current period's interest rate differential will decay substantially over the next 'n' periods, which means that there will be a very small influence on $Pr(t+n)$ when the current period interest rate differential changes. In this case, the $- 2E[\mu] \ dPr(t+n)/dID(t)$ term on the rhs of (9.12) is negative, but very small. On the other hand, this term will be negative and larger in absolute value as the size of 'n' decreases, because the interest rate differential will have less time to decay.

To repeat, increase in the current period's interest rate differential increases the expected value of the differential 'n' periods into the future. Thus, the $- dE[ID(t+n)]/dID(t)$ term on the rhs of (9.12) is also negative. As before, however, it will approach zero as 'n' approaches infinity. All of this means that in all circumstances the regressive expectations prediction error will be **negatively** related to the current period's interest rate differential. This relationship, however, becomes progressively smaller in absolute value as the time horizon, 'n', increases. Hence, the model will always yield a β coefficient that is less than plus unity, but this coefficient will approach plus unity (because the rhs of (9.12) approaches zero) as 'n' grows larger.

At the other extreme, if the time horizon is only one time interval, i.e., $n = +1$ in (9.12), then the one period rate of decay in the interest rate differential is apt to be extremely low. Therefore, the $- dE[ID(t+n)]/dID(t)$ term in (9.12) will be approximately minus unity. When this is combined with the negative $- 2 \ E[\mu] \ dPr(t+n)/dID(t)]$ term in (9.12), the result is that the rhs of (9.12) is less than minus unity. **Therefore, when the duration of one time interval is extremely brief, the model generates an exchange rate prediction error that is negatively correlated with and more volatile than the interest rate differential, as is requires in order to obtain a negative value for** β **in the FDB literature.**

9.6.3 Short Term Rationality

Next, consider the rationality of extrapolative short run exchange rate expectations. Rewrite (9.6a) as

$$E[ds(t+k+1)] = (1-\psi)^{k+1} \Delta s_0 + 2\mu \{1 - Pr[R2/R2]\} \qquad (9.13)$$

Recall that (9.13) assumes that the market has been drifting downward in regime 2 for k periods from period t to period $t+k$. This has occurred because a positive shock to the interest rate differential induced an instantaneous jump from regime 1 to regime 2 in period t of $\Delta s_0 < 0$. Also, it assumes that the spot rate lies below its fundamental value, the interest rate differential is constant, and no destabilizing short term speculation exists.

We seek the conditions under which it is Muth rational to expect this downward drift in the spot rate away from its fundamental value to continue for another period, i.e., for the rhs of (9.13) to be negative. This requires the negative term, $(1-\psi)^{k+1} \Delta s_0$, to dominate the positive term given by $2\mu\{1 - Pr[R2/R2]\}$. This is more likely if: (a) the downward drift has not lasted very long, i.e., 'k' is not large; (b) μ is relatively small; (c) the positive interest rate differential is large; and (d) the weight given to fundamentals in the regressive expectations of LT-speculators, ψ, is low.

Condition (a) suggests that it becomes less likely that an endogenous movement in the spot rate will continue as the age of this drift increases. Hence, it will be optimal to bet that a short term drift will continue as quickly as possible after such a drift has been identified. Also, if the risk premium, μ, decreases during nonvolatile periods, then condition (b) suggests that an endogenous drift is more likely to continue if the exchange rate has been relatively tranquil in the recent past.

Condition (c) is tied up with two influences on the exchange rate from an increase in the interest rate differential. First, a large positive interest rate differential increases the absolute value of Δs_0, the initial exogenous discontinuous jump in the spot rate. This, in turn, raises the speed of the ensuing downward drift in the spot rate, i.e., it gives the drift more momentum. Second, a large positive interest rate differential increases the conditional probability of remaining in regime 2, which in turn makes it more likely that an endogenous drift will continue. Finally, it becomes more likely that condition (d) exists if LT-speculators have a relatively brief time horizon. Conditions (a), (b), and (c) appear to be empirically testable.

In sum, under reasonable conditions, it can be perfectly rational to expect a short term drift in the exchange rate away from its fundamental value to continue for at least one more time period. This is true even if no destabilizing speculation occurs. If so, then it will be rational to bet **against** the fundamentals in the short run. In such a case, profits can be earned by betting in the short run against any stabilizing FX intervention by the Fed or Treasury, as in puzzle #7. Also, clearly extrapolative expectations can be appropriate in the very short run, as in puzzle #8.

Finally, the analysis above suggests that if the interest rate differential is significantly nonzero now, but it is correctly expected to decay substantially over the time horizon of LT-speculators, then it can be perfectly rational to bet **against** the fundamentals in the short run, and to bet **on** them in the long run. In such a case, the model is consistent with the empirical finding that positive profits could have been earned by betting in the short run against US intervention, and by betting with the intervention in the long run, provided that such intervention generally worked against movements in the spot rate away from its fundamental value.

9.7 OBSERVATIONS AND COMPLICATIONS

9.7.1 The Lack of a Closed Form Solution

This section briefly explores several aspects of our modern FX market theory of the exchange rate. First, the total model has not been solved formally, but only piece by piece. This is similar to what is true with regard to models dealing with 'currency crises'.[14] In the latter, as well as here, multiple equilibria exist, thereby making it impossible to obtain a closed-form solution for the model. This suggests that simulations of our FX model might prove to be very useful.

9.7.2 Noise Traders

The second topic deals with the addition of 'noise traders' to the model along the lines suggested by DeLong, *et al.* (1990) and used by Mark and Wu (1998). Noise traders are defined here as short term speculators who randomly have a hunch about the near term movement in the spot rate, and who speculate accordingly on a short term basis. This implies that noise traders randomly buy or sell FX on a short term basis.

The easiest way to incorporate noise trader activities into our model is to redefine the random shock term, $v(t)$, in (8.8a). Previously, this represented any temporary shocks to the fundamental balance of payments. Now assume that $v(t)$ also includes the normally distributed random and temporary FX market sales, $v(t) > 0$, or purchases, $v(t) < 0$, of noise traders. Such shocks shift the J-curve to the right with noise trader sales of FX and to the left with noise trader purchases of FX.

The FX market activities of noise traders increase the variance of random shifts in the J-curve, which in turn makes regime switching more likely and long swings in the spot rate less likely. To explain, assume that the spot rate has been drifting downward in regime 2, and is currently at point d in

Figure 9.3. Any negative shock to the J-curve in excess of the distance cd will end the downward drift via a switch up to regime 1.

Since the existence of noise traders raises the variance of random temporary shocks to the J-curve, it becomes more likely that a negative shock will occur that is sufficiently large to induce a regime switch. This, in turn, implies that the probability of remaining in regime 2 decreases. Thus, noise traders reduce the duration of endogenous drifts in the spot rate, and increase the number of discontinuous jumps in the exchange rate, thereby **increasing** the short run volatility of the exchange rate. However, in the process, they decrease the probability of a long swing, which means that noise traders **reduce** the long run volatility of the exchange rate.

9.7.3 Heterogeneous Expectations and a Nonconstant Risk Premium

The third issue concerns the simplifying assumption that the Γ curve is perfectly elastic once it becomes profitable for LT-speculators either to buy or sell FX. This is a consequence of the assumptions that: (a) all LT-speculators have homogeneous exchange rate expectations, and (b) agents are willing to take a progressively larger position in FX without any increase in the risk premium on it. This property of the model leads to the conclusion that shifts in the J-curve exert no direct effect on the exchange rate, provided that the FX market does not switch regimes. Consequently, changes in the net FX position of short term speculators have no effect on the exchange rate. This property of the model is at odds with what one would expect to be true.

In an attempt to remedy this deficiency in the model, maintain the assumption of homogenous exchange rate expectations, but drop the assumption that the Γ curve is perfectly elastic at s1 and s2. Instead, assume that LT-speculators require a progressively higher expected rate of return in order to induce them to increase their FX position. This gives a negatively sloped Γ curve (not shown anywhere). However, the assumption of homogeneous exchange rate expectations means that the discontinuous kinks in Γ still exist at s1 and s2.

If the Γ curve has a negative slope, then clearly shifts in the J-curve will alter the equilibrium value for the exchange rate. Consequently, variations in the net speculative activity of short term speculators will move the spot rate in the direction in which these speculators are betting. For example, if they become net sellers of FX, then the J-curve will shift to the right, thereby depreciating FX, just as short term speculators are betting.

Next assume that LT-speculators have heterogeneous exchange rate expectations, but retain the assumption that the Γ curve is perfectly elastic once all LT-speculators have entered the market. Let s^e_i represent what the ith agent believes will be the value for the spot rate in period $t+n$. In this case, each agent will buy or sell FX when they believe it is profitable to do so, according to (8.7a) and (8.7b). However, if regressive exchange rate expectations differ, then there will be a different buying point, $s2_i$, and a selling point $s1_i$, for each agent. In this situation, the Γ curve will no longer have two 90 degree kinks in it. Rather, it will have two rounded portions, as in Figure 9.4, in the ranges for the spot rate at which progressively more LT-speculators enter the market.

The selling and buying points for the ith agent are given by: $s^e_i - ID(t) \pm \mu$. Figure 9.4 assumes that agent-a enters the FX market at: (i) point a, where the agent sells FX when the spot rate is $s1_a$, or (ii) point a', where the agent buys FX when the spot rate is $s2_a$. Also, agent-b enters the market at: (i) point b, where the agent sells FX at spot rate $s1_b$, or (ii) at point b', where the agent buys FX at spot rate $s2_b$. Similarly, agent-c enters the market at points c and c', at exchange rates s_{1c} and $s2_c$. In each case, the difference between the buying and selling points is assumed to equal 2μ.

In the situation depicted in Figure 9.4, the FX market still has an unstable equilibrium that is bounded by two stable equilibria. Figure 9.4 is drawn such that short run equilibria can conceivably exist in the rounded portions of the Γ curve. Therefore, the FX market model can generate values for the spot rate that lie between the two extremes of $s1_a$ and $s2_c$ in Figure 9.4.

Finally, note that in Figure 9.4, the magnitude of any discontinuous jump in the spot rate (when the market switches regimes) can be greater or less

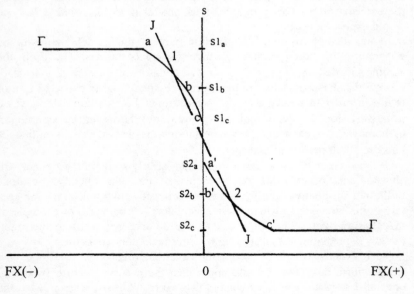

Figure 9.4 Heterogeneous exchange rate expectations

than 2μ. For example, if the market jumps from point 'a' in regime 1 to point c' in regime 2, then the magnitude of this instantaneous appreciation of home money is larger than 2μ. On the other hand, if the market jumps from point c in regime 1 to point a' in regime 2, then this instantaneous appreciation of home money is less than 2μ.

9.8 SUMMARY

1. Drifts in the spot rate away from its fundamental value do not require destabilizing speculation. All that is needed is for stabilizing speculation to begin at a spot rate that is progressively farther away from the fundamental rate, as will happen if long term expectations are regressive.
2. Any initial short term drift in the spot rate can end abruptly via: (a) random shocks to the fundamental balance of payments; (b) exogenous shocks to the interest rate differential; (c) changes in the expected future exchange rate.
3. A long swing in the exchange rate becomes more likely as the absolute value of the interest rate differential increases, and as short term speculators bet on the continuation of an existing trend.
4. A short term drift can end if a nonzero interest rate differential decays over time. The decay: (a) increases the probability of a regime switch, and (b) tends to offset and can even reverse the endogenous drift, without a regime switch. This property of the model appears to be consistent with 'delayed overshooting'.
5. The model suggests that any long swing in the exchange rate is likely to be reversed eventually. This is true because continuous movements in the spot rate in the same direction eventually alter the trade balance, and progressively increase the probability of a regime switch.
6. The model is consistent with the forward discount bias because an increase in the interest rate differential makes it more likely that a downward drift in the spot rate will begin and/or will continue. The magnitude of the often estimated β coefficient will vary over time with the size of the risk premium, i.e., the algebraic value for β will be lower during turbulent periods. The forward discount bias will not exist for extremely low frequency data if the interest rate differential decays substantially from one long time interval to another, and/or if the weight given to fundamentals in regressive expectations is very high for long time horizons.
7. Heteroskedastic and leptokurtic frequency distributions for exchange rate variations exist with high frequency data but not for lower frequency data, because regime switching and/or short term drifts in the

spot rate exist in short run data, but tend to cancel in longer run data. The model can generate volatility clusters, puzzle #5, if a regime switch induces a substantial volume of profit taking.

8. Regressive expectations will be Muth rational in the long run if the mean value for the interest rate differential over all possible states of the world is zero. In this case, the modern FX market model yields an exchange rate whose rational expectations value approaches the fundamental rate in the long run.

9. The model generates an exchange rate prediction error that is negatively correlated with the current period interest rate differential, and this is consistent with the FDB. If the rate of decay in the interest rate differential is low, and/or if the duration of one time interval is extremely brief, then the prediction error in the very short run will be negatively correlated with and more volatile than the interest rate differential. This is consistent with a negative value for the β coefficient in the FDB literature.

10. Extrapolative expectations can be Muth rational in the short run if: (a) the interest rate differential is strongly nonzero, and/or (b) an existing drift in the spot rate has not existed for very long. In this case, it will be profitable to bet that a short term drift in the exchange rate will continue for at least one more time period.

11. If the interest rate differential is significantly nonzero now, but if it decays to zero in the long run, then it can be rational: (a) to bet against the fundamentals in the short run, but (b) to bet on them in the long run. This makes the model consistent with puzzle #7, if US government FX intervention always 'leans against the wind'.

12. Noise traders increase the variability in the J-curve, which raises the probability of discontinuous regime switching in the FX market. This increases exchange rate volatility in the short run. However, the existence of noise traders makes it less likely that a short term drift in the spot rate will develop into a long swing

13. If it takes a progressively larger risk premium to induce LT-speculators to increase their position in the FX, then the activities of short term speculators will alter the exchange rate in the direction in which they speculate.

14. Also, if long term exchange rate expectations are heterogeneous, then, for any given position of the Γ curve, the level of the exchange rate can assume many values between those associated with the buying and selling points with homogeneous expectations. Furthermore, with heterogeneous expectations, the magnitude of discontinuous jumps in the spot rate can vary, even if μ is constant and is the same for each speculator.

15. The modern FX market model generates the following potentially empirically testable conclusions: (a) short term drifts in the exchange rate will be larger if: the initial exogenous shock to the spot rate is larger, and/or if the weight given to fundamentals is smaller; (b) the probability that a short term drift will continue decreases as the duration of the drift increases, and this probability increases as the absolute value of the interest rate differential rises; (c) the duration of long swings in the exchange rate will be larger in countries with smaller long run trade elasticities; (d) the algebraic value of the β coefficient in the FDB literature falls during periods in which the exchange rate has been more volatile; also it rises as the duration of one time interval increases; and (e) volatility clusters are more likely as the time spent in a particular regime increases.

NOTES

1. Algebraically, FX market equilibrium exists if: $J(\ ) = -\Gamma$. This is equivalent to: $J(\ ) - (Cs - Cd) - \Omega(t) = -\Gamma - (Cs - Cd) - \Omega(t)$. The lhs of this expression is the fundamental balance of payments, and the rhs takes account of all speculative activities, including profit taking by LT-speculators.
2. This occurs because the positive interest rate differential will not decay completely to zero over 'n' periods, for all values of 'n' less than infinity.
3. See Baillie and Bollerslev (1994), Bekaert and Hodrick (1992), and Bekaert (1995) as well as the discussion associated with assumption #6 in section 8.3.1.
4. This is true even if short term destabilizing speculation is taking place, provided that the magnitude of such speculation is not increasing over time.
5. To obtain (9.5c), start with the condition $-(j_2/j_1)(1-\psi)\Delta s_o < (1-\psi)^{k+j}\Delta s_o$. Recall that $\Delta s_o < 0$, and rewrite this expression as $-(j_2/j_1) > (1-\psi)^k$ from which (9.5c) follows directly.
6. See Goldstein and Khan (1985, table 4.3) for a summary of the estimates for 14 leading countries.
7. An unlikely but nevertheless conceivable exception to this conclusion exists. The limit to a long swing in the exchange rate as given by (9.2c) is: $\Delta s_o/\psi$. Consequently, there is an upper limit to how much the trade balance and fundamental balance of payments can deteriorate in response to a long swing. If the initial value for the fundamental balance of payments exceeds this limit, then the J-function will never become negative in regime 2 via endogenously induced deteriorations in the trade balance. However, even in this unlikely case, the probability of a regime switch (which ends the long swing) via an exogenous shock to the J-curve gradually increases over time.
8. The events in (a) and (b) affect the position of the Γ curve, and, hence, the value for the spot rate, regardless of the regime in which the market is operating.
9. The $dPr[R2 \mid R2]/dID(t+k)$ term will vary over time if the J-curve is not linear, and if the FX market equilibrium position moves over time to many positions on the J-curve.
10. Westerfield (1977) did the original work on this subject. See Booth and Glassman (1987) for other early references.
11. Mandelbrot (1963) first observed that stock and commodity price changes have frequency distributions that are leptokurtic. Studies by Barnes and Downes (1973), and Fielitz and Rozelle (1983) confirmed this. Note that the observed leptokutosis in stock and commodity market are undoubtedly caused by dynamic forces that generate more volatile movements in the prices of these assets than in the fundamentals that affect them.

However, there is no logical reason why these dynamic forces have to be the same as those that drive the FX market.

12. Notice that the assumption that the risk premium is constant has been dropped.

13. An increase in the interest rate differential shifts the Γ curve downward. This: (a) increases the size of a shift to the left in the J-curve that is needed to induce a jump from regime 2 to regime 1, and (b) reduces the size of a shift to the right in the J-curve that is needed to induce a jump from regime 1 to regime 2. Both consequences increase the probability of being in regime 2.

14. See Garber and Svensson (1995) for an excellent survey of the early literature on this subject.

References

Abuaf, Niso and Philipe Jorion (1990), 'Purchasing Power Parity in the Long Run', *Journal of Finance*, **45** (1), 157–74.

Akgiray, V. and Geoffrey. G. Booth (1988), 'Mixed Diffusion-Jump Process Modeling of Exchange Rate Movements', *Review of Economics and Statistics*, **70** (4), 631–7.

Akgiray, V., G. Geoffrey Booth, and Bruce Seifert (1998), 'Distribution Properties of Latin American Black Market Exchange Rates', *Journal of International Money and Finance*, **7** (1), 3–48.

Aldcroft, Derek H. and Michael J. Oliver (1998), *Exchange Rate Regimes in the Twentieth Century*, Cheltenham, U.K. and Northhampton, MA, U.S.A.: Edward Elgar.

Alexander, Sidney S. (1952), 'Effects of a Devaluation on the Trade Balance', *International Monetary Fund Staff Papers*, **3**, 263–78.

Alexander, Sidney S. (1959), 'Effects of a Devaluation: A Simplified Synthesis of Elasticities and Absorption Approaches', *American Economic Review*, **49** (1), 23–42.

Allen, Helen and Mark P. Taylor (1990), 'Charts, Noise, and Fundamentals in the London Foreign Exchange Market', *Economic Journal*, **100** (400), 49–59.

Backus, D., P. Kehoe, and F. Kydland (1992), 'International Real Business Cycles', *Journal of Political Economy*, **100** (4), 745–75.

Baillie, Richard T. and Tim Bollerslev (1989), 'The Message in Daily Exchange Rates: A Conditional Variance Tale', *Journal of Business and Economic Statistics*, **7** (3), 297–305.

Baillie, Richard T. and Tim Bollerslev (1994), 'The Long-Memory of the Forward Premium', *Journal of International Money and Finance*, **13** (5), 309–324.

Baillie, Richard T. and Tim Bollerslev (2000), 'The Forward Premium Anomaly is Not as Bad as You Think', *Journal of International Money and Finance*, **19** (4), 471–88.

Baldwin, Robert E. (1968), 'The Role of Capital Goods Trade in the Theory of International Trade', *American Economic Review*, **58** (4), 943–44.

Ball, Clifford A., and Antonio Roma (1993), 'A Jump–Diffusion Model for the European Monetary System', *Journal of International Money and Finance*, **12** (5), 475–92.

Balvers, Ronald J. and Jeffrey H. Bergstrand (1997), 'Equilibrium Real Exchange Rates: Closed Form Theoretical Solutions and Some

Empirical Evidence', *Journal of International Money and Finance*, **16** (3), 345–66.

Bank for International Settlements (1998), 'Central Bank Survey of Foreign Exchange and Derivatives Market Activity in April 1998: Preliminary Global Data', *Press Release*, Basle: Bank for International Settlements.

Bardhan, P.K. (1967), 'Optimum Foreign Borrowing', in *Essays in the Theory of Optimal Economic Growth*, ed. by Karl Shell, Cambridge, MA: MIT Press.

Barnea, A. and D. H. Downes (1973), 'A Re-Examination of the Empirical Distribution of Stock Price Changes', *Journal of the American Statistical Association*, **68** (342), 348–50.

Bates, David S. (1996), 'Jumps and Stochastic Volatility: Exchange Rate Processes Implicit in Deutsche Mark Options', *The Review of Financial Studies*, **9** (1), 69–107.

Baum, Christopher F., John T. Barkoulas, and Mustafa Caglayan (2001), 'Nonlinear Adjustment to Purchasing Power Parity in the Post-Bretton Woods Era', *Journal of International Money and Finance*, **20** (3), 379–99.

Baxter, Marianne (1994), 'Real Exchange Rates and Real Interest Rates: Have We Missed the Business Cycle Relationship?', *Journal of Monetary Economics*, **33** (1), 5–38.

Baxter, Marianne (1995), 'International Trade and Business Cycles', in Grossman and Rogoff (1995), 180–64.

Baxter, Marianne and Mario Crucini (1993), 'Explaining Saving–Investment Correlations', *American Economic Review*, **83** (3) 416–36.

Bekaert, G. (1995), 'The Time Variation of Expected Returns and Volatility in Foreign Exchange Markets', *Journal of Business and Economic Statistics*, **13** (4), 397–408.

Bekaert, G. and R. J. Hodrick (1992), 'Characterizing Predictable Components in Excess Returns on Equity and Foreign Exchange Markets', *Journal of Finance*, **47** (2), 467–509.

Bhandari, Jagdeep S. (1981), 'Exchange Rate Overshooting Revisited', *The Manchester School of Economic and Social Studies*, **49** (2), 165–72.

Blanchard, Oliver (1983), 'Debt and the Current Account Deficit in Brazil', in *Financial Policies and the World Capital Market: The Problem of Latin American Countries*, ed. by Pedro Aspe Armella, Rudiger Dornbusch, and Maurice Obstfeld, Chicago: University of Chicago Press.

Bollerslev, T. and M. Melvin (1994), 'Bid–Ask Spreads and Volatility in the Foreign Exchange Market', *Journal of International Economics*, **36** (3), 355–72.

Boothe, Paul and Deborah Glassman (1987), 'The Statistical Distribution of Exchange Rates: Empirical Evidence and Economic Implications', *Journal of International Economics*, **22** (3), 29–319.

Branson, William H. (1983), 'Macroeconomic Determinants of Real Exchange Risk', in *Managing Foreign Exchange Risk*, ed. by R.J. Herring, Cambridge: Cambridge University Press, ch. 1.

Branson, William H. and H. Halttunen (1979), 'Asset Market Determination of Exchange Rates: Initial Empirical and Policy Results', in *Trade and Payments Under Flexible Exchange Rate*, ed. by J.P. Martin and A. Smith, London: Macmillian, pp. 55–85.

Branson, William H. and Dale Henderson (1985), 'The Specification and Influence of Asset Markets', in *Handbook of International Economics: Volume II*, ed. by Ronald A. Jones and Peter B. Kenen, Amsterdam: North-Holland, pp. 749–93.

Buiter, Willem H. (1980), 'Walras' Law and All That: Budget Constraints and Balance Sheet Constraints in Period Models and Continuous Time Models', *International Economic Review*, **21** (1), 1–16.

Buiter, Willem H. and Jonathan Eaton (1981), 'Keynesian Balance of Payments Models: Comment', *American Economic Review*, **71** (4), 784–95.

Burnham, James B. (1991), 'Current Structure and Recent Developments in Foreign Exchange Markets', in *Recent Developments in International Banking and Finance*, ed. by Sarkis J. Khoury, Amsterdam: North-Holland, pp. 123–53.

Calvo, Guillermo A. (2000), 'Balance of Payments Crises in Emerging Markets: Large Capital Inflows and Sovereign Government', in *Currency Crises*, ed. by Paul Krugman, Chicago: The University of Chicago Press, pp. 71–104.

Chakraborty, Debashish, David Luan, and Norman C. Miller (1996), 'Sterilization, International Reserve Flow Reversals, and Monetary Autonomy in the Bretton Woods System', *Indian Economic Journal*, **44** (3), 22–43.

Chakraborty, Debashish and Norman C. Miller (1988), 'Economic Growth and the Balance of Payments', *Journal of Economic Development*, **13** (2), 57–79.

Chang, Chen Fu (1976), 'Liquidity Preference and Loanable Funds Theories: A Synthesis', *Australian Economic Papers*, **15** (27), 302–7.

Chen, Chan-nan, Ching-Chang Lai, and Tien-wang Tsaur (1988a), 'Capital Mobility, Trade Balance Elasticity, and Exchange Rate Dynamics', *Southern Economic Journal*, **55** (2), 211–14.

Chen, Chan-nan, Ching-Chang Lai, and Tien-wang Tsaur (1988b), 'The Loanable Funds Theory, and the Dynamics of Exchange Rates: The Mundell Model Revisited', *Journal of International Money and Finance*, **7** (2), 221–29.

Chen, Shikuan (2000), 'Endogenous Real Exchange Rate Fluctuations in an Optimizing Open Economy Model', *Journal of International Money and Finance*, **19** (2), 185–205.

Cheung, Yin-Wong and Menzie D. Chinn (1999a), 'Traders, Market Microstructure, and Exchange Rate Dynamics', *NBER Working Paper 7416*, Cambridge, MA.

Cheung, Yin-Wong and Menzie D. Chinn (1999b), 'Macroeconomic Implications of the Beliefs and Behavior of Foreign Exchange Traders', *NBER Working Paper 7417,* Cambridge, MA.

Cheung, Yin-Wong and Menzie D. Chinn (2001), 'Currency Traders and Exchange Rate Dynamics: A Survey of the US Market', *Journal of International Money and Finance*, **20** (4), 439–71

Cheung, Yin-Wong, Menzie D. Chinn, and Ian W. Marsh (2000), 'How Do UK-Based Foreign Exchange Dealers Think Their Market Operates?', *NBER Working Paper 7524*, Cambridge, MA.

Cheung, Yin-Wong and K.S. Lai (2000), 'On the Purchasing Power Parity Puzzle', *Journal of International Economics*, **52** (2), 321–30.

Chinn, M.D. and R.A. Meese (1994), 'Banking on Currency Forecasts: How Predictable is a Change In Money?', *Journal of International Economics*, **38** (1), 161–78.

Christiano, L., M. Eichenbaum, and C. Evans (1996), 'The Effects of Monetary Policy Shocks: Evidence from the Flow of Funds', *Review of Economics and Statistics*, **78** (1), 16–34.

Christiano, L., M. Eichenbaum, and C. Evans (1998), 'The Effects of Monetary Policy Shocks: What Have We Learned and to What End?', *NBER Working Paper 6400*, Cambridge, MA.

Clark, Peter B. and Ronald MacDonald (1999), 'Exchange Rates and Economic Fundamentals: Methodological Comparison of BEERs and FEERs', in *Equilibrium Exchange Rates,* ed. by R. MacDonald and Jerome Stein, Boston: Kluwer Academic Press, ch. 10.

Connally, Michael and Stephen Ross (1970), 'A Fisherian Approach to Trade, Capital Movements, and Tariffs', *American Economic Review*, **60** (3), 478–84.

Copeland, Laurence S. (1994), *Exchange Rates and International Finance*, 2nd ed, Workingham, England: Addison-Wesley, ch. 8.

Corden, W. Max (1994), *Economic Policy, Exchange Rates, and the International System*, Oxford: Oxford University Press.

Corsetti, Giancarlo, Paolo Pesenti, and Nouriel Roubini (1998), 'Paper Tigers? A Model of the Asian Crisis', Paper Presented at the NBER-Bank of Portugal International Seminar on Macroeconomics, Lisbon.

Crownover, Collin, John Pippenger, and Douglas Steigerwald (1996), 'Tests for Absolute Purchasing Power Parity', *Journal of International Money and Finance*, **15** (5), 783–96.

Cumby, R.E. and F.S. Mishkin (1986), 'The International Linkage of Real Interest Rates: The European-U.S. Connection', *Journal of International Money and Finance*, **5** (1), 5–23.

Darby, Michael (1986), 'The Internationalization of American Banking and Finance: Structure, Risk, and World Interest Rates', *Journal of International Money and Finance*, **5** (4), 403–28.

Davis, George K. and Norman C. Miller (1996), 'Exchange Rate Mean Reversion from Real Shocks Within An Intertemporal Equilibrium Model', *Journal of International Money and Finance*, **15** (6), 947–67.

Deardorff, Alan V. (1981), 'The Inadequacy of Keynesian Balance of Payments Models: Comment', *American Economic Review*, **71**, (4), 774–77.

DeLong, B., A. Shleifer, L. Summers, and R. Waldman (1990), 'Noise Trader Risk in Financial Markets', *Journal of Political Economy*, **98** (3), 703–38.

Devereux, M.B. (2000), 'How Does a Devaluation Affect the Current Account?', *Journal of International Money and Finance*, **19** (6), 833–51.

Dewachter, Hans (2001), 'Can Markov Switching Models Replicate Chartist Profits in the Foreign Exchange Market?', *Journal of International Money and Finance*, **20** (1), 25–41.

Diebold, Francis X., Steve Husted and Mark Rush (1991), 'Real Exchange Rates under the Gold Standard', *Journal of Political Economy*, **99** (6), 1252–71.

Dluhosch, Barbara, Andreas Freytag, and Malte Kruger (1996), *International Competitiveness and the Balance of Payments: Do Current Account Deficits and Surpluses Matter?*, Cheltenham, UK: Edward Elgar.

Dooley, Michael P. and S. Schafer (1984), 'Analysis of Short-Run Exchange Rate Behavior: March, 1973 to November, 1981', in *Floating Exchange Rates and the State of World Trade Payments*, ed. by D. Bigman and T. Taya, Cambridge, MA: Ballinger Press, pp. 43–69

Dornbusch, Rudiger (1976), 'Expectations and Exchange Rate Dynamics', *Journal of Political Economy*, **84** (6), 1161–76.

Dornbusch, Rudiger (1980), *Open Economy Macroeconomics*, New York: Basic Books.

Dornbusch, Rudiger (1983), 'Real Interest Rates, Home Goods, and Optimal External Borrowing', *Journal of Political Economy*, **91** (1), 141–53.

Dornbusch, R., S. Fischer, and P.A. Samuelson (1977), 'Comparative Advantage, Trade, and Payments in a Ricardian Model with a Continuum of Goods', *American Economic Review*, **67** (5), 823–39.

Edwards, Sebastian (2001), 'Does The Current Account Matter?', *NBER Working Paper 8275*, Cambridge, MA.

Eichenbaum, Martin and Charles L. Evans (1995), 'Some Empirical Evidence on the Effects of Shocks to Monetary Policy on Exchange Rates', *Quarterly Journal of Economics*, **110** (4), 975–1009.

Engel, Charles (1994), 'Can the Markov Switching Model Forecast Exchange Rates?', *Journal of International Economics*, **36** (1), 151–65.

Engel, Charles (1996), 'Why is There a Forward Discount Bias? A Survey of Recent Evidence', *Journal of Empirical Finance*, **3** (2), 123–91.

Engel, Charles and Jeffrey Frankel (1984), 'Why Interest Rates React to Money Announcements', *Journal of Monetary Economics*, **13** (1), 31–9.

Engel, Charles and J. D. Hamilton (1990), 'Long Swings in the Dollar: Are They in the Data and Do Markets Know It?', *American Economic Review*, **80** (4), 689–713.

Engel, Charles, M. Hendrickson, and J. Rogers (1997), 'Intra-National, Intra-Continental, and Intra-Planetary PPP', *NBER Working Paper 6069*, Cambridge, MA.

Engle, Robert F. (1995), 'Autoregressive Conditional Heteroskedasticity with Estimates of the Variance of U.K. Inflation', in *ARCH: Selected Readings*, Oxford and New York: Oxford University Press, pp. 1–23.

Fair, Ray C. (1982), 'Estimated Output, Price, Interest Rate, and Exchange Rate Linkages Among Countries', *Journal of Political Economy*, **90** (3), 507–35.

Feldstein, Martin (1983), 'Domestic Saving and International Capital Movements in the Long Run and the Short Run', *European Economic Review*, **21** (1–2), 129–51.

Feldstein, Martin and C. Horioka (1980), 'Domestic Saving and International Capital Flows', *Economic Journal*, **90** (358), 314–29.

Ferguson, J. David and William R. Hart (1980), 'Liquidity Preference or Loanable Funds: Interest Rate Determination in Market Disequilibrium', *Oxford Economic Papers*, **32** (1), 57–70.

Fernandez de Cordoba, Gonzalo and Timothy J. Kehoe (2000), 'Capital Flows and Real Exchange Rate Fluctuations Following Spain's Entry in the European Community', *Journal of International Economics*, **51** (1), 49–78.

Fieleke, Norman (1982), 'National Saving and International Investment', in *Saving and Government Policy*, Conference Series no. 25, Boston: Federal Reserve Bank of Boston.

Fielitz, B.D. and J.P. Rozelle (1983), 'Stable Distribution and the Mixtures of Distributions Hypotheses for Common Stock Returns', *Journal of the American Statistical Association*, **78** (381), 28–36.

Fisher, Irving (1930), *The Theory of Interest*, New York: Macmillan.

Fleming, J.M. (1962), 'Domestic Financial Policies Under Fixed and Floating Exchange Rates', *International Monetary Fund Staff Papers*, **9** (3), 369–79.

Flood, Mark D. (1991), 'Microstructure Theory and the Foreign Exchange Market', *Federal Reserve Bank of St. Louis Review*, **73** (6), 52–70.

Flood, Robert P. and Andrew K. Rose (1996), 'Fixes: Of the Forward Discount Puzzle', *Review of Economics and Statistics*, **78** (4), 748–52.

Flood, Robert P. and Mark P. Taylor (1995), 'Exchange Rate Economics: What's Wrong with the Conventional Macro Approach?', in *The Microstructure of Foreign Exchange Markets*, ed. by J. A. Frankel, G. Galli, and A. Giovannini, Chicago: University of Chicago Press, pp. 261–302.

Foley, Duncan K. (1975), 'On Two Specifications of Asset Equilibrium in Macroeconomic Models', *Journal of Political Economy*, **83** (2), 303–24.

Frankel, Jeffrey A. (1993), *On Exchange Rates*, Cambridge, MA: MIT Press.

Frankel, Jeffrey A. and Rudiger Dornbusch (1993), 'The Flexible Exchange Rate System: Experiences and Alternatives', in *International Finance and Trade*, ed. by Silvio Borner, London: Macmillan Press, 1988; reprinted in Frankel (1993), ch.3.

Frankel, Jeffrey A. and Kenneth Froot (1986), 'Understanding the US Dollar in the Eighties: The Expectations of Chartists and Fundamentalists', in Frankel (1993), ch. 14.

Frankel, Jeffrey A. and Kenneth Froot (1989), 'Forward Discount Bias: Is It Exchange Risk Premium?', *Quarterly Journal of Economics*, **104** (1), 139–61.

Frankel, Jeffrey A. and Kenneth Froot (1990a), 'Chartists, Fundamentalists, and Trading in the Foreign Exchange Market', *American Economic Review*, **90** (1), 180–5.

Frankel, Jeffrey A. and Kenneth Froot (1990b), 'Chartists, Fundamentals, and the Demand for Dollars', in *Private Behavior and Government Policy in Interdependent Economies*, ed. by A. Courakis, and Mark Taylor, Oxford: Clarendon Press, pp. 73–126.

Frankel, Jeffrey A., G. Galli, and A. Giovannini (1995), *The Microstructure of Foreign Exchange Markets*, Chicago: University of Chicago Press.

Frankel, Jeffrey A. and Andrew K. Rose (1995), 'Empirical Research on Nominal Exchange Rates', in Grossman and Rogoff (1995), 1689–1729.

Frenkel, Jacob, A., and Harry G. Johnson, eds. (1976), *The Monetary Approach to the Balance of Payments,* London: Allen Unwin.

Frenkel, Jacob A. and Assaf Razin (1992), *Fiscal Policies and the World Economy: An Intertemporal Approach*, 2nd ed Cambridge, MA: MIT Press.

Frenkel, Jacob A., Assaf Razin, and Efraim Sadka (1991), *International Taxation*, Cambridge, MA: MIT Press.

Frenkel, Jacob A. and Carlos A. Rodriguez (1982), 'Exchange Rate Dynamics and the Overshooting Hypothesis', *IMF Staff Papers*, **29** (1), 1–29.

Froot, Kenneth and Kenneth Rogoff (1995), 'Perspectives on PPP and Long Run Real Exchange Rates', in Grossman and Rogoff (1995), ch. 32.

Froot, Kenneth and Richard H. Thaler (1990), 'Anomalies: Foreign Exchange', *Journal of Economic Perspectives*, **2** (2), 179–92.

Fujii, Eiji and Menzie D. Chinn (2000), 'Fin De Siecle Real Interest Parity', *NBER Working Paper 7880*, Cambridge, MA.

Garber, Peter M. and Lars E.O. Svensson (1995), 'The Operation and Collapse of Fixed Exchange Rate Regimes', in Grossman and Rogoff (1995), ch. 36.

Gencay, R. (1999), 'Linear, Non-linear, and Essential Foreign Exchange Rate Prediction with Simple Technical Trading Rules', *Journal of International Economics*, **47** (1), 91–107.

Gertler, Mark and Kenneth Rogoff (1990), 'North-South Lending and Endogenous Domestic Capital Market Inefficiencies', *Journal of Monetary Economics*, **26** (2), 245–66.

Glen, Jack D. (1992), 'Real Exchange Rates in the Short, Medium, and Long Run', *Journal of International Economics*, **33** (1), 147–66.

Glick, Reuben and Kenneth Rogoff (1995), 'Global versus Country-Specific Productivity Shocks and the Current Account', *Journal of Monetary Economics*, **35** (1), 159–92.

Goldstein, Morris and Mohsin S. Khan (1985), 'Income and Price Effects in Foreign Trade', in *Handbook of International Economics, Volume 2*, ed. by Ronald W. Jones, and Peter B. Kenen, Amsterdam: North-Holland, pp. 1041–1105.

Gordon, Roger H. and Hal Varian (1989), 'Taxation of Asset Income in the Presence of a World Security Market', *Journal of International Economics*, **26** (3), 205–26.

Gourinchas, Pierre-Olivier and Aaron Tornell (1996), 'Exchange Rate Dynamics and Learning', *NBER Working Paper 5530*, Cambridge, MA.

Grossman, Gene M. and Kenneth Rogoff (1995), *Handbook of International Economics: Volume III*, Amsterdam: Elsevier.

Hahn, Frank H. (1977), 'The Monetary Approach to Balance of Payments', *Journal of International Economics*, **7** (3), 231–49.

Hamada, K. (1969), 'Optimal Capital Accumulation by an Economy Facing an International Capital Market', *Journal of Political Economy*, **77** (4), 684–97.

Harberger, Arnold (1950), 'Currency Depreciation, Income, and the Balance of Trade', *Journal of Political Economy*, **58** (1), 47–60.

Heller, H. Robert (1974), *International Monetary Economics*, Englewood Cliffs, NJ: Prentice-Hall.

Henderson, Dale (1984), 'Exchange Market Intervention Operations: Their Role in Financial Policy and Their Effects', in *Exchange Rate Theory and Practice*, ed. by John Bilson and Richard C. Marston, Chicago: University of Chicago Press, pp. 359–98.

Hicks, John R. (1986), 'Loanable Funds and Liquidity Preference', *Greek Economic Review*, 8 (2), 125–31.

Hogan, Kedreth C. Jr, and Michael T. Melvin (1994), 'Sources of Meteor Showers and Heat Waves in The Foreign Exchange Market', *Journal of International Economics*, 37 (3–4), 23–47.

Hsieh, David A. (1991), 'Implications of Observed Properties of Daily Exchange Rate Movements', *Journal of International Financial Markets, Institutions, and Money*, 1 (1), 61–71.

International Monetary Fund (1997), *International Financial Statistics*, May.

Isard, Peter and Hamid Faruqee, eds. (1998), *Exchange Rate Assessment: Extensions of the Macroeconomic Balance Approach.* Washington, DC: International Monetary Fund.

Johnson, Harry G. (1961), 'Towards a General Theory of the Balance of Payments', in H.G. Johnson, *International Trade and Economic Growth: Studies in Pure Theory,* Cambridge, MA: Harvard University Press, pp. 153– 68.

Jorion, Philippe (1988), 'On Jump Processes in the Foreign Exchange and Stock Markets', *Review of Financial Studies*, 1 (4), 427–45.

Jorion, Philippe (1996), 'Does Real Interest Parity Hold at Longer Maturities?', *Journal of International Economics*, 40 (1-2), 105–26.

Kaminsky, Graciela (1993), 'Is There a Peso Problem? Evidence from the Dollar/Pound Exchange Rate, 1976–1987', *American Economic Review*, 83 (3), 450–72.

Karacaoglu, Girol (1985), 'Liquidity Preference, Loanable Funds, and Exchange Rate and Interest Rate Dynamics', *Journal of Macroeconomics*, 7 (1), 69–83.

Komiya, R. (1969), 'Economic Growth and the Balance of Payments: A Monetary Approach', *Journal of Political Economy*, 77 (1), 35–48.

Koraczyk, R. (1985), 'The Pricing of Forward Contracts for Foreign Exchange', *Journal of Political Economy*, 93 (2), 346–68.

Kouri, P.J.K. and M.G. Porter (1974), 'International Capital Flows and Portfolio Equilibrium', *Journal of Political Economy*, 82 (3), 443–67.

Krasker, W.S. (1980), 'The "Peso Problem" in Testing Forward Exchange Markets', *Journal of Monetary Economics*, 6 (2), 269–76.

Krugman, Paul R. (1995), 'What Do We Need to Know About the International Monetary System?', in *Understanding Interdependence*, ed. by Peter B. Kenen, Princeton N J: Princeton University Press, ch. 13.

Krugman, Paul and Maurice Obstfeld (1994), *International Economics*. 3rd ed, New York: Harper-Collins.

Kuska, Edward A. (1978), 'On the Almost Total Inadequacy of Keynesian Balance of Payments Theory', *American Economic Review*, **68** (4), 659–70.

Kuska, Edward A. (1982), 'On the Adequacy or Inadequacy of Keynesian Balance of Payments Theory: A Reply', *American Economic Review*, **72** (4), 887–98.

Laidler, David (1984), 'The "Buffer Stock" Notion in Monetary Economics', *Economic Journal*, **94** (Supplement), 17–34.

Laursen, S. and Lloyd Metzler (1950), 'Flexible Exchange Rates and the Theory of Employment', *Review of Economics and Statistics*, **32** (4), 281–90.

Leahy, Michael P. (1995), 'The Profitability of US Intervention in the Foreign Exchange Markets', *Journal of International Money and Finance*, **14** (6), 823–44.

LeBaron, B. (1999), 'Technical Trading Rule Profitability and Foreign Exchange Intervention', *Journal of International Economics*, **49** (1), 125–43.

Leontief, Wassily (1933), 'The Use of Indifference Curves in the Analysis of Foreign Trade', *Quarterly Journal of Economics*, **47** (3), 493–503.

Leontief, Wassily (1958), 'Theoretical Note on Time-Preference, Productivity of Capital, Stagnation, and Economic Growth', *American Economic Review*, **48** (1), 105–11.

Levin, Jay (1986), 'Trade Flow Lags, Monetary and Fiscal Policy, and Exchange Rate Overshooting', *Journal of International Money and Finance*, **5** (4), 485–95.

Lewis, Karen K. (1989), 'Changing Beliefs and Systematic Rational Forecast Errors with Evidence from Foreign Exchange', *American Economic Review*, **79** (4), 621–36.

Lewis, Karen K. (1993), 'What Can Explain the Apparent Lack of International Consumption Risk Sharing?', Manuscript, Wharton School of Business.

Lewis, Karen K. (1995), 'Puzzles in International Financial Markets', in Grossman and Rogoff (1995), ch. 37.

Lothian, James R. and Mark P. Taylor (1996), 'Real Exchange Rate Behavior: The Recent Float from the Perspective of the Past Two Centuries', *Journal of Political Economy,* **104** (3), 488–509.

Luan, David and Norman C. Miller (1978), 'A Monetary Approach to International Capital Flows Applied to the United States: A Note', *Journal of Money, Credit, and Banking*, **7** (1), 87–90.

Lucas, Robert E. (1982), 'Interest Rates and Currency Prices in a Two Country World', *Journal of Monetary Economics*, **10** (3), 335–59.

Lui, Yu-Hon and David Mole (1998), 'The Use of Fundamental and Technical Analyses by Foreign Exchange Dealers: Hong Kong Evidence', *Journal of International Money and Finance*, **17** (3), 535–45.

Lyons, Richard K. (1993), 'Tests of Microstructural Hypotheses in the Foreign Exchange Market', *NBER Working Paper 4471*, Cambridge, MA.

Lyons, Richard K. (1995a), 'Foreign Exchange Volume: Sound and Fury Signifying Nothing?', in Galli, and Giovannini, eds., 1995.

Lyons, Richard K. (1995b), 'Tests of Microstructural Hypothesis in the Foreign Exchange Market', *Journal of Financial Economics*, **39** (2–3), 321–51.

Lyons, Richard K. (1997), 'A Simultaneous Trade Model of the Foreign Exchange Hot Potato', *Journal of International Economics*, **42** (3–4), 278–98.

Lyons, Richard K. (1998), 'Profits and Position Control: A Week of Foreign Exchange Dealing', *Journal of International Money and Finance*, **17** (1), 97–115.

Lyons, Richard K. and Andrew K. Rose (1995), 'Explaining Forward Exchange Bias ... Intraday', *Journal of Finance*, **50** (4), 1321–29.

MacDonald, Ronald (1988), *Floating Exchange Rates: Theories and Evidence*, London: Unwin-Hyman.

MacDonald, Ronald and Ian W. Marsh (1996), 'Currency Forecasters are Heterogeneous: Confirmation and Consequences', *Journal of International Money and Finance*, **15** (5), 665–85.

MacDonald, Ronald and Mark P. Taylor (1993), 'The Monetary Approach to the Exchange Rate: Rational Expectations, Long Run Equilibrium, and Forecasting', *International Monetary Fund Staff Papers*, **40** (1), 89–107.

MacDonald, Ronald and Mark P. Taylor (1994), 'The Monetary Model of the Exchange Rate: Long run Relationships, Short Run Dynamics, and How to Beat a Random Walk', *Journal of International Money and Finance,* **13** (3), 276–90.

Malz, Allan M. (1996), "Using Option Prices to Estimate Realignment Probabilities in the European Monetary System: The Case of Sterling-Mark', *Journal of International Money and Finance*, **15** (5), 717–48.

Mandelbrot, B.B. (1963), 'The Variation of Certain Speculative Prices', *Journal of Business*, **36** (4), 394–419.

Mark, Nelson C. (1995), 'Exchange Rates and Fundamentals: Evidence on Long-Horizon Predictability', *American Economic Review*, **85** (1), 201–18.

Mark, Nelson C. and Yangru Wu (1998), 'Rethinking Deviations from Uncovered Interest Parity: The Role of Covariance Risk and Noise', *Economic Journal*, **108** (451), 1686–1706.

McCallum, Bennett (1994), 'A Reconsideration of the Uncovered Interest Parity Relationship', *Journal of Monetary Economics*, **33** (1), 105–32.

McGregor, Peter G. (1988), 'The Demand for Money in a Period Analysis Context, the Irrelevence of the Choice of Market, and the Loanable Funds–Liquidity Preference Debate', *Australian Economic Papers*, **27** (50), 136–41.

Meese, Richard A. and Kenneth Rogoff (1983a), 'Empirical Exchange Rate Models of the Seventies', *Journal of International Economics*, **14** (1), 3–24.

Meese, Richard A. and Kenneth Rogoff (1983b), 'The Out-of-Sample Failure of Empirical Exchange Rate Models', *Exchange Rates and International Macroeconomics*, ed. by J. Frenkel, Chicago, University of Chicago Press, pp. 67–112.

Melvin, Michael (1983), 'Vanishing Liquidity Effect of Money on Interest: Analysis and Implications for Policy', *Economic Inquiry*, **21** (2), 188–202.

Meredith, Guy and Menzie Chinn (1998), 'Long-Horizon Uncovered Interest Parity', *NBER Working Paper 6797*, Cambridge, MA.

Michael, P., A. R. Nobay, and D. A. Peel (1997), 'Transactions Costs and Nonlinear Adjustment in Real Exchange Rates: An Empirical Investigation', *Journal of Political Economy*, **105** (4), 862–79.

Miller, Norman C. (1968), 'A General Equilibrium Theory of International Capital Flows', *Economic Journal*, **78** (310), 312–20.

Miller, Norman C. (1970), 'A General Equilibrium Theory of International Capital Flows: Reply', *Economic Journal*, **80** (319), 747–49.

Miller, Norman C. (1972), 'The Balance of Payments Composition Problem', *Canadian Journal of Economics*, **5** (2), 237–56.

Miller, Norman C. (1978), 'Monetary Versus Traditional Approaches to the Balance of Payments', *American Economic Review*, **68** (2), 406–11.

Miller, Norman C. (1980), 'Offset and Growth Coefficients for Five Industrial Countries: 1960-1970', *Review of Economics and Statistics*, **62** (3), 329–38.

Miller, Norman C. (1981), 'Keynesian Balance of Payments Models: Comment', *American Economic Review*, **71**, (4), 778–83.

Miller, Norman C. (1986a), 'The Structure of Open Economy Macro Models', *Journal of International Money and Finance*, **5** (1), 75–89.

Miller, Norman C. (1986b), 'A General Approach to the Balance of Payments and Exchange Rates', *Journal of International Economic Integration*, **1** (1), 89–126.

Miller, Norman C. (1992), 'Cash-in-Advance, Buffer-Stock Monetarism, and the Loanable Funds Liquidity Preference Debate in an Open Economy', *Journal of Macroeconomics*, **14** (3), 487–507.

Miller, Norman C. (1993), 'Short-Run Disequilibrium and Long-Run Deviations From Purchasing Power Parity', *Journal of Post Keynesian Economics*, **15** (3), 443–50.

Miller, Norman C. (1995), 'Towards a Loanable Funds/Amended Liquidity Preference Theory of the Exchange Rate and Interest Rate', *Journal of International Money and Finance*, **14** (2), 225–45.

Miller, Norman C. and Sherry S. Askin (1976), 'Monetary Policy and the Balance of Payments in Brazil and Chile', *Journal of Money, Credit, and Banking*, **8** (2), 227–38.

Miller, Norman C. and Marina v. N. Whitman (1970), 'A Mean-Variance Analysis of United States Long Term Portfolio Foreign Investment', *Quarterly Journal of Economics*, **84** (2), 175–96.

Miller, Norman C. and Marina v.N. Whitman (1972), 'The Outflow of Short-Term Funds from the United States: Adjustments of Stocks and Flows', in *International Mobility and Movement of Capital*, ed. by Fritz Machlup, Walter Salant, and Lorie Tarshis, New York: Columbia University Press, pp. 253–86.

Miller, Norman C. and Marina v.N. Whitman (1973), 'Alternative Theories and Tests of US Short Term Foreign Investment', *Journal of Finance*, **28** (5), 1131–50.

Mishkin, Frederick (1984), 'Are Real Interest Rates Equal Across Countries? An Empirical Investigation of International Parity Conditions', *Journal of Finance*, **39** (5), 1345–58.

Mundell, Robert A. (1962), 'The Appropriate Use of Monetary and Fiscal Policy Under Fixed Exchange Rates', *International Monetary Fund Staff Papers*, **9** (1), 70–77.

Mussa, Michael (1979), 'Empirical Regularities in the Behavior of Exchange Rates and Theories of the Foreign Exchange Market', in *Policies for Employment Prices and Exchange Rates*, ed. by Karl Brunner and Allen H. Meltzer, New York: North-Holland, pp. 9–57.

Neely, Christopher J. (1998), 'Technical Analysis and the Profitability of U.S. Foreign Exchange Intervention', *Federal Reserve Bank of St. Louis Review*, **80** (4), 3–17.

Neely, Christopher J. and Paul A. Weller (2001), 'Technical Analysis and Central Bank Intervention', *Journal of International Money and Finance*, **20** (7), 949–70.

Nieuland, Fred, W. Verschoor, and C. P. Wolff (1991), 'EMS Exchange Rates', *Journal of International Financial Markets, Institutions, and Money*, **1** (2), 21–21.

Obstfeld, Maurice (1982), 'Aggregate Spending and the Terms of Trade: Is There a Laursen–Metzler Effect?', *Quarterly Journal of Economics*, **97** (2), 251–70.

Obstfeld, Maurice (1990), 'The Effectiveness of Foreign-Exchange Intervention: Recent Experiences, 1985–1988', in *International Policy Coordination and Exchange Rate Fluctuations*, ed. by W. H. Branson,

J.A. Frenkel, and M. Goldstein, Chicago: University of Chicago Press, pp. 197–237.

Obstfeld, Maurice (1995), 'International Capital Mobility in the 1990s', in *Understanding Interdependence: The Macroeconomics of the Open Economy*, ed. by Peter B. Kenen, Princeton, NJ: Princeton University Press, pp, 201–61.

Obstfeld, Maurice and Kenneth Rogoff (1995a), 'The Intertemporal Approach to the Current Account', in Grossman and Rogoff (1995), ch. 34.

Obstfeld, Maurice and Kenneth Rogoff (1995b), 'Exchange Rate Dynamics Redux', *Journal of Political Economy*, **103** (3), 624–60.

Obstfeld, Maurice and Kenneth Rogoff (1996), *Foundations of International Macroeconomics*, Cambridge, MA: MIT Press.

Obstfeld, Maurice and Kenneth Rogoff (2000), 'The Six Major Puzzles in International Macro–Economics: Is There a Common Cause?', *NBER Working Paper 7777*, Cambridge, MA.

Obstfeld, Maurice and A. Taylor (1997), 'Nonlinear Aspects of Goods-Market Arbitrage and Adjustment: Hechscher's Commodity Points Revisited', *Journal of the Japanese and International Economies*, **11** (4), 441–79.

O'Connell, P.G. (1998), 'The Overvaluation of Purchasing Power Parity', *Journal of International Economics*, **44** (1), 1–19.

O'Connell, P.G. and S. Wei (1997), 'The Bigger They Are, the Harder They Fall: How Price Differences Across U.S. Cities Are Arbitraged', *NBER. Working Paper 6089*, Cambridge, MA.

Osler, C. L. (1998), 'Short Term Speculators and the Puzzling Behavior of Exchange Rates', *Journal of International Economics*, **45** (1), 37–58.

Papell, David (1997), 'Searching for Stationarity: Purchasing Power Parity under the Current Float', *Journal of International Economics*, **43** (3–4) 313–32.

Patinkin, Don (1958), 'Liquidity Preference and Loanable Funds: Stock and Flow Analysis', *Economica*, **25** (100), 300–18.

Penati, Alessandro (1983), 'Expansionary Fiscal Policy and the Exchange Rate', *International Monetary Fund Staff Papers*, **30**, (3), 542–69.

Peterson, T. and Lars Svensson (1985), 'Current Account Dynamics and the Terms of Trade: Harberger–Laursen–Metzler Two Decades Later', *Journal of Political Economy*, **93** (1), 43–65.

Pippenger, John (1996), 'Misalignment and Real Variability Before, During, and After Bretton Woods', University of California, Santa Barbara Working Paper, Santa Barbara, CA.

Pippenger, John (1998), 'Modeling Foreign Exchange Markets: Stock Versus Flow', University of California, Santa Barbara: Working Paper, # 8–98, Santa Barbara, CA.

Rabin, Alan A. (1979), 'A Note on the Link Between Balance of Payments Disequilibrium and the Excess Demand for Money', *Southern Economic Journal*, **45** (4), 1233–38.

Rabin, Alan A. and Leland B. Yeager (1979), 'Monetary Approaches to the Balance of Payments and Exchange Rates', in *Economic Perspectives*, ed. by Maurice B. Ballabon, London: Harwood.

Rabin, Alan A. and Leland B. Yeager (1982), 'Monetary Approaches to the Balance of Payments and Exchange Rates, *Essays in International Finance # 148*, Princeton, NJ: Princeton University Press.

Radelet, Steven and Jeffrey Sachs (2000), 'The Onset of the East Asian Financial Crisis', in *Currency Crisis*, ed. by Paul Krugman, Chicago: University of Chicago Press, pp. 105–62.

Razin, Assaf (1995), 'The Dynamic-Optimizing Approach to the Current Account: Theory and Evidence', in *Understanding Interdependence: The Macroeconomics of The Open Economy*, ed by Peter B. Kenen, Princeton, NJ: Princeton University Press, ch. 5.

Razin, Assaf, Efraim Sadka, and Chi-Wa Yuen (1996), 'Tax Principles and Capital Inflows: Is It Efficient to Tax Nonresident Income?', *NBER Working Paper 5513*, Cambridge, MA.

Robichek, E. Walter (1981), 'Some Reflections About External Public Debt Management', *Estudios Monetarios VII,* Santiago, Chile: Banco Central de Chile.

Robinson, Joan (1937), 'The Foreign Exchanges', in her *Essays in the Theory of Employment*, London: Cambridge University Press.

Rogoff, Kenneth (1996), 'The Purchasing Power Parity Puzzle', *Journal of Economic Literature*, **34** (2), 647–68.

Rose, Andrew K. (1991), 'The Role of Exchange Rates in a Popular Model of International Trade', *Journal of International Economics*, **30** (3–4), 301–16.

Rose, Andrew K. and Janet L. Yellen (1989), 'Is There a J-Curve?', *Journal of Monetary Economics*, **24** (1), 53–68.

Sachs, Jeffery D. (1981), 'The Current Account and Macroeconomic Adjustment in the 1970s', *Brookings Papers on Economic Activity*, **1** (1), 201–68.

Sachs, Jeffery D. (1982), 'The Current Account in the Macroeconomic Adjustment Process', *Scandinavian Journal of Economics*, **84** (2), 147–59.

Sachs, Jeffery D. (1983), 'Aspects of the Current Account Behavior of OECD Economies', in *Recent Issues in the Theory of Flexible Exchange Rates,* ed. by Emil Claasen and P. Salin, Amsterdam: North-Holland.

Sarno, Lucio (2001), 'Toward a New Paradigm in Open Economy Modeling: Where Do We Stand?', *Federal Reserve Bank of St Louis Review*, **83** (3), 21–36.

Sargent, Thomas (1987), *Macroeconomic Theory*, Cambridge, MA: MIT Press.

Schinasi, G. and P.A.V.B. Swamy (1989), 'The Out-of-Sample Forecasting Performance of Exchange Rate Models When Coefficients are Allowed to Change', *Journal of International Money and Finance*, **8** (3), 375–90.

Smith, Peter R. (1980), 'Liquidity Preference Versus Loanable Funds: A Brief Revival', *Australian Economic Papers*, **19** (3–4), 215–18.

Stein, Jerome (1994), 'The Natural Real Exchange Rate of the US Dollar and Determinants of Capital Flows', in Williamson (1994), pp. 133–75.

Stockman, Alan C. (1980), 'A Theory of Exchange Rate Determination', *Journal of Political Economy*, **88** (4), 673–98.

Stockman, Alan C. (1987), 'The Equilibrium Approach to Exchange Rates', *Federal Reserve Bank of Richmond Economic Review*, **73** (1), 12–30.

Stockman, Alan C. and L. Tesar (1995), 'Tastes and Technology in a Two-Country Model of the Business Cycle: Explaining International Comovements', *American Economic Review*, **85** (1), 168–85.

Stokes, Houston H. and Hugh Newburger (1979), 'The Effect of Monetary Changes on Interest Rates: A Box–Jenkins Approach', *Review of Economics and Statistics*, **61** (4), 534–48.

Summers, Lawrence (1988), 'Tax Policy and International Competitiveness', in *International Aspects of Fiscal Policies*, ed. by Jacob Frenkel, Chicago: University of Chicago Press.

Svensson, Lars (1983), 'Oil Prices, Welfare and the Trade Balance', *Quarterly Journal of Economics*, **99** (4), 649–72.

Svensson, Lars and Assaf Razin (1983), 'The Terms of Trade and the Current Account: The Harberger–Laursen–Metzler Effect', *Journal of Political Economy*, **91** (1), 97–125.

Sweeney, Richard J. (1986), 'Beating the Foreign Exchange Market', *Journal of Finance*, **41** (1), 163–82.

Taylor, Mark P. (1990), *The Balance of Payments: New Perspectives on Open-Economy Macroeconomics*, Aldershot, UK and Brookfield, US: Edward Elgar.

Taylor, Mark P (1995), 'The Economics of Exchange Rates', *Journal of Economic Literature*, **33** (1), 13–47.

Taylor, Mark P. and L. Sarno (1998), 'The Behavior of Real Exchange Rates During the Post–Bretton Woods Period', *Journal of International Economics*, **46** (2), 281–312.

Throop, Adrian W. (1993), 'A Generalized Uncovered Interest Parity Model of Exchange Rates', *Federal Reserve Bank of San Francisco Economic Review*, **2** (2), 3–16.

Tobin, James (1983), 'Comment on Domestic Saving and International Capital Movements in the Long Run and the Short Run' by M. Feldstein, *European Economic Review*, **21** (1–2), 153–56.

Tsiang, S.C. (1958), 'A Theory of Foreign-Exchange Speculation under a Floating Exchange System', *Journal of Political Economy*, **66** (5), 399–418.

Tsiang, S.C. (1980), 'Keynes' Finance Demand for Liquidity, Robertson's Loanable Funds Theory, and Friedman's Monetarism', *Quarterly Journal of Economics*, **94** (3), 467–91.

Visser, Hans (1986), 'Loanable Funds Theory versus Liquidity Preference Theory', *De Economist*, **134** (1), 109–10.

Visser, Hans (2000), *A Guide to International Monetary Economics*, 2nd ed, Cheltenham, UK: Edward Elgar.

Webb, L. Roy (1970), 'The Role of International Capital Movements in Trade and Growth: The Fisherian Approach', in *Studies in International Economics*, ed. by I.A. McDougall and R.H. Snape, Amsterdam: North-Holland, ch. 13.

Westerfield, J. M. (1977), 'An Examination of Foreign Exchange Risk Under Fixed and Floating Rate Regimes', *Journal of International Economics*, **7** (2), 181–200.

Willett, Thomas D. and Francesco Forte (1969), 'Interest Rate Policy and External Balance', *Quarterly Journal of Economics*, **83** (2), 242–62.

Williamson, John, ed. (1994), *Estimating Equilibrium Exchange Rates*, Washington, DC: Institute for International Economics.

Williamson, John (1994), 'Estimates of FEERS', in Williamson, ed. (1994), pp. 177–243.

Wolff, C.C.P. (1987), 'Time Varying Parameters and the Out-of-Sample ForecastingPerformance of Structural Exchange Rate models', *Journal of Business and Economic Statistics*, **5** (1), 87–97.

Wu, Yangru (1996), 'Are Real Exchange Rates Nonstationary? Evidence From a Panel-Data Test', *Journal of Money, Credit, and Banking*, **28** (1), 54–63.

Index